Presidential Powers

If the President does it, it is not illegal.

—Richard Nixon

Presidential
Powers

Harold J. Krent

NEW YORK UNIVERSITY PRESS
New York and London

NEW YORK UNIVERSITY PRESS
New York and London
www.nyupress.org

Library of Congress Cataloging-in-Publication Data
Krent, Harold J.
Presidential powers / Harold J. Krent.
p. cm.
Includes bibliographical references and index.
ISBN 0-8147-4782-5 (cloth : alk. paper)
 1. Executive power—United States. 2. Presidents—United States.
I. Title.
JK516.K73   2004
352.23'5'0973—dc22   2004017315

New York University Press books are printed on acid-free paper,
and their binding materials are chosen for strength and durability.

Manufactured in the United States of America
10 9 8 7 6 5 4 3 2 1

Contents

during Time of War   141

C. Emergency Measures to Protect
Governmental Personnel and Property   149

4   Presidential Immunities and Privileges   161
     A. Immunity from Suit   162
     B. Executive Privilege   173

5   The Pardon Power   189
     A. Congressional Interference   194
     B. General Separation of Powers Concern   196
     C. Pardon Based on Legal Disagreement   199
     D. Scope of Judicial Review   201
     E. Conditional Pardons   205

     Conclusion   215

     Notes   219

     Bibliography   261

     Index   269

     About the Author and Acknowledgments   279

Acronyms and Abbreviations

ABA   American Bar Association

ABM   anti-ballistic missile

APA   Administrative Procedure Act

ASAT   antisatellite

CIA   Central Intelligence Agency

DOJ   Department of Justice

EEOC   Equal Employment Opportunity Commission

EPA   Environmental Protection Agency

FAA   Federal Aviation Agency

FALN   Fuerzes Armedas Liberacion Nacional

FBI   Federal Bureau of Investigation

FDR   Franklin Delano Roosevelt

FEC   Federal Election Commission

FOMC   Federal Open Market Committee

FTC   Federal Trade Commission

GAO   Government Accounting Office

HHS   Department of Health and Human Services

ICC   Interstate Commerce Commission

IEEPA   International Emergency Economic Powers Act

INF   Intermediate Nuclear Forces

IRS   Internal Revenue Service

JCAH   Joint Committee on Accreditation of Hospitals

LBJ   Lyndon Baines Johnson

NAFTA   North American Free Trade Agreement

NATO   North American Treaty Organization

NSA   National Security Agency

OLC   Office of Legal Counsel

OMB   Office of Management and Budget

RUDs   reservations, understandings, and conditions

SDI   Strategic Defense Initiative

SEC   Securities and Exchange Commission

TWEA   Trading with the Enemy Act

WTO   World Trade Organization

Introduction

Presidential powers can be viewed through many prisms. Political scientists, for instance, have catalogued presidential actions to gain a picture of the authorities that prior presidents have in fact exercised.[1] Some presidents earn higher marks for administration, some for leadership, and some for vision. Such descriptions of presidential powers are incredibly important.

Understanding presidential powers from a constitutional perspective is much more difficult. There is no readily definable list of attributes or authorities. Article II itself is quite vague, never defining the "executive" power with specificity. The discrete powers granted to the president, such as the authority to enter into treaties, serve as commander in chief, and appoint superior officers, do not define the precise contours of what presidents can or should do. Moreover, presidential power under Article II readily can clash with the powers of Congress under Article I and the judiciary under Article III. Although some believe that the text itself definitively answers the vast majority of contemporary issues concerning presidential powers, most are of the view that the constitutional language presents only a starting point that must be complemented by considerations of the overall structure of the Constitution, the underlying purposes of those who drafted Article II and ratified the Constitution, and historical practice.

Nowhere in the Constitution, for instance, does it specify whether Congress or the president can remove executive branch officials. The Constitution also is silent as to whether the Senate or president can terminate treaties. Nor does it mention whether judges can review presidential actions for conformance with constitutional requirements. Resolution of such questions must stem from considerations of history and structure.

Although the debates surrounding the Constitutional Convention supply little detail, they reinforce the overall concept of a vigorous chief executive. We know that the Founders wished to scale back the executive powers of a monarch but also intended the executive to be a counter-weight to legislative powers that many believed had expanded danger-ously in the years following the Revolutionary War.[2] The lack of an ex-ecutive branch helped precipitate the fall of government under the Arti-cles of Confederation, and some state legislatures had exercised almost unchecked powers in the years leading up to the Convention.

Considerations of that background along with the emerging constitu-tional structure thereafter have persuaded most commentators that the Constitution does not define unique powers for each branch. As an ex-ample, only Congress has the power to pass laws, but presidents partici-pate in legislation by offering bills for Congress to consider, by vetoing legislation, and then by filling in the gaps in laws when applying or en-forcing them in particular contexts. Similarly, although the function of judges under Article III is to interpret and apply the law in resolving cases and controversies, presidents must interpret the law in carrying out the terms of both treaties and statutes. Presidents determine which treaties are best for the nation, but so does the Senate. The Constitution therefore does not set aside particular functions and label them "executive" or "legislative," but rather prescribes a relational framework under which all the branches must act.

The constitutional system of separation of powers, therefore, turns not on separating functions but on creating a system of checks and balances. The Constitution places restraints on how each branch must act, includ-ing the executive. The executive branch can enforce only those laws that Congress enacts; it can bind the nation to treaties only should two-thirds of the Senate concur; and it can spend only sums appropriated by Con-gress. Understanding the basic constitutional structure of overlapping powers permits headway in answering the bewildering array of contem-porary questions concerning executive power.

When challenges to the exercise of presidential powers arise, judges may be called upon to set limits or accommodate the powers of the exec-utive branch with other constitutional powers and values. The judicial system, whether through criminal or civil cases, provides a critical means of monitoring executive branch governance. Suits challenging whether presidential actions comport with congressional directives may preserve congressional prerogatives. Suits by individuals and firms also can ensure that presidential acts do not violate individual rights. Moreover, judges may augment accountability to both Congress and the public by directing presidents to divulge critical information in their control that either Congress or private parties need for compelling reasons.

But many such disputes never reach court. Under Article III of the Constitution, judges can resolve only "cases and controversies," and conflicts among the branches often do not under current doctrine meet that requirement. No individual or entity may suffer the personal, tangible harm necessary to satisfy the constitutional test. A congressional demand for information from the executive branch may never ripen into a cognizable case or controversy. Moreover, even when a case or controversy exists, courts have been loathe to intervene in cases in which they feel powerless or particularly ill-equipped to participate, particularly in matters of foreign affairs. Accordingly, challenges over presidential decisions to introduce troops or abrogate treaties have been dismissed. Courts have termed many such challenges "political questions," suggesting that redress can be obtained only through the political process.

As a consequence of both the case or controversy requirement and the political question doctrine, much law of presidential powers develops through the political give-and-take among the branches. Conflicts among the branches may be resolved under the shadow of existing judicial precedents, but each nonjudicial resolution creates its own historical precedent that may guide presidents, members of Congress, and even courts in the future.

History therefore plays a prominent role in answering some of the questions left open in the Constitution. Some of the historical practice—undeclared wars, expenditure of unappropriated funds, refusal to disclose confidential memoranda to Congress and courts—is quite difficult to reconcile with the constitutional text and structure. Presidents' historical exercise of particular authorities does not by itself preclude questions as to the constitutionality of the prior practice: that "an unconstitutional action has been taken before surely does not render that same action any less unconstitutional at a later date."[3] Nonetheless, historical practice influences contemporary interpretation of Article II, for each president builds on the contemporary understanding of presidential powers existing when assuming office.

To resolve many contemporary questions of presidential powers, one must consider the text, the structure of the Constitution, any judicial precedents, and history. Although a clear picture has not emerged, many of the lingering questions concerning the scope and propriety of Article II presidential powers in various contexts hinge on resolution of three potentially overlapping determinants of the president's role within the Constitution's separation of powers framework.

Presidential Initiative

By vesting extensive authority in one chief executive, the constitutional system stresses the need for vigorous presidential leadership. Particularly in times of war or fiscal emergency, assertive presidential action may be critical to protect the country. Presidents Jefferson, Lincoln, and Franklin Roosevelt demonstrated such verve in confronting crises. But, in times of comparative peace as well, initiative may be important to ensure the continued progress of the nation. The focus on initiative derives not only from the history leading up to enactment of Article II but also from the specific decision to vest the "executive" power in a single executive. Moreover, the public seemingly has welcomed presidential initiative throughout much of our nation's history.

Presidential Accountability to Congressional Policymaking

At the same time, however, presidential initiative threatens to infringe a second goal of our system of separated powers, which is to ensure Congress's ability to set the framework for national policy and determine within broad constraints how that policy should be implemented. Congress, for instance, determines which agencies should exist, which agencies are to exercise particular functions, and how much they can spend. Battles over control of the so-termed independent agencies reflect the clash between Congress's prerogative to establish policy and presidential efforts to establish control over the executive branch and thereby preserve greater flexibility for executive action. The president under Article II, in other words, must bow to Congress's Article I lawmaking and appropriation authorities in executing the law.

Presidential accountability to Congress also is critical because Congress must determine if the president is carrying out legislative policy faithfully and effectively. Congress's monitoring efforts may include investigations, oversight hearings, and requests for presidential documents.

Without such information, Congress may fashion poor policy in subsequently legislating for the nation, whether in crafting welfare programs, setting criminal fines, or establishing environmental regulation. Moreover, by changing the terms of authority delegated to the president or his subordinates, Congress can pressure presidents to adhere to congressional instructions more closely. Impeachment looms as the ultimate oversight mechanism.

Presidential Accountability to the Public

As a final goal, the president should be accountable not only to Congress but to the public as a whole for his exercise of both constitutional and delegated authority. The determination to make presidents electorally accountable—both by virtue of the electoral college and by virtue of the now finite terms in office—suggests that presidential actions be sufficiently transparent so that they can be judged by the electorate. Citizens should be able to assess the president's leadership and track record in exercising presidential prerogatives and in carrying out congressional direction. The public should be able to distinguish the roles of Congress and the executive branch in shaping U.S. policy so that the president can be judged for his own actions. Even if the president is serving a second term in office or does not intend to stand for reelection, voter antipathy to his conduct in office may be visited upon his party and close associates.

At times, these three goals of our system reinforce one another. For instance, presidential commissions of inquiry may embody presidential initiative while ensuring that the president remains accountable to Congress and the public for any subsequent change in policy. The report and recommendations of a commission may dovetail with congressional priorities, and even if not, the commission will leave any policy change to Congress. Similarly, a congressional measure designed to require the president to announce any pardon publicly would make the president's actions more transparent and understandable by the public. When the three goals coincide, the particular governmental action is almost assuredly constitutional. On the other hand, when the goals conflict—as more often is the case—the question of constitutionality is more problematic. Congressional efforts to allocate power to executive branch officials outside the president's control, for instance, while furthering congressional policymaking may obscure to the public which officials should be accountable for what particular actions. Or, presidential efforts to shield information from private parties, while bolstering presidential initiative, may undermine presidential accountability to both Congress and the public. No formula for ascertaining constitutionality in such contexts is possible.

In short, our system has achieved only modest success in telling us when presidential initiative should trump the president's need to be accountable to Congress, or when Congress's ability to set broad policy parameters should trump presidential efforts to make the executive branch more accountable to the public. Studying the three factors, therefore, will not by itself generate answers to concrete questions. It can, however, illuminate the crosscurrents underlying evolution of presidential powers. Clashes among the three goals play out differently in distinct doctrinal contexts as the succeeding chapters chart.

History

Any exegesis of presidential powers under Article II starts with the colonists' perception and experience under British control. Their existence was shaped by the rule of the British sovereign as well as by colonial governors.

Under the British system, the monarch was accountable to the parliament, both the aristocratic House of Lords and the more democratic House of Commons. The king could not legislate but did enjoy an absolute veto over any parliamentary measure. The king could also declare war but was dependent upon Parliament for the funds to equip and train armies. The king's pardon power was absolute except for cases of impeachment.

Kings also appointed governors in the colonies. Governors typically enjoyed rights to convene and dissolve assemblies, and to veto any objectionable legislative measure.[4] They, too, were dependent upon the colonial legislatures for funding. Governors could call out troops only in emergencies necessitated by hostilities with Indian tribes. They also typically exercised the pardon power and appointment power over judicial and administrative offices within the colony.

Differences among the colonies nonetheless existed. A family dynasty ruled New Hampshire; North Carolina experienced long periods of anarchy.[5] Rhode Island and Connecticut elected their own governors. The king's Privy Council in London oversaw the work of the colonial governments, and enjoyed the right to veto laws it found problematic. In turn, colonial governments faced difficulty in repealing laws that the Crown had approved.

As hostilities between London and the colonies increased, colonists placed most of the blame on corrupt or narrow-minded governors and ministers of the Crown. They apparently believed that a constitutional monarchy was best tailored to their needs, and that the monarch would be receptive to their concerns. Indeed, colonists responded to the repeal of the Stamp Act with renewed faith in the Crown.[6] When King George III finally unambiguously denounced the colonists and ordered their repression, the reaction was one of surprise and betrayal. As hostilities continued, resentment toward the Crown and the system of monarchy increased.

That sense of betrayal precipitated a strong anti-executive reaction. Thomas Paine in *Common Sense* wrote that the monarchy was "exceedingly ridiculous."[7] The monarchy allowed individuals of modest or limited abilities too much power and, over time, British monarchs had "swallowed up the power and eaten out the virtue of the [republican] house of commons."[8]

The Declaration of Independence elaborated upon Paine's theme, accusing King George of imposing "an absolute Tyranny over these States."[9] The document listed a series of grievances. For instance, it charged that King George had "refused his Assent to Laws, the most wholesome and necessary for the public good";[10] that he "has abdicated Government here, by declaring us out of his Protection and waging War against us";[11] that he "has plundered our seas, ravaged our Coasts, burnt our towns, and destroyed the lives of our people";[12] that he "has constrained our fellow Citizens taken Captive on the high Seas to bear Arms against their Country, to become the executioners of their friends and Brethren";[13] and that he "has excited domestic insurrections amongst us, and has endeavored to bring on the inhabitants of our frontiers, the merciless Indian Savages, whose known rule of warfare, is an undistinguished destruction of all ages, sexes and conditions."[14] The colonists fought the Revolutionary War in part to escape from the despotism of a too powerful monarch.

Almost all of the states after the War of Independence stripped governors of authority. Only in New York did the governor retain significant powers. For instance, Pennsylvania established a unicameral legislature with no chief executive. Instead, a twelve-person council elected for three-year terms appointed certain officers and granted pardons. The state's Constitution restricted the council to one clerical employee. Executive authority was vested in the legislature alone. As one critic of the legislature lamented, had the supreme power instead "been lodged in the hands of one man, it would have been less dangerous to the safety and liberties of the community."[15]

Governors existed in other states but with limited influence. Most were elected by legislatures for only one-year terms, but even they could not appoint many of what we today would consider executive officials.[16] None of the governors possessed a veto power, and only the governors of Delaware and North Carolina could issue pardons. The Massachusetts legislature deviated from the norm in the other states by proposing that the state's chief executive be vested with greater authority, but Massachusetts citizens rejected the proposal. Thomas Jefferson reflected about Virginia's comparable experience that "[a]n elective despotism was not the government we fought for, but one which should not only be founded on free principles, but in which the powers of government should be so divided and balanced among several bodies of magistracy, as that no one could transcend their legal limits, without being effectually checked and restrained by the others."[17] As Madison later summarized in the Federalist Papers about the period after the Declaration of Independence, "The legislative department is everywhere extending the sphere of its activity and drawing all power in its impetuous vortex."[18]

At the same time, the Continental Congress kept most executive-type powers for itself. It largely attempted to conduct the war, raise money, and negotiate internationally through committees. Congress under the Articles of Confederation could "appoint such other committees and civil officers as may be necessary for managing the general affairs of the united states under their direction."[19] By nearly everyone's estimation, the committees' conduct of government affairs was abysmal—inefficiency and graft abounded.

Under the Articles of Confederation, the drafters declined to create a distinct executive branch. There was no chief executive, and the power to appoint officials, declare war, negotiate treaties, and grant pardons remained vested in the legislature. Congress, however, established four departments—foreign affairs, finance, war, and marine—and set one person to have full control over each. As an example, Congress directed

Robert Livingston as secretary of foreign affairs to correspond with foreign ministers and to provide information to Congress at its request. For the first time, some administration existed outside Congress itself. The drafters placed a premium on executive accountability to congressional policymaking. Yet the government remained hard-pressed to keep the nation solvent, let alone protect American shipping overseas.

Other inefficiencies plagued Congress. Most notably, the Articles of Confederation placed no power in the central government to tax or to coerce compliance from the states. Two-thirds of the states had to agree before any law could go into effect, and any emendation of the articles had to be unanimous. No power existed to regulate commerce among the newly independent states in the confederation. Despite the myriad problems, more and more individuals pointed to the lack of a chief executive as one of the shortcomings of the governmental system. Legislative efforts to print paper money and repudiate debts in states such as Rhode Island convinced others that legislatures were not to be trusted.[20] Moreover, civil unrest in a number of states—typified by Shays' Rebellion—sparked fears of lawlessness. Sentiment for a more centralized executive increased.

The stage was set for a greater executive role when the Constitutional Convention convened. Not surprisingly, members of the convention reflected a wide range of views, from those who thought the Articles of Confederation had it right, to those who sympathized with a monarchy. Nor was the development of Article II in any way linear. Proposals for a plural executive alternated with proposals for greater centralization. Roger Sherman uniquely pressed that Congress should be able to determine the size of the executive as experience might dictate. James Madison championed a Council of Revision, under which a president and members of the judiciary jointly would have exercised a veto power. Despite the great range of proposals, almost all agreed that greater executive initiative was needed. A key turning point came with embrace of the electoral college system relatively late in the deliberations, which liberated the office of the chief executive from the newly created Congress, with the exception of impeachment. For the first time, a chief executive would be accountable, at least in part, to the citizenry. Then, with a consensus building that the executive should be singular, the duties to be exercised by the president fell into place.

Article II provides then, as it does now, in principal part that "the President shall be Commander in Chief of the Army of the United States;"[21] that "he shall have Power to grant Reprieves and Pardons for Offenses against the United States, except in Cases of Impeachment;"[22] that "He shall have Power, by and with the Advice and Consent of the Senate to make Treaties, provided two thirds of the Senators present concur; and he shall nominate, and by and with the Advice and Consent of the Senate, shall appoint Ambassadors, other public Ministers and Consuls, Judges of the supreme Court, and all other Officers of the United States . . . but the congress may by Law vest the Appointment of such inferior Officers, as they think proper, in the President alone, in the Courts of Law, or in the Heads of Departments."[23] Toward the end of Article II, the Framers also provided that the president "shall take Care that the Laws be faithfully executed."[24] Moreover, at the very head of Article II, the Framers provided that the "executive Power shall be vested in a President of the United States of America,"[25] although the significance and extent of that grant was unclear.

Many have argued that the Vesting Clause itself represents a substantial grant of executive power. The Vesting Clauses in Articles I and III limit power to that "herein granted" in the remainder of the Articles; the Vesting Clause in Article II is not similarly cabined. Rather, by vesting "executive power" in the president, Article II plausibly granted the president all of the then understood category of executive power, including authority over both foreign and domestic policy,[26] limited only by the specific exceptions elsewhere in the Constitution.

Despite the ambiguity of the language in Article II, the president was made independent of Congress and granted substantial powers to counteract the failings of the state governments and federal government under the Articles of Confederation. A strong president could restrain legislative excesses and limit legislative graft. Although the president therefore was to exercise considerable initiative, the magnitude of the authority vested in the president was never worked out, and the Framers clearly intended to avoid vesting the new president with anything resembling kinglike powers.

The Constitutional Convention recommended that Congress send the new document to state ratification conventions and bypass the amendment procedures under the Articles of Confederation, which would have required approval by Congress and the legislatures of all thirteen states. Congress agreed, and declared that the new Constitution would go into effect once accepted by nine of the thirteen states. Ratification, however, was not guaranteed, and the debates over the wisdom of the new Constitution raged. Indeed, Rhode Island did not ratify the Constitution until almost three years after the convention ended, well into George Washington's first term as president.

Disagreement over the executive power did not occupy center stage. Rather, most of the debates concerned the allocation of power between the states and Congress and between large and small states. Nonetheless, there were many, like Patrick Henry, who voiced concerns about the shift toward monarchial power: "Your President may easily become King. . . . If your American chief, be a man of ambition . . . how easy it is for him to render himself absolute."[27] Others more narrowly questioned the propriety of the appointment and veto power, or the wisdom of linking the president to the Senate in the foreign relations field.

Proponents of the new Constitution across the country took up the challenge, defending the office of the presidency as a much more restrained, nuanced creation than its British forebear. In particular, Alexander Hamilton in the Federalists Papers embraced the need for an energetic president distinct from the legislature, but one who nevertheless was subject to checks and balances of public electoral approval, congressional purse strings, and even judicial review. Hamilton stressed the ways in which the presidency differed from a monarchy: electoral basis; limited term in office; possibility of impeachment; limited veto; lack of an ability to create offices and raise armies. He also emphasized the dangers of legislatures run amok. At the Pennsylvania ratifying convention, James Wilson stressed the importance of the Constitution's decision to vest the executive power in one individual: "[W]e well know what numerous executives are. We know there is neither vigor, decision, nor responsibility in them."[28] And, Edmund Randolph at the Virginia Convention commented, "All the enlightened part of mankind agree that the superior dispatch, secrecy, and energy with which one man can act, renders it more politic to vest the power of executing the laws in one man."[29] Details as to the extent of presidential supervision of law administration remained fuzzy—Article II was a work in progress. Ratification of the Constitution created a new office of the presidency whose ambit would have to be fleshed out with succeeding generations.

As the subsequent chapters chart, presidents themselves have disagreed over the extent of executive authority under Article II. Their words and deeds manifest contrasting theories of presidential power. The following analysis is quite summary, but even so it reflects that some presidents have sought to defend exercises of initiative not only on expansive interpretations of the constitutional text but also on pragmatic need. Vigorous action may be required to seize strategic international advantage or to steer the nation away from danger. Other presidents, however, have endeavored to remain more accountable to Congress. Although presidential power unquestionably has expanded over the generations, the progress has not been consistent—the scope of presidential power turns on the resistance exerted by the other branches as well as on the philosophies and personalities of those serving in office.

George Washington possessed the advantage of being the first officeholder—he defined the office through every political step he took. As he related, "There is scarcely any part of my conduct which may not hereafter be drawn into precedent."[30] He did not seek to push any particular vision of the presidency, but he believed in energetic leadership over both foreign policy and domestic affairs. His dispatch of troops to quell the Whiskey Rebellion and his formulation of the Neutrality Proclamation in particular demonstrate his view. To Washington, the president had to respond to challenges from outside or inside the country, and it simply was not critical to be able to justify each step by reference to the constitutional text.

Alexander Hamilton defended Washington's actions in more theoretical terms, arguing that Article II did not fully define executive powers: "The difficulty of a complete enumeration of all the cases of executive authority, would naturally dictate the use of general terms, and would render it improbable, that a specification of certain particulars was designed as a substitute for those terms. . . . The enumeration ought therefore to be considered, as intended merely to specify the principal articles implied in the definition of executive power; leaving the rest to flow from the general grant of that power."[31] Washington, however, remained more circumspect.

Moreover, some presidents who, as a theoretical matter, believed in a more limited presidency, expanded presidential power once in office. Thomas Jefferson is a case in point. Prior to the election of 1800, he had written that the constitutional vesting of executive power should be construed narrowly, lest the executive swallow the legislative power of setting national policy. Yet, he transformed the very nature of the young nation through the Louisiana Purchase, despite the fact that he lacked prior congressional authorization. He viewed the opportunity as essential, even if not in strict accordance with constitutional direction.[32] In a letter, he commented to Senator John C. Breckenridge regarding Congress that "I pretend to no right to bind you; you may disavow me and I must get out of the scrape as I can; I thought it my duty to risk myself for you."[33] To Jefferson, congressional acquiescence after the fact sufficed.

Andrew Jackson expanded the notion of executive power further still. His brand of populism suggested that he could appeal over the heads of Congress to the people for support of his policies. He viewed himself as a "tribune" of the people.[34] For instance, he utilized the veto power more than had his predecessors and waged a long battle against the Bank of the United States. He did not hesitate to clash with Congress over policy. Jackson also showed contempt for the Supreme Court, reportedly reacting to a Court opinion recognizing greater rights for Indian tribes by retorting, "Well, John Marshall has made his decision, now let him enforce it."[35] Indeed, he believed it was his constitutional duty to interpret the Constitution for himself: "The opinion of the judges has no more authority over Congress than the opinion of Congress has over the judges, and on that point the President is independent of both."[36] Finally, his view of the presidency led him to become an ardent defender of the union—the people had vested power in him, not in the states.

President James Polk later elaborated that "the President represents in the executive department the whole people of the United States, as each member of the legislative department represents portions of them.[37] Polk, like Jackson before him, seized the policymaking initiative from Congress whenever possible, pushing forward both international and domestic objectives.[38] Both men stressed accountability to the people, not their representatives.

President Lincoln famously expanded executive power during the Civil War. He viewed his role as president foremost to save the Union, niceties in the Constitution notwithstanding. His expansion of the army when Congress was not in session, suspension of habeas corpus, declaration of a blockade against Southern ports, and emancipation of the slaves all increased Union power, irrespective of the lack of congressional authorization. He justified his actions on the ground that "measures otherwise unconstitutional might become lawful by becoming indispensable to the preservation of the Constitution through the preservation of the nation" and queried whether it were "possible to lose the nation and yet preserve the Constitution?"[39] President Lincoln believed that his primary obligation was to the people, not Congress or the Constitution. Whether Lincoln would have asserted such powers in the absence of such a crisis is unclear.

Presidents after Lincoln were not able to exercise such expansive authority, and indeed, Congress almost removed his successor, Andrew Johnson, for exercising too much initiative in office. Subsequent presidents, such as Ulysses S. Grant and Chester B. Arthur, paid closer heed to congressional priorities. To them, accountability to Congress was key. Grant viewed the office in administrative terms—he was willing for Congress to take the initiative.[40]

The presidency of Theodore Roosevelt ushered in a new era of presidential activism. Roosevelt demonstrated initiative in both the foreign and domestic arenas. For instance, he helped build the Panama Canal, invaded Santo Domingo, and blocked economic development on federal lands, all without congressional authorization. Unlike other presidents, however, he more self-consciously defended his exercise of broad powers, at least after his term in office was completed. Under his "stewardship" concept of executive power,

> every executive officer . . . was a steward of the people bound actively and affirmatively to do all he could for the people, and not to content himself with the negative merit of keeping his talents undamaged in a napkin. I declined to adopt the view that what was imperatively necessary for the Nation could not be done by the President unless he could find some specific authorization to do it. My belief was that it was not only his right but his duty to do anything that the needs of the Nation demanded. . . .[41]

Roosevelt used the office as a pulpit from which to press his agenda of conservation and international activism.

The views of Roosevelt's successor, William Howard Taft, developed in almost the opposite direction from those of Jefferson, whose forceful actions in office belied his prior cautious views on executive power. As president, Taft backed off his predecessor's theory of broad executive power untethered to the constitutional text. He remarked that he found Roosevelt's beliefs jarring in a republic because the use of "undefined" powers could swallow up personal liberties.[42] He explained, "The true view of the Executive functions is, as I conceive it, that the President can exercise no power which cannot be fairly and reasonably traced to some specific grant of power or justly implied and included within such express grant as proper and necessary to its exercise."[43] Later, however, as a Supreme Court justice, he helped graft more expansive views of executive authority onto Article II itself.[44]

President Wilson, and particularly Presidents Harding and Coolidge, were more restrained in the use of executive authority. President Harding largely deferred to Congress,[45] and President Coolidge rarely tried to push Congress one way or the other, writing that he "never felt it was

[his] duty to attempt to coerce Senators or Representatives."[46] For these chief executives, presidential initiative should be suppressed to ensure accountability.

The advent of the Great Depression, however, helped convince first President Hoover and then President Franklin Roosevelt to wield greater authority. FDR's actions included seeking and obtaining a series of legislative measures affording him significant authority to create jobs and manage the economy. In his first inaugural address, he commented that the Constitution "is so simple and practical that it is possible always to meet extraordinary needs by changes in emphasis and arrangement without loss of essential form."[47] He did not hesitate to pack the Supreme Court when it balked at his economic measures, for he wanted to save the Constitution "from hardening of the judicial arteries." He pursued almost unilateral action in helping the Allies in their war efforts against Germany despite the more neutral stance of Congress, and he was little interested in preserving civil liberties along the way—"Rights come after victory, not before."[48]

Although Presidents Eisenhower and Carter professed greater respect for Congress,[49] the remaining generation of presidents who have followed FDR have all asserted presidential authority vigorously. For instance, President Truman resolved that he would not allow labor-management disputes to "immediately endanger the safety of our fighting forces abroad and weaken the whole structure of our national security."[50] President Truman's Justice Department subsequently argued that the president represented the "sole organ" of foreign relations.[51] Truman's successors have all taken critical foreign policy steps, from Vietnam to the Iran-Contra affair, in the absence of congressional authorization and at times in the teeth of congressional reluctance. All, as well, have endeavored to centralize executive authority through internal executive agency regulations, thereby making themselves more accountable to the people for executive branch actions. President Nixon pursued both domestic (internal surveillance)[52] and foreign affairs (Cambodia)[53] initiatives that lacked congressional authorization, and were doubtless in violation of both statutes and the Constitution. Nixon followed Lincoln's precepts that presidents must take actions to preserve the nation, and that such steps should be deemed constitutional. Nixon later quipped, "When the President does it, that means that it is not illegal."[54]

Moreover, Presidents Reagan, the first George Bush, Clinton, and George W. Bush abided by Nixon's assertions of expansive executive power. In foreign affairs, they all dispatched troops without congressional authorization, and they all claimed the need to operate under a veil of secrecy. The Iran-Contra affair, which defined the Reagan administration, only epitomized these more recent presidents' view of executive power.[55] Moreover, they were willing to use the courts as venues for vetting increased assertions of executive privilege. In their view, the need for initiative plainly outweighed concerns for accountability either to Congress or more directly to the people.

Presidents themselves, therefore, have disagreed over how to balance initiative with accountability to Congress and the public. Part of their disagreement no doubt turned on how much leverage they had over Congress—if Congress was acquiescent, there was little need for initiative. Part of the disagreement, however, also turned on political philosophy: presidential actions have manifested different views of how magisterial the presidency should be.

The tension between initiative and accountability to both the Congress and the public has played out in many doctrinal areas. Understanding these conflicts can help make sense out of an otherwise seemingly arbitrary set of contemporary constitutional law doctrines. This book first addresses the president's role in administering the nation's laws, investigating the degree to which Article II prevents Congress from limiting presidential control over criminal and civil enforcement of the law, including supervision over agency rulemaking and litigation. The book subsequently turns to the foreign policy context, inquiring whether the balance between initiative and accountability veers more toward the president when international relations are at stake. In related vein, the book next explores whether presidents should be able to tap a reservoir of authority in an emergency to protect the public, not just when faced with foreign threats but with domestic ones as well. The remaining chapters examine the tension between initiative and accountability in more discrete aspects of presidential authority, including the degree to which the Congress and the public can demand information from the president and the scope of the president's pardon power.

1

The President's Power to Execute
the Laws Passed by Congress

A. Presidential Participation in the
Legislative Process—The Veto Power

Before addressing the president's powers to enforce the law, a short detour is necessary. The president plays a fundamental role not only in administering the law but also in helping Congress decide what needs to be administered. When civics courses teach that Congress makes law, the president enforces the law, and judges interpret law, they miss the critical function that the Constitution assigns to the president in the lawmaking process: Congress must present all bills to the president for his approval before the bills can become law. The Constitution provides that "[e]very Bill which shall have passed the House of Representatives and the Senate, shall, before it become a Law, be presented to the President of the United States; If he approve he shall sign it, but if not he shall return it, with his Objections to that House in which it shall have originated. . . ."[1] Congress can override a president's veto only by vote of two-thirds of each house.

The veto power affords the president a potent weapon to influence legislation. As Madison commented, the veto power permits the president "to restrain the Legislature from encroaching on the other coordinate departments, or on the rights of the people at large, or from passing laws unwise in their principle, or incorrect in their form."[2] The power to block legislation also permits presidents to shape, if not control, the legislative agenda. The threatened use of a veto itself can cause Congress to revise or abandon planned legislation. Moreover, the Constitution provides that the president can "recommend to [Congress's] Consideration such Measures as he shall judge necessary and expedient."[3] Indeed, presidents customarily propose a substantial portion of the policies that ultimately become legislation. Presidents and their subordinates identify needs and find legislative sponsors to champion the proposals. The Constitution clearly contemplates, therefore, that the president is to take part in the legislative process.

Early presidents, however, exercised the veto sparingly. Vetoes were to be deployed only in the rare case in which Congress passed a law that the chief executive thought unconstitutional or outrageous for some other reason. Washington, for instance, vetoed only two bills (the first attempted to apportion representatives), and neither Adams used the veto at all. Zachary Taylor articulated the cautious view of many early presidents when he said that the personal opinion of the president "ought not to control the action of Congress upon questions of Domestic policy."[4] Even President Warren Harding almost a century later pledged during the election of 1920 not to be a leader in legislation.[5]

President Andrew Jackson, however, recognized the veto's promise in setting national policy. He issued twelve vetoes, none of which was overridden by a fractured Congress. Most notably, he vetoed a bill rechartering the Bank of the United States. President John Tyler vetoed a subsequent effort to recharter the bank twice, sparking a wave of protests, including death threats. His subsequent veto of a tariff measure prompted Representative John Minor Botts to introduce an impeachment resolution charging the president "with the high crime and misdemeanor of withholding his assent to laws indispensable to the just operation of the government."[6] Tyler's successors became less hesitant in using the veto, whether to block legislation concerning economic policy, rights of private citizens, or Reconstruction after the Civil War.[7] By the end of the nineteenth century, President Cleveland had exercised the veto almost six hundred times. FDR issued more vetoes than any other twentieth-century president.

In stressing the importance of the president's veto power, the Supreme Court commented in *INS v. Chadha*: "The President's role in the lawmaking process also reflects the Framers' careful efforts to check whatever propensity a particular Congress might have to enact oppressive, improvident, or ill-considered measures."[8] And, the exercise of a veto tells only part of the story, for the threatened exercise of a veto molds legislation in far more contexts.[9]

The incidence of vetoes depends on not only a president's willingness to take political heat but also his relationship to Congress as a whole. In the context of a divided government, the exercise of vetoes becomes far more important politically. Truman, Eisenhower, and Reagan, for instance, vetoed major economic and labor legislation passed by hostile majorities in Congress. On some occasions, use of a veto may reflect a presidential failure to achieve goals through persuasion and politicking.

Congress, of course, can take a number of actions to counter the president's veto power. Principally, it can group so many items together in one package, called an omnibus bill, that the president may hesitate to veto the bill for fear of throwing the baby out with the bathwater. Much legislation currently runs hundreds of pages, so the risk—from a president's perspective—of vetoing one offending paragraph is that hundreds of pages of beneficial legislation may never be enacted. The problem is particularly acute with appropriations bills. If Congress ties policy to appropriations, then the government may shut down if the president wishes to veto the unrelated legislative policy initiative.

Presidents have long advocated a line item veto to counteract the power of omnibus bills, as exists in many states. In that way, presidents can pick and choose which congressional provisions to approve. They can disapprove of so-termed pork and yet retain socially beneficial legislation. Presidents such as Buchanan and Grant refused to fund all of the projects specified in omnibus appropriations bills, and FDR, Truman, Eisenhower, LBJ, and Nixon in the twentieth century followed suit.[10] In a bipartisan effort, Congress in 1996 passed the Line Item Veto Act to accord the president the power to cancel legislative items that he believed were wasteful.[11] The Supreme Court, however, ultimately struck down the act.[12] It explained that no constitutional provision authorized such veto power, and that such executive power would in effect afford presidents the power to rewrite legislation by selecting which provisions to enforce.

Overall, despite the practice of omnibus bills, vesting the veto power in the president provides the executive with a lever to pry concessions and help influence the shape of legislation.[13] As Judge McGowan remarked, "A presidential veto can moderate legislation for the national good or skew legislation toward the President's personal agenda. Each of these results is desirable. Since the veto clearly contemplates presidential participation in the difficult task of legislating, there is no good reason why the President should don blinders and ignore the full range of his policy, and even political, interests."[14] Thus, although we understandably speak as if Congress were solely responsible for legislation, the president plays a subsidiary role, shaping the laws that he subsequently must enforce and administer.

B. Degree of Centralized Control over Law Enforcement

Article II vests the president with the power to enforce and administer the laws enacted by Congress. Although the precise scope of the authority is not delineated, the language of Article II seemingly embraces some form of unitary executive by vesting "the executive Power"[15] in a president; assigning the president the responsibility to "take Care that the Laws be faithfully executed;"[16] and directing the president to appoint all principal officers of the United States.[17] The text suggests that the president must exercise at least some hierarchical control: how else can he "take care that the laws be faithfully executed"? The "take care" clause presupposes some ability to ensure that laws are enforced: as the Supreme Court has stated, "The Constitution does not leave to speculation who is to administer the laws enacted by Congress; the President, it says, 'shall take Care that the Laws be faithfully executed,' personally and through officers whom he appoints."[18] When Congress delegates authority directly to the president, therefore, Article II requires the president to execute those responsibilities faithfully, whether in the civil or criminal law context.

Indeed, the first Congress provided for military pensions "under such regulations as the President of the United States may direct,"[19] and it authorized executive officers to license "any proper person" to engage in trade with Indian tribes under "such rules and regulations as the president shall prescribe."[20] The first Congress evidently found that it could function more effectively through delegation of tasks to the president himself. Subsequent Congresses have delegated an array of additional responsibilities, including the power to impose and lift tariffs, impound funds in limited contexts, investigate crimes, and declare national emergencies. The president in those situations must be able to discharge the responsibilities delegated by Congress.

In the vast majority of contexts, however, Congress assigns duties not to the president directly but to other officials within the executive branch. Congress, particularly in the twentieth century, created a huge bureaucratic structure and lodged the responsibility in executive branch officials to administer a welter of regulatory requirements as well as to enforce crimes. Congress has created hundreds of administrative agencies, vested them with enormous and complicated authority, and staffed them with hundreds of thousands of employees. Congress has left agency heads with vast discretion. For instance, Congress has delegated the open-ended authority to set "fair and equitable" prices to agencies during wartime,[21] and to the Federal Communications Commission the power to award broadcast licenses according to "the public interest."[22] Moreover, Congress has directed officials within the executive branch to protect the public, whether from a terrorist threat abroad or from a narcotics threat within.

Congress under Article I enjoys the authority to determine the identity of the delegate who is to discharge administrative and law enforcement authority. Does Article II, whether by vesting "executive" power in the president or by requiring the president to "take Care that the Laws be faithfully executed" mandate presidential control over administrative or law enforcement authority delegated to officials other than the president? Would that presidential control help the public trace executive branch actions more directly to the president, enhancing presidential accountability?

Much of the contemporary debate over the scope of presidential control over administrative and enforcement authority turns on the advisability of a centralized or unitary executive. Many fear the dangers from too strong of an executive, but others are more concerned that a fragmented executive might become too weak to assert the nation's interests forcefully and effectively. Considerations of constitutional text, history, and judicial doctrine fail to depict a clear picture of presidential power over authority delegated by Congress to the executive branch.

The idea of a unitary executive is neither new nor radical. The Framers rejected several proposals to split the executive,[23] prompting opponents to assert that a unitary executive was a "feotus of monarchy."[24] There have been adherents of a strong centralized executive ever since, from George Washington to Theodore Roosevelt to Ronald Reagan. Arguments today for greater centralized control based on the unitary executive ideal coalesce around two virtues: accountability to the public, and the requisite initiative to exert effective leadership in administering the federal government.

According to proponents of a strong executive, the constitutional structure stresses accountability to the public in order to secure individual liberty. In this context, accountability suggests that individuals and firms should be able to trace particular governmental actions to governmental officials who are responsible in some way to the electorate, whether through direct election or other means of voicing voter disapproval. From this vantage point, Articles I, II, and III delineate powers that the branches are to exercise so as to clarify the lines of constitutional authority. The president stands responsible for all discharge of criminal and civil law enforcement, and is judged by his or her performance on election day. To be sure, voters cannot always call the president to account for one particular issue, given that they vote for a candidate based upon that candidate's entire record. And, the president may not stand for reelection. Nonetheless, the political process remains open to air misgivings about presidential leadership, and as those concerns mount in importance, they may become determinative at election time. At a minimum, even if a president does not face political repercussions, his party may.

This is not to suggest that the president must personally craft all foreign and domestic policy initiatives. Congress can create new offices pursuant to the Necessary and Proper Clause and delegate responsibility to particular government officials.[25] But, from the perspective of those advocating a unitary executive, the president must be able to superintend that policy in order not to fragment and dissipate accountability. As Alexander Hamilton noted in the Federalist Papers (No. 70),

> It often becomes impossible, amidst mutual accusations, to determine on whom the blame or the punishment of a pernicious measure . . . ought really to fall. . . . The circumstances which may have led to any national miscarriage or misfortune are sometimes so complicated that where there are a number of actors who may have had different degrees and kinds of agency . . . it may be impracticable to pronounce to whose account the evil which may have been incurred is truly chargeable.[26]

Liberty is gained to the extent that one electorally accountable official stands responsible for law implementation efforts. With a plural executive, responsibility may be shrouded, and the costs of determining who is responsible for what increase.

On the other hand, the desire for a strong unitary executive may be more an invention of twentieth-century thinkers than of the constitutional plan. Congress has a legitimate interest in determining how delegated authority should best be exercised, and that interest arguably includes the identity and independence of the officer selected to wield that power. Congress over the past two centuries has delegated authority to officers independent of the president, and the president has never exerted close control over all law enforcement nor over administration of governmental policy. Indeed, presidents did not exercise close control over federal employees when they numbered only a few hundred,[27] and presidents now cannot supervise subordinates extensively because the number has exceeded a million.[28] A strong conception of a unitary executive, therefore, runs afoul of historical precedent and Congress's discretion under Article I to provide for what it determines is the best mechanism, consistent with other constitutional restraints, of implementing congressional directives.

The following section examines the controls that the president can wield under Article II, consistent with contemporary doctrine, to ensure that the authority delegated by Congress is carried out in a way sensitive to his policy priorities. Those favoring centralized presidential control over administrative authority and hence greater presidential initiative view any restrictions on the president's authority to appoint and remove officials with suspicion. Others argue that independent officers are needed to carry out congressional instructions faithfully and to ensure that the president remain more accountable to Congress. Over time, courts have established a relatively clear framework for assessing the level of control that the president under the Constitution must be able to exercise. Courts have held that, although the president has plenary authority to exercise the functions delegated directly to him, he has only limited power to influence the authority delegated to other executive branch officials. The courts thus have rejected a strong version of a unitary executive and hence have limited the president's ability to exercise initiative.

Given the pervasive delegations by Congress, the president can maintain formal control for law administration principally through the power to appoint and remove executive officials. The appointment power is rooted in Article II, and the structure of Article II permits the president to appoint, with some restrictions, all principal officers of the United States, whether holding offices in "executive" agencies or in the so-termed independent agencies. The president's appointment authority has not generated much controversy, except when trying to ascertain the line between superior and inferior officers and in unusual situations when Congress has specified qualifications for the officeholder. Presidents have argued, and courts have agreed, that the president's removal authority is (largely) derivative of the power to appoint. Consensus has emerged that the president possesses the power to remove all principal officers. No agreement, however, has been reached either on which officers the president must be able to remove at will and, for the others, what type of reasons constitute "cause" for dismissal.

C. The President's Appointment Power

The Constitution provides that the president "shall nominate, and by and with the Advice and Consent of the Senate, shall appoint Ambassadors, other public Ministers and Consuls, Judges of the supreme Court, and all other Officers of the United States, whose Appointments are not herein otherwise provided for, and which shall be established by Law."[29] The Framers plainly rejected the option of legislative appointment, as had been practiced in some colonies,[30] and proposed (to some extent) in the "Virginia Plan" discussed at the Convention.[31] As George Reed of Delaware commented, "[T]he legislature was an improper body for appointments. Those of the state legislatures were a proof of it. The Executive being responsible would make a good choice."[32]

On the other hand, the Constitution limits the presidential power by rejecting the British precedent allowing the king to create new offices. Congress creates offices and only then is it up to presidents to nominate individuals to fill those positions. Moreover, the Constitution provides that "the Congress may by Law vest the Appointment of such inferior Officers, as they think proper, in the President alone, in the Courts of law, or in the Heads of Departments."[33] The Appointments Clause represents one of the many instances in the Constitution of blended powers: the president takes the initiative but is checked by the Senate, ensuring some measure of accountability.

The mere act of appointment and necessity of senatorial approval raise the public awareness of the nominee's policy positions. As Alexander Hamilton argued in the Federalist Papers, "[T]he circumstances attending an appointment . . . would naturally become matters of notoriety: and the public would be at no loss to determine what part had been performed by the different actors."[34] Furthermore, he noted, "The blame of a bad nomination would fall upon the president singly and absolutely. The censure of rejecting a good one would lie entirely at the door of the Senate."[35]

A president's nomination of an officer represents a critical means by which he can influence the administration of the laws. Presidents can appoint individuals who share their values and social priorities. The president's ability to take the initiative in criminal and civil law enforcement hinges in part on the presence of officers to follow his bidding. Through the power to appoint officers of the United States, presidents can serve the public by ensuring accountability for the exercise of delegated authority.

Of course, the appointment process does not guarantee that the president will always agree with the appointee's decisions. Presidential appointment of Supreme Court justices in particular demonstrates that predicting the course of an individual's career is not a science. President Eisenhower's selection of William Brennan[36] as well as the first President Bush's selection of Justice Souter highlight the risk that agents can deviate from the policy preferences of their principals.[37] Nonetheless, despite the occasional surprises, presidents, to a large extent, can ensure that the laws will be carried out in a manner sensitive to their priorities by selecting the individuals to carry out those responsibilities. It is certainly no surprise that presidents appoint an overwhelming majority of members of their own political parties to governmental offices.[38]

The Senate has used its power to reject presidential appointees both because of characteristics of the nominee[39] and hostility toward the president. The Senate rejected one of President Washington's choices for a naval position, with no explanation.[40] Washington noted that "[a]s the President has a right to nominate without assigning his reasons, so has the Senate a right to dissent without giving theirs."[41] Moreover, the Senate has rejected nominations for partisan reasons, as manifested by Washington's failure to ensure approval for his nominee, John Rutledge, for appointment to the Supreme Court in 1795.[42] The Senate blocked four of President John Tyler's cabinet choices and four of his choices for the Supreme Court.[43] Presidents Garfield and Hayes as well fought with the Senate over their nominations to executive offices.[44] The very presence of the consent power influences presidential selection: presidents realize that they must nominate individuals who can gain the Senate's trust. The battles over Supreme Court nominees during the last three decades of the twentieth century illustrate the continuing senatorial power.

The Senate, however, has never insisted on a separate power to "advise" presidents in their selection of officers. Although presidents have often solicited the views and recommendations of individual senators, they have not afforded the Senate as a whole any formal role prior to nomination.[45] Presidents have deferred, though, to preferred choices of senators from their own parties to fill certain federal positions, a practice termed senatorial courtesy.

Not every individual employed by the government must be appointed in conformance with the Appointments Clause. In the words of the Court in *Buckley,* the clause covers only those individuals who exercise "significant authority pursuant to the laws of the United States."[46] The Court had previously in *United States v. Hartwell* explained that the Appointments Clause is triggered only by appointment to an office: "An office is a public station, or employment, conferred by the appointment of government. The term embraces the ideas of tenure, duration, emolument, and duties."[47] Congress, therefore, can appoint individuals to serve on commissions that exercise advisory functions without running afoul of the Appointments Clause. In addition, it can appoint its own officers, such as Librarian of Congress or Senate Legal Counsel, as long as the powers exercised do not bind those outside the legislative branch. Moreover, consistent with *Buckley* and *Hartwell,* Congress can provide for competitive hiring under a civil service system throughout government, as long as the murky line between employee and inferior officer is followed.

The fuzzy line between officers and employees is illustrated by the status of special tax judges serving on the United States Tax Court. The special judges serve as subordinates to the regular tax judges and cannot issue a final judgment. Accordingly, they might be considered to be "employees," and thus no constitutional problem could arise as to their appointment. Nonetheless, Congress created the office by statute, and vested the power to appoint the judges in the chief judge of the United States Tax Court, which is an Article I tribunal—its judges do not have the salary and tenure protections granted judges under Article III of the Constitution. In light of that special status, the tax judges arguably could have been considered "inferior" officers within the meaning of Article II. As inferior officers, they could be appointed by the president, heads of departments, or courts of law. If the appointment did not conform to the constitutional procedure, the entire tax court system would have had to be revamped.

In a Supreme Court test questioning the propriety of the tax judges' appointment, all the justices agreed that the special tax judges exercised significant authority and thus were officers who could be appointed only pursuant to the procedures in Article II. Five justices voted to uphold the appointments because the chief judge of the U.S. Tax Court should be considered a head of a department and therefore could appoint inferior officers. Four justices—disagreeing with that assessment—would have upheld the appointment on the ground that the Tax Court should be considered a court of law and hence able to appoint inferior officers.[48] The difficulty in characterizing various congressionally created offices—the chief judge of the Tax Court as well as the special tax judges—makes application of the Appointments Clause more problematic.

The disputes that have arisen under the Appointments Clause largely concern four issues. First, courts have been vigilant in striking down congressional efforts to make appointments directly or indirectly. Second, there have been knotty cases in which courts have struggled to draw the line between superior officers, whom only the president can appoint, and inferior officers, whose appointment Congress can vest not in itself but in the courts of law or in heads of departments. Third, Congress in numerous contexts has prescribed restrictive qualifications for particular officeholders, such as political party affiliation or membership in a particular group. Although seldom the subject of litigation, at some point such congressional restrictions undermine the executive's ability to control administration of the laws. Finally, no consensus has been reached on what constitutes a congressional recess entitling a president to make an appointment without the need for the Senate's consent.

1. The Supreme Court has held any (direct) congressional usurpation of the appointment power to be particularly pernicious. In *Buckley v. Valeo* the Court considered a broad-ranging constitutional challenge to the Federal Election Campaign Act of 1971,[49] including the provision prescribing composition of the Federal Election Commission.[50] Under the act, the president appointed two members of the commission subject to confirmation by both the Senate and the House.[51] The Speaker of the House and the president pro tempore of the Senate appointed the remaining four voting members of the commission.[52] In striking down the two arrangements, the Court noted that the "debates of the Constitutional Convention, and the Federalist Papers, are replete with expressions of fear that the Legislative Branch of the National Government will aggrandize itself at the expense of the other two branches."[53] Because of the commission's enforcement and rulemaking responsibilities in regulating campaign finance, the Court concluded that its members had to be appointed in the constitutionally prescribed manner. Accordingly, the Court held that Congress could not, consistent with Article II, vest confirmation authority in the House for the two members, or vest appointment authority directly in Congress as to the remaining four.[54]

Similarly, in *Metropolitan Washington Airports Authority v. Citizens for the Abatement of Aircraft Noise* the Court struck down Congress's efforts to retain policy influence in administration of the airports surrounding Washington, D.C. Congress ceded control over the airports to a newly created authority established by a compact between the District of Columbia and State of Virginia.[55] Congress subjected authority decisions to veto by a board of review consisting of nine members of Congress purportedly serving "in their individual capacities as representatives of users of the Metropolitan Washington Airports."[56] Congress in essence appointed its own members to the board. The Court determined that the board, through its exercise of the veto power, wielded administrative authority and therefore invalidated the congressional appointment role. The Board of Review, according to the Court, was "a blueprint for extensive expansion of the legislative power."[57]

In response to the Court's decision to invalidate congressional participation on the Board of Review in the *Airports Authority* case, Congress reconstituted the board to include congressional nominees instead of members of Congress and gave the board the power to delay measures of the Airports Authority as opposed to the veto previously exercised. In resolving a subsequent challenge in court, the court of appeals set that arrangement aside as well, concluding that Congress still violated the Appointments Clause because of the congressional designation of members. It found no constitutional distinction between the power to veto and the power to delay—viewing both as executive-type authority—or between the appointment of members of Congress to the board and appointment of congressional nominees. Congress can have no direct say in the appointment power,[58] for otherwise Congress could too easily blunt executive initiative in enforcing the law.

2. The difficulty in drawing a line between superior and inferior officers is illustrated in the independent counsel case *Morrison v. Olson.*[59] Under the former Ethics in Government Act, when the attorney general determined that there were "reasonable grounds to believe that further investigation or prosecution" of a senior executive branch official "is warranted,"[60] then he or she had to apply to a special court made up of Article III judges that would appoint an independent counsel.[61] Members of Congress also could have requested that an independent counsel be appointed by the special court.[62] In either case, the special court also exercised the responsibility to define the independent counsel's jurisdiction.[63] If the independent counsel were considered a superior officer, then the act plainly contravened the president's appointment authority under Article II because the president had no direct role

in the appointment. On the other hand, if the independent counsel were considered only an inferior officer, then Congress arguably would have respected the constitutional structure by vesting that appointment in the courts of law.

As the Court in *Morrison* said, "[T]he Framers provided little guidance into where [the line between inferior and principal officers] should be drawn."[64] Two means of demarcation can be ascertained: the first by looking at the importance of the function and the second by looking at whether the officer was subordinate to another.

The Court chose the first approach. It noted that the independent counsel could perform only "certain, limited duties" under the act connected to prosecution, so that the office could not be understood to formulate government-wide policy.[65] Moreover, because the independent counsel could act only within the restricted jurisdiction provided by the special court, his or her office could be considered temporary in that the appointment covered "a single task."[66] In addition, the Court noted that the act permitted the attorney general to remove an independent counsel for "good cause," which thus made the counsel in a sense subordinate to the attorney general.[67] In light of the limited nature of the functions and the removal provisions, the Court concluded that the independent counsel was an inferior officer who could be appointed by the courts of law or heads of departments.[68]

In dissent, Justice Scalia lambasted the majority's conclusion that the independent counsel was only an inferior officer. Justice Scalia stressed the prosecutorial might wielded by the independent counsel and noted that all agency officials—not just the independent counsel—operated within limited jurisdiction. Indeed, he noted that some independent counsels served in office longer than cabinet officials. Moreover, to Justice Scalia, the fact that the act subjected the independent counsel to removal for cause could not distinguish that office from the many heads of agencies similarly removable for cause—such as SEC commissioners—who were clearly superior officers. Perhaps more important, Justice Scalia chided the majority for its ad hoc assessment of the importance of the office. Rather, he believed that the proper definition of an inferior officer is whether that officer is "*subordinate* to any officer in the Executive Branch."[69] Because Congress intended the independent counsel, as the name suggests, to act independently of all other executive branch officials, Scalia concluded that the appointments provision violated the Constitution.

The line between superior and inferior officers has yet to be drawn clearly, but *Morrison* suggests that courts will look to the importance and scope of the duties exercised by the officer. The Supreme Court, however, chose a slightly different tack in *Edmond v. United States*.[70] There, in considering whether judges on the Coast Guard Court of Criminal Appeals should be considered principal or inferior officers, the Court focused largely on the question of supervision. According to the Court, "'[I]nferior officers' are officers whose work is directed and supervised at some level by others who were appointed by presidential nomination with the advice and consent of the Senate."[71] Because the Coast Guard judges could be removed without cause by the judge advocate general of the Coast Guard,[72] and because the Court of Appeals for the Armed Forces exercised appellate review over their decisions,[73] the Court concluded that the judges were inferior officers who could be appointed by department heads.[74] There is no certainty, however, how future challenges will be resolved.

A subsidiary question arises for inferior officers: Can such officers be appointed by heads of departments in other branches? For instance, in the independent counsel case, the Court confronted the problem that the independent counsel was appointed by an entity outside the executive branch, raising the question whether Congress could direct heads of departments to appoint inferior officers within the judiciary, or whether it could direct the judges to appoint inferior officers within the agencies. No limitation on cross-branch appointments exists in the constitutional text. On the other hand, it would be unseemly, if not a violation of the separation of powers, to permit the attorney general to appoint law clerks assisting judges, or judges to appoint the deputy director of the FBI. Each branch might not be able to perform its assigned functions vigorously. In considering a challenge to the judicial appointment of election commissioners a century before, the Supreme Court had held that cross-branch appointments should be upheld as long as there was no "incongruity" between the functions normally performed by the courts and the performance of their duty to appoint in the particular context.[75] Based on that standard, the Court in the independent counsel case concluded that, in light of the conflict of interest facing the executive branch, it would be appropriate for the special court to appoint an independent counsel investigating allegations of wrongdoing by senior executive branch officials.[76]

A similar issue arises under a statute that directs courts to appoint a U.S. attorney, the chief federal prosecutor in a geographic jurisdiction, under certain conditions in the event of a vacancy.[77] First, if U.S. attorneys are considered principal officers, then the fallback appointment mechanism is invalid. Second, even if the U.S. attorneys are inferior officers, it is not clear whether judicial appointment should be considered "congruous" as discussed in the independent counsel case. On the one hand, judicial appointments may be efficient and ensure no lapse in prosecutorial activity. Moreover, presidents have the right to remove all such officers at will. On the other hand, no special conflict of interest arises necessitating independent appointment; indeed, courts can appoint U.S. attorneys only when a vacancy exists after a certain period of time. Judicial impartiality may be compromised by judicial appointment of such prosecutors; judges may defer too much to the prosecutor whom they appointed.[78] Thus, if a judicial appointment of a U.S. attorney were challenged, other courts would have to determine the congruity of the appointment.

3. A third set of issues concerns Congress's effort to specify the characteristics and terms of persons holding government offices. Some restrictions cannot be considered objectionable. Congress oftentimes prescribes qualifications for officeholders as part of its responsibility to determine how laws should be implemented. For instance, Congress has directed that international trade commissioners must have "qualifications requisite for developing expert knowledge of international trade problems."[79] Similarly, the solicitor general must be "learned in the law."[80] Indeed, the Judiciary Act passed in 1789 provided that each of the government's attorneys be "a meet person, learned in the law,"[81] and that lower court judges had to reside in the district for which they were appointed.[82]

Other restrictions, however, are more problematic. Congress has directed that some multimember commissions are to be staffed by a particular mixture of Republicans and Democrats,[83] and that some offices are to be occupied by representatives of particular interest groups such as unions.[84] Moreover, Congress has provided that some officers, such as governors of the Federal Reserve Bank, serve fourteen-year terms[85] and that the director of the FBI serve a ten-year term in office,[86] which deprives most presidents of the opportunity to make an appointment. In different ways, all of these congressional restrictions, by limiting the president's choices in filling particular positions, curtail the president's ability to shape the administration of the laws. Moreover, through such requirements, the House of Representatives gains a voice in the appointments process.

Congress presumably can impose reasonable restraints on the president's choice of whom to appoint to various offices. Those qualifications seem ancillary to Congress's unquestioned authority to create and disband agencies. In delegating authority, Congress can select which office should carry out the delegated tasks, and what the qualifications of officeholders should be. Presidents generally have acquiesced in such restrictions, but while abiding by congressional direction, they have claimed the discretion to depart from such restrictions if the situation so warrants.[87]

No judicial case has arisen testing the limits of Congress's power to restrict the president's appointment power by imposing too stringent qualifications. The lack of a test case is not surprising. If the president decides to abide by the restrictions, no justiciable case seems possible. No one can prove that the president would have selected a different official if the qualifications had been removed. Conversely, the president has little incentive to flout congressional will when the Senate can block any appointment it deems unwise. The congressional limitation, therefore, likely will not cause the requisite injury in fact to give rise to a justiciable controversy, even if unconstitutionally restricting the president's appointment authority. (A disappointed appointee can never show that the president would have appointed and the Senate would have ratified his or her appointment but for the restriction). If the president ignores the restrictions, a case conceivably could arise if the Senate then ratified the president's choice. Anyone who later claims injury in fact due to that officer's action might assert that the officer was appointed counter to legitimate congressional direction. This situation, however, has never arisen.

Using the cross-branch appointments doctrine previously discussed as an analogy, congressional restrictions upon the appointment power would be constitutional as long as the qualifications—whether political affiliation or educational pedigree—were not "incongruous" in light of the duties exercised by the officer.[88] Antinepotism requirements, for instance, may dovetail closely with the purposes for which judicial appointments are made.[89] At some point, however, Congress's restriction of options would violate the Appointments Clause, irrespective of the relevance of the qualifications imposed. For instance, if Congress directed the president to appoint as head of the IRS the leader of "an organization that represents the largest number of Internal Revenue Service employees" then only one person would fit that description. If Congress so limited the president's choice, it would be exercising a power clearly denied it under the Constitution. Congress must leave at least some room for choice to the president, and the qualifications must be germane to the delegated authority.[90] Moreover, in the prior example, the fit between the qualifications imposed and the duties to be exercised is weak—the head of an employee union may not be the right person to serve as IRS commissioner.

In order to attain political balance, Congress has directed that some offices be filled by a mixture of Republicans and Democrats. No more than three of the six commissioners on the International Trade Commission can be from the same political party.[91] Analogous restraints govern appointment of members of the National Mediation Board and the Federal Election Commission (among others).[92] In some contexts, restricting offices to individuals of particular political party affiliation would be unconstitutional. If Congress provided that a Democrat had to be appointed to an assistant attorney general position for each Republican appointed to an office with that rank, the constitutional problem would be clear: Congress cannot deprive the president of the ability to appoint individuals close to him to key policymaking positions. Otherwise, presidents could not exercise the requisite initiative in enforcing the law. Indeed, Congress's determination that no more than five of the nine judges on the Article III Court of International Trade can be from any one party[93] likely infringes too much on the president's appointment power, given the attenuated link between party affiliation and the qualities requisite for serving in the independent Article III judiciary. In general, however, the multimember commissions must be considered as exceptions, due to the mix of legislative and judicial functions they exercise.[94]

Congress's determination that some positions should be occupied by representatives of interest groups at times also may be problematic. Congress cannot accomplish its goal of representing different interests on multimember boards without imposing significant restrictions on the president's appointment authority. Consider that Congress has directed interest groups to be represented on a variety of multimember commissions, principally those that serve in an advisory capacity.[95] In the IRS Oversight Act, Congress directed the president to appoint an "individual who is a full-time Federal employee or a representative of employees" to the Oversight Board, which performs duties that cannot be considered merely advisory.[96] As long as substantial choice remains, however, the congressional restriction would pass constitutional muster: Congress can serve pluralistic values by ensuring wide-ranging membership on at least multimember agencies.

Similarly, term restrictions generally should be considered reasonable as well. Congress presumably creates fourteen-year terms for the governors of the Federal Reserve because it believes that stability is critical for the exercise of some administrative functions. That congressional restriction could well be considered consistent with the unique financial nature of the functions exercised; a long term could be "congruous" with the purposes for which the office was created. Establishing a similar term for the attorney general or secretary of agriculture, however, might deprive the president of the ability to carry out his constitutionally assigned functions, even if he could remove such officers at will.

Congress, moreover, should not be able to extend the term of an officer, at least one who is not subject to the president's plenary removal authority. Otherwise, Congress could effectively circumvent the president's Article II authority by dint of adding years to the term. Although minor alterations to a term might be appropriate in order to stagger terms of commissioners, for instance, congressional reappointments to an office can run afoul of the limitations discussed in *Buckley*. Similarly, if Congress grafted onto an existing office entirely unrelated functions, then it would in essence have bypassed the president's appointment authority.[97] By adding new duties, Congress in effect could create a new office.[98]

Finally, under the Constitution, presidents presumably lack the discretion *not* to appoint officers to a congressionally created office. No timeline can be imposed, but delay at some point becomes tantamount to a failure to nominate. Otherwise, presidents could frustrate the legislative design in creating the office in the first instance. Indeed, a district court on one occasion not so gently reminded President Nixon that he had "no discretion to decide if the Council should or should not be constituted" by failing to appoint anyone to the legislatively created entity.[99]

In short, Congress has acted in numerous contexts to restrict the president's appointment authority. Presidents largely have acquiesced. At some point, however, expansion of the current restrictions would violate the president's appointment authority, which is one of the critical means through which the president can shape administrative authority to ensure that he exercises initiative in enforcing the laws passed by Congress.

4. The Constitution also vests the president with the "Power to fill up all Vacancies that may happen during the Recess of the Senate, by granting Commissions which shall expire at the End of their next Session."[100] That power plainly extends to intersession recesses. The Framers evi-

dently tried to prevent the Senate from thwarting a president's adminis-tration of the law by going into recess when vacancies existed. Moreover, given that the Senate in the early years of the nation's history typically was in recess for half of a year, the president as a matter of efficiency needed to fill offices before the Senate returned. Even today, the Senate customarily recesses for at least six weeks between sessions. The Senate can always reject the nominee when the president resubmits the name for a more permanent appointment "at the end of [the] next Session."[101]

Congress, however, has attempted to shape the president's recess ap-pointment authority through legislation. For instance, the Federal Vacan-cies Reform Act of 1998 purports to delimit how presidents can make temporary appointments.[102] When an officer dies, resigns, or is otherwise unable to discharge his or her functions, then the president must select from (1) a Senate-confirmed first assistant to the vacant officer; (2) a Sen-ate-confirmed officer who works in an executive agency; or (3) a career civil servant who has who has worked for the agency in which the va-cancy exists for at least ninety of the past 365 days.[103] In addition, the act provides that, if the president appoints an officer in any other manner during a recess, then the vacant office must remain open.[104] This most re-cent effort to cabin the president's recess appointment power arguably cannot be reconciled with the terms and import of Article II. Congress can retaliate if it believes the president is abusing the recess appointment authority, but it cannot refuse to permit the president to make a funda-mental choice among qualified candidates.

There is some question, however, as to whether the Clause applies to vacancies that occur when the Senate has gone into a short recess before the end of a session.[105] The constitutional question is whether such an "intrasession" recess satisfies Article II's condition that there be a "Recess of the Senate." On the one hand, such recesses may last weeks, though not months, so that the president, as in the case of intersession recesses, must still act to ensure that government officials can discharge legisla-tively delegated tasks and enforce the law faithfully. On the other hand, presidents could circumvent the Senate's power to consent by making controversial appointments once the Senate announced a short recess.

Presidents largely desisted from making appointments during intrases-sion recesses until the second half of the twentieth century. President Tru-man made twenty appointments during four intrasession recesses; Presi-dent Eisenhower made nine such recess appointments; President Nixon, eight; President Carter, seventeen; and President Reagan, seventy-three.[106] Presidents have adopted a flexible interpretation of the constitutional term "recess." An attorney general opinion states that the pivotal issue is "whether in a practical sense the Senate is in session so that its advice and consent can be obtained."[107] Any recess, therefore, could satisfy the constitutional preconditions to an appointment.

President Carter's appointment of John McGarry to the Federal Election Commission after a brief Senate recess illustrates the potential for abuse. The Senate previously had failed twice to act on Carter's nomination of McGarry. Intrasession recess appointments, therefore, can circumvent the Senate's constitutional role. Not surprisingly, the Senate has protested such appointments. For instance, the Senate passed a nonbinding resolution during the Reagan presidency, providing that recess appointments should be restricted to "a formal termination of a session of the Senate, or to a recess of the Senate, protracted enough to prevent it from discharging its constitutional function of advising and consenting to executive nominations. . . . No recess appointments should be made [during intrasession recesses] of less than thirty days."[108] The president's power to appoint officers during recesses before the end of a session therefore remains highly questionable. But, because there has been scant litigation over recess appointments, the Supreme Court has yet to clarify the bounds of the president's Article II recess appointment authority.

Through the appointments power, the president can ensure that there is a group of officers who can help him discharge his constitutionally assigned tasks. Congress's efforts to restrain presidential choice can blunt presidential initiative, for there are few tasks that the president can carry out on his own. The Supreme Court has precluded Congress from appointing officers itself, but issues still arise as to the extent of congressional influence permitted under Article II.

D. The President's Removal Authority

The power to remove officers represents the other formal means by which presidents can influence their subordinates' ongoing exercise of power and ensure unified, vigorous execution of the law. The power to remove an official is emblematic of a continuing relationship between the president and subordinate officials and, in the public eye, links the conduct of those officials to the presidency itself. The removal power therefore has attributes of both enhancing presidential initiative and ensuring that the public can hold the president accountable for executive branch actions. As an incident of functional control, the removal and appointment powers work together: if the president can remove officials at will the appointment power is less critical; conversely, the removal power is more important if the president's control over appointments is less direct.

Yet, the Constitution omits any discussion of the removal authority. The respective roles of Congress and the president are not specified; accordingly, Congress and the president have jockeyed over the years to ascertain the limits of each's authority.[109] If presidents can freely remove any officer at will, then the president might be able to frustrate Congress's policy objectives. But, if the president cannot remove such officers, the prospect for presidential initiative and for making executive branch actions more transparent to the public dims. The three overall determinants of presidential power—initiative, accountability to Congress, and accountability to the public—cannot be reconciled in the removal context.

At least three dimensions of the clash exist. First, the Court's doctrine today allows the president to exercise plenary removal authority over most senior executive officers, irrespective of congressional desires. The Constitution implicitly recognizes that the president, in order to exercise close control over law administration, must be able to remove a small category of executive officials for any reason at all. Second, Congress may limit the president's ability to remove other executive officers, so that the officers can be removed only "for cause." Third, Congress itself can play no role in removing federal officers, just as it can exercise no direct say in the original appointment.

History

Soon after ratification of the Constitution, the newly elected Congress debated the organization of the new government. Congress first considered the structure of the Department of Foreign Affairs, and proposed that the secretary of foreign affairs be subject to removal by the president. Some thought that, given the Senate's role in consenting to the president's appointment of officers, the Senate should also have a role in removing all officers so appointed. Indeed, Hamilton had so opined in the Federalist Papers.[110] Other members of Congress disagreed, believing that it was up to Congress as a whole to regulate the status of the heads of agencies that it created. Still others believed that the president under the Constitution had the right to remove the officer for any reason whatsoever.[111] In a closely contested vote, Congress granted the president the plenary removal authority over the secretary of foreign affairs.[112] But, the statutory direction did not reveal which members of Congress thought that the Constitution vested that power in the president and which members assigned that right to the president as a matter of policy.

To confuse the historical issue more, Congress established the Department of the Treasury in a different way. Congress did not denominate the Treasury as an "executive department," as it had for Foreign Affairs; Congress specified in greater detail the duties that the secretary of the Treasury was to carry out than it had for the prior office; and Congress shielded one office within the Treasury, the comptroller, from presidential direction.[113] Congress evidently linked that department much more closely to Congress than to the president. Congress also insulated the head of the Post Office three years later from close presidential direction and control.[114] In any event, John Adams was the first president to exercise the removal authority, dismissing Secretary of State Timothy Pickering in 1800.[115]

When creating the Second Bank of the United States some twenty years later, Congress conferred even greater independence on that federal instrumentality. Although some can quibble whether the bank should be considered an agency, Congress permitted the president to appoint (and remove) only five of the bank's twenty-five directors. Despite the independence, directors of the bank made critical decisions of monetary policy that bound the nation. Accordingly, the president might not have been able to take vigorous steps in adjusting national monetary policy as conditions warranted. And, during this same period, Congress vested considerable authority in state officials to enforce federal law, and those state officials remained immune from the reach of the president's appointment and removal authority.[116]

History does not reveal any clear clues as to the constitutional scope of the president's removal authority. Tradition suggests that presidents were to exercise removal authority, but it also suggests that Congress could immunize some important executive officials from his removal authority.

1. The Constitutional Requirement to Vest a Degree of Removal Authority in the President

Despite the fact that the Constitution does not explicitly authorize the president to remove any officers, the Supreme Court has long recognized that the president should be able to remove all principal officials. As the Court noted in *Myers* at the outset of the twentieth century, "Article II grants to the President the executive power of the Government, the power of appointment and removal of executive officers—a conclusion confirmed by his obligation to take care that the laws be faithfully executed."[117] Although Congress at times might have good reasons to insulate particular executive officials from the president's removal authority, the president must have the power to remove such officers at least if the officers are incompetent or neglectful of their duties. The president cannot superintend administration of the law effectively if he cannot, as a last resort, threaten to discharge officials. Government officials, like the rest of us, try to please those who control their tenure in office.

Thus, even when Congress in creating an office does not specify how the officeholder is to be removed, the president may exercise the authority to remove that officer. We have followed Congress's decision of 1789 in creating a Department of Foreign Affairs to determine that presidents must have the power to discharge principal officers. The scope of that removal authority, however, has remained in dispute, and much of the contemporary debate turns on when Congress can limit the president's removal authority to only specified contexts.

With respect to inferior officers, however, the president does not need to wield the removal authority himself. Rather, the appointing authority—the heads of departments or the courts of law—may exercise the discretion to remove the official. As the Supreme Court summarized, "[W]hen Congress, by law, vests the appointment of inferior officers in the heads of departments, it may limit and restrict the power of removal."[118] The president's control over administration of the laws may not be impaired even if he personally cannot fire individuals serving under officials whom he can discharge. The president can manage indirectly through officials whom he can control.

2. THE PRESIDENT'S PLENARY REMOVAL AUTHORITY

Presidents have long argued that, in order to exercise their authority effectively, they must be able to remove at will any executive officer exercising significant authority under the laws of the United States, and that all inferior officers exercising significant authority must be subject to plenary removal by a principal officer, if not the president himself. Although President John Adams kept Washington's cabinet intact, Thomas Jefferson removed many Federalist officials from office in order to create greater policy uniformity within his government.[119] Congress can vest the president with the power to remove officers at will, but can Congress limit the president's removal authority if it deems such restrictions in the public interest?

Presidents have asserted that the power to remove officers for congressionally specified reasons such as "good cause" did not sufficiently protect their interests for a number of reasons. First, to the extent good cause is limited to neglect of duties or misconduct, then subordinate officers can refuse to abide by the president's priorities or programs and escape discipline. Presidents have argued that they cannot accomplish their constitutionally assigned tasks if subordinate officials can ignore any presidential directive they find displeasing. Second, the "good cause" limitation suggests the availability of judicial review to test whether the discharge was in fact for good cause. That review can undermine the needed control wielded by the chief executive; judges should not be able to probe whether the reasons proffered by the president were pretextual and, even if not, whether they satisfied the good cause standard. For the past two centuries, presidents and Congress have tussled over Congress's ability to shield particular officers from at-will discharge. Indeed, the very definition today of the so-termed independent agencies turns on whether the head of the agency is "independent" of the president's plenary removal authority and therefore cannot be removed from office but for cause.

Debate over this fundamental principle almost led to the removal of President Andrew Johnson from office. The Reconstruction Congress became more and more enraged at the conciliatory gestures that Johnson showed to the South. It passed the Tenure of Office Act that forbade Johnson from dismissing any executive official without the consent of the Senate.[120] Johnson vetoed the measure, but the House and Senate overrode the veto with the necessary two-thirds votes. Although not the first Congress to attempt to limit the president's removal power, the Reconstruction Congress used this lever aggressively, presumably wishing to prevent the Democrat Johnson from firing Republican officeholders. President Johnson nonetheless believed the restriction unconstitutional and fired Secretary of War Edwin Stanton, who had been closely allied with the Radicals, without complying with the statute's terms.[121] Johnson asserted that having taken his oath of office, he could not comply with a law he deemed unconstitutional, and he asserted that the discharge could expedite resolution of the question by the Supreme Court.[122]

Johnson's discharge of Stanton was the event for which many in Congress had waited. The House impeached the president for flouting the congressional restriction. Debate was intense. His foes came within one vote of convicting him in the Senate, the closest that any president has ever come to removal from office through a vote in the Senate. Johnson's opponents may have seized upon the discharge of Stanton as a pretext, but the episode reveals a deep tension between Congress and the president over presidential power to remove senior officers. Disputes erupted as well during the administrations of Garfield, Hayes, and Cleveland.[123] President Cleveland, for instance, discharged the U.S. attorney from Alabama and refused Congress's request for information as to what justified the dismissal. The Senate passed a resolution condemning Cleveland's refusal to cooperate, and he responded that those in the Senate have no right "to sit in judgment upon the exercise of my exclusive discretion and executive function, for which I am solely responsible to the people."[124]

Three Supreme Court cases in the twentieth century highlight the continuing struggle for power between Congress and the President. The cases affirm President Johnson's view in vetoing and flouting the Tenure of Office Act, but as a group they also refute presidential claims for expansive removal authority. Hopes for presidential initiative have been tempered by concern that presidents remain accountable to congressional policymaking. As a consequence, the public cannot hold presidents as accountable for the actions of their subordinates.

First, in *Myers v. United States* the Supreme Court addressed whether the president could exercise plenary removal authority over a postmaster.[125] In 1876 Congress had provided that "[p]ostmasters of the first, second, and third classes shall be appointed and may be removed by the President with the advice and consent of the Senate."[126] As in the Tenure of Office Act, Congress conditioned the president's removal authority on consent of the Senate. The Supreme Court upheld the president's action: several paths were plausible. For instance, it might have held that Congress could not itself participate in removal of a federal official, but that Congress could limit the president's power by placing "good cause" restrictions on the dismissal or subjecting the dismissal to judicial review.

Chief Justice (and former president) Taft, however, used the occasion to paint a picture of expansive executive authority under Article II. According to the Court in a lengthy opinion, the president must be able to fire at will all officers exercising administrative authority:

The ordinary duties of officers prescribed by statute come under the general administrative control of the President by virtue of the general grant to him of the executive power, and he may properly supervise and guide their construction of the statutes under which they act in order to secure the unitary and uniform execution of the laws which Article II of the Constitution evidently contemplated. . . .[127]

The opinion continued that, in light of the president's "own constitutional duty of seeing that the laws be faithfully executed," the president must be able to remove an officer "on the ground that the discretion regularly entrusted to that officer by statute has not been on the whole intelligently or wisely exercised."[128] Viewed another way, "Each head of a department is and must be the President's alter ego in the matters of that department where the President is required by law to exercise authority."[129] Because the postmaster administered the laws passed by Congress, the Court upheld the postmaster's discharge.[130]

Less than ten years later, the Supreme Court did a partial about-face in passing on the propriety of President Franklin Roosevelt's discharge of William E. Humphrey as a federal trade commissioner.[131] Shortly after taking office, Roosevelt fired Humphrey. Although Roosevelt arguably could have fired Humphrey for incompetence and misconduct given Humphrey's record, Roosevelt chose to ground the discharge on the fact that the two of them did not "go along together on either policies or the administering of the Federal Trade Commission."[132] The statute permitted the president to remove a sitting commissioner only for "inefficiency, neglect of duty, or malfeasance in office."[133]

In a short opinion, *Humphrey's Executor v. United States,* the Court cut back on former Chief Justice Taft's reasoning in *Myers.* In the Court's view, the *Myers* reasoning made sense only when an officer exercised purely "executive" duties, such as the postmaster in question. If the officer exercised a mixture of executive and either legislative or judicial functions, according to the Court, then Congress could shield that officer from the president's plenary removal authority. In contrast to the postmaster, the "Federal Trade Commission is an administrative body created by Congress to carry into effect . . . specified duties as a legislative or as a judicial aid. Such a body cannot in any proper sense be characterized as an arm or an eye of the executive."[134] Agencies issuing rules acted in a legislative-type capacity, and agencies presiding over adjudications acted in a judicial-type capacity. Given that so many officials engage in either rulemaking or adjudication, the Court's decision curtailed the breadth of *Myers* significantly. Indeed, under the reasoning in *Humphrey's Executor,* Congress could always shield an officer from removal by providing that the officer exercise some quasi-legislative or quasi-judicial duties.

Despite *Humphrey's Executor,* President Reagan pushed for greater executive authority over agency heads in many respects, including the power to remove them at will. He believed that centralization and coordination of executive affairs was impossible without the plenary power to remove officials, much as former President Taft had argued in the *Myers* decision. Given the close link between administration policy and agency rules in particular, he argued that *Humphrey's Executor* should be revisited, and some lower courts were supportive. He authorized attorneys in the Justice Department to make broader arguments in support of Article II authority in a variety of contexts that, if accepted, would have threatened the continued existence of independent agencies.

The issue came to a head in the independent counsel case *Morrison v. Olson.*[135] Congress in creating the Office of Independent Counsel provided that the independent counsel could be removed by the attorney general only for cause, and subjected that determination to judicial review. President Reagan argued that such independence flew in the face not only of Article II's grant of executive power over prosecution but also of the Court's opinion in *Humphrey's Executor,* which seemingly had held that the president should be able to wield plenary removal authority over all officers exercising purely executive functions. And, as a functional matter, given the independent counsel's importance in determining whom to subpoena and what evidence to collect, control was important to ensure some accountability to the public. Historically, all had viewed prosecution as a quintessentially executive function, and thus if the president could fire the postmaster general, he (or his delegate, the attorney general) should be able to fire the independent counsel for any reason whatsoever. Politics might counsel caution, as President Nixon learned when his discharge of the special prosecutor, Archibald Cox, during the Watergate investigation, sparked a firestorm in the press and placed added pressure on his administration.[136] But any reluctance to fire an executive official, according to President Reagan, should stem from similar political constraints as opposed to the Constitution.

In response, the Court abandoned the lines drawn in *Humphrey's Executor* to adopt a more general balancing test. The question, according to the Court, was not whether the officer exercised executive- or legislative-type duties but, rather, whether in light of the removal provisions, the president remained capable of exercising his constitutionally assigned functions—whether the president retained "sufficient control over the independent counsel to ensure that the President be able to perform his constitutionally assigned duties."[137] Indeed, the Court acknowledged that "[t]here is no real dispute that the functions performed by the independent counsel are 'executive' in the sense that they are law enforcement functions that typically have been undertaken by officials within the Executive Branch."[138] In applying the test, the Court noted that the independent counsel's jurisdiction was narrow, its impact upon government-wide policy modest, and that the attorney general could remove the official for any misconduct.

> Notwithstanding the fact that the counsel is to some degree "independent" and free from executive supervision to a greater extent than other federal prosecutors, in our view these features of the Act give the Executive Branch sufficient control over the independent counsel to ensure that the President is able to perform his constitutionally assigned duties.[139]

In subsequent cases, therefore, Congress can shield executive officials from removal if it has a good enough reason and if the president remains capable of discharging his constitutionally assigned duties. Congressional insertion of a "good cause" restriction on removal of the attorney general would be suspect because, even though Congress might want to ensure that the attorney general provide unbiased legal advice, the president needs to rely closely upon the attorney general in discharging his constitutional responsibilities. Restriction placed on the removal of the head of the Environmental Protection Agency, however, would likely be constitutional if Congress should so choose. The Court has decided that the Constitution does not enshrine centralization of executive authority in a president as a preeminent value. Rather, the presidential interest in centralizing authority must be accommodated with Congress's policy-making interest in determining the degree of independence that officers should possess in order to discharge administrative duties effectively. *Morrison v. Olson* embraces the role of independent agencies, even those discharging what historically have been considered purely executive duties.

Congress's bill to create an IRS Oversight Board triggered an unusual question of whether Congress can direct some private entity to share in the removal authority. Under the proposed bill, once a representative of the Internal Revenue Service employees was terminated from "membership, or other affiliation with the organization" he or she would be removed from the Oversight Board.[140] Thus, although the president enjoyed the plenary authority to remove the representative, that authority was shared in part with the employee organization itself. Should the organization rescind the representative's membership or other affiliation with the organization, then he or she would have been removed from office.

Although Congress eliminated the disputed provision, the issue raised is whether Congress can vest some removal authority in a private group outside the president's control. Each exercise of delegated authority by the IRS Oversight Board would have been in part overseen by the employee group. And, the authority of the board extended well beyond the interests of the employee group. A private group's exercise of the removal authority affords it too much say in implementation of the laws governing the entire nation. As the Court stated in *Humphrey's Executor,* "[I]t is quite evident that one who holds his office only during the pleasure of another, cannot be depended upon to maintain an attitude of independence against the latter's will."[141]

As an analogy, if Congress determined that the solicitor general must be a member of the American Bar Association, and that the solicitor general may be removed from office if the ABA canceled the solicitor general's membership, a similar constitutional difficulty would arise. A private group would have excessive influence over the solicitor general's actions. The solicitor general would recognize that any step taken at odds with official ABA positions could jeopardize his tenure in office. The fact that the president also could exercise removal authority would not be a sufficient safeguard, for any successor in office would owe allegiance to the private group or face dismissal. The solicitor general would have to please two masters, and the continuing loyalty to the private group undermines the presidential control that the Supreme Court found essential in *Morrison.* Exercise of the removal authority by anyone other than the president, therefore, cannot easily be squared with our system of separated powers.

In short, the president must be able to exercise plenary removal authority over all principal officers when most critical to discharging his constitutionally assigned functions and exercising initiative in law enforcement. The power to remove enhances the president's accountability to the public for his administration's actions, while limiting congressional influence. The category of such officers presumably extends to his cabinet, but perhaps not much beyond. The president must be able to remove all other principal officers at least for cause, and inferior officers must be removable by the president or appointing authority for cause as well. Congress, however, if it so chooses, can vest the president with greater removal authority.

The remaining pivotal issue is how to define the "good cause" requisite for removing most executive branch officials. A good cause standard prevents a president from firing an official for arbitrary or vindictive reasons, and forces disclosure of the motivations. The president must be able to articulate legitimate grounds justifying the discharge. Personal dislike will not do.

If the concept of "good cause" is capacious enough to include disagreements with the executive's priorities or policies, however, then much of the debate over the removal provision comes to very little—the power to remove for cause would still constitute a formidable tool to ensure centralization and coordination of overall governmental authority. Presidents could exact allegiance to their programs by threatening to discharge any official who blocks their progress. To be sure, judicial review might prompt greater caution, but presidents nonetheless would be on strong ground in discharging officials who disagree with their agendas, much as President Franklin Roosevelt had attempted with the FTC commissioner.

Recent courts, however, have suggested that the "good cause" needed for removal tracks the traditional categories of neglect of duties or misconduct. Disagreement over policies and procedures would not be a sufficient reason to remove an officer. Neither would most forms of insubordination. Accordingly, good cause currently remains a significant barrier to close presidential control, ensuring continued existence of independent agencies. Few cases, however, have arisen, and thus elaboration of what constitutes sufficient neglect of duties or incompetence to give rise to cause for dismissal must await future developments.

3. Congressional Role in Removal

As President Johnson's attempted veto of the Tenure of Office Act and the Court's decision in *Myers* suggest, Congress itself cannot exercise any formal role in removing executive branch officials. Once Congress delegates authority, all such formal supervision must be exercised by the president or heads of departments. Congress can hold hearings, modify the delegation, or even abolish an office, but it cannot initiate any steps to remove an executive officer. Otherwise, Congress would act as both the lawmaker and law enforcer.

The critical case at the end of the twentieth century is *Bowsher v. Synar*.[142] Under the Gramm-Rudman-Hollings Act, Congress authorized the comptroller general, based upon economic forecasts proposed by the Office of Management and Budget (OMB) and the Congressional Budget Office, to specify the spending reductions necessary to keep the budget deficit within the limits set by Congress.[143] The act directed the president then to issue a sequestration order in a manner "consistent with the [comptroller general's] report in all respects."[144] If the comptroller general were considered an executive branch official, the delegation would be consistent with the Constitution as long as the president could remove the official for cause.

The Court, however, concluded that the comptroller general should be considered an officer of the legislative branch and therefore could not perform the budget-cutting functions under the act. To the Court, the key factor lay in Congress's prior decision to make the officer removable at its instigation for any one of several reasons. According to the Court, "Congress cannot reserve for itself the power of removal of an officer charged with the execution of the laws,"[145] which included the comptroller general's administrative duties under the act. As the Court noted, "Once an officer is appointed, it is only the authority that can remove him . . . that he must fear and, in the performance of his functions, obey."[146] Furthermore, the majority made it clear that "once Congress makes its choice in enacting legislation, its participation [and those of its agents] ends. Congress can thereafter control the execution of its enactments only indirectly—by passing new legislation."[147] Because the "structure of the Constitution does not permit Congress to execute the laws; it follows that Congress cannot grant to an officer under its control what it does not possess."[148] Although the comptroller general could have exercised the budget-cutting duties if the Court excised the offending congressional removal provision, the Court concluded that Congress and not the courts should determine the comptroller general's future status. Direct congressional involvement in removal of officers muddies the lines of authority; officers should be subject to presidential supervision instead to ensure that agency action can be traced to the president and the president held accountable by the people for the exercise of authority by executive branch officials.

In addition to the appointment and removal authority, presidents can, of course, rely on a host of political means to exert authority. They can bank on party or personal loyalty, or the prestige of the office. A telephone call or visit from an influential donor may do the trick. Presidents, moreover, may be able to exact fealty by pledging some other benefit to the officeholder. Not surprisingly, many presidents successfully have enlisted independent officers in their policy initiatives. Conversely, some presidents will be unable to coordinate agency efforts even with the power to remove. They may not have the requisite political or personal skills. At a minimum, the exercise of the removal power exacts a potentially high political cost. Presidents have desisted from discharging officials for fear of public backlash. The formal power to remove, therefore, tells only part of the story.

Nonetheless, in the absence of the powers to appoint and remove officers, many presidential efforts to coordinate agency power would fail. Those two formal means remain an essential part of the tool kit that presidents can use to persuade officers to follow the presidentially preferred path and thereby enable the president to exercise initiative in administering the laws passed by Congress. Under contemporary constitutional doctrine, presidents may use the appointment and removal powers to help ensure coordinated executive branch policy, but each means of control is far from completely effective, and the Supreme Court has imposed limits to prevent greater control, which has undermined, to a certain extent, the public's ability to hold the president accountable for actions of executive branch officials.

E. Presidential Controls under Article II over Rulemaking and Litigation

To this point, this book has examined how the president pursues policy priorities through subordinate officials in the executive branch. He can control their actions principally through the formal powers of appointment and removal, which are only crude tools to ensure coordination of policy, particularly in light of the congressional restrictions discussed above.

To ensure greater initiative in administering the law, presidents increasingly have sought to coordinate agency rulemaking and litigation. Through formal and informal rulemaking, agencies issue the thousands of rules each year that control individual and firms' conduct across the nation. Agency rules govern almost every nook and cranny of our existence, including grazing fees, safety in the workplace, sentencing guidelines, and regulation of telecommunications. And, through litigation, agencies help formulate doctrines that courts adopt to set precedents for future cases. Although presidents can shape the exercise of power by heads of "executive" agencies far more than "independent" agencies, they can attempt to influence the exercise of delegated authority by all agency heads. Judicial analysis in the few cases that have arisen has not yielded any clear understanding of what steps the president can take to shape subordinates' exercise of administrative power.

1. RULEMAKING

Presidents have long attempted to coordinate executive branch rulemaking in a variety of ways. They have suggested regulatory priorities, requested agencies to pursue specific tasks, and at times even directed agencies to adopt particular positions in areas of great political visibility. In a former era with little congressional delegation and few agencies, the need to coordinate agency rulemaking was not pressing. Agencies engaged in minimal policymaking. What agency business there was could be overseen by other methods. For instance, Presidents Washington and Jefferson apparently required each agency head to circulate correspondence to the president's office prior to mailing. Jefferson noted that Washington, by reviewing all correspondence, "was always in accurate possession of all facts and proceedings in every part of the Union, and to whatsoever department they related; he formed a central point for the different branches; preserved an unity of object and action among them."[149] No White House staff existed until after the Civil War.

As the central government expanded in the late nineteenth century, the need for coordination became more acute. Agencies issued more and more rules in setting policy within their jurisdictions. Party or personal loyalty did not guarantee effective control over rulemaking. For instance, President Theodore Roosevelt created a commission in 1903 to recommend ways to coordinate the scientific work accomplished by federal agencies.[150] Although Congress declined to act on its recommendations,

Roosevelt persevered and established another commission with a broader scope to study administrative reforms more generally. Congress even more adamantly refused to act, complaining of the executive's efforts to wrest "an authority previously the exclusive and unchallenged domain of Congress."[151] Congress first acquiesced in the need for greater executive centralization in passing the Budget and Accounting Act in 1921,[152] creating the office of comptroller general, and empowering the president to submit an annual budget to Congress. But, control over rulemaking remained elusive.

With the increase in broad delegations during the New Deal and the proliferation of agencies, the challenges of coordination became much more acute. Both FDR and Truman suggested numerous steps to streamline and reorganize the executive branch, and Congress agreed to many of the recommendations. Agencies through rulemaking made extensive law, and presidents intent on tackling social problems wished to exert more influence on the burgeoning rulemaking. Presidential influence promised greater coordination among agencies and forged a closer link in the public's eye between the president and agency rulemaking. Indeed, given the staggering hundreds of billions of dollars spent on regulation each year, any effort by a president to distance himself from significant agency rules would be curious, if not unprincipled.

Absent coordination, agency rules may suffer from several drawbacks. They may be duplicative, conflict with one another, or undercut other agencies' rules. In addition, the lack of coordination may impair efficiency; one agency may not know of another's innovative program, or may miss the opportunity to coordinate buying or selling programs with other agencies. Moreover, to the extent that agency rules are the product of interest-group pressure, a second look from a president or other coordinating entity in the executive branch might dampen the effectiveness of such lobbying. Further, each agency may have parochial interests in fashioning rules that are not shared with the public at large. A centralized clearinghouse can make sure that rules of all agencies are harmonized to the extent possible.

Congress, of course, may provide for centralized review of agency rulemaking. However, in the absence of such a mechanism, what source of authority can presidents turn to if Congress specifically delegates the power to promulgate rules to the secretary of transportation or the administrator of the Environmental Protection Agency, and not to the president? Indeed, as in other contexts, Congress may wish to insulate the agency from presidential influence in shaping rules to minimize the potential for a conflict of interest. Can the president claim authority under Article II to take steps to ensure centralization of administrative authority?

a. The Executive Order Mechanism Of all contemporary methods used to coordinate agency rulemaking, the executive order has been the most important. Although some executive orders stem from authority delegated by Congress, most arise from the president's inherent authority under Article II to manage the executive branch. As the D.C. Circuit recently explained: "Article II, § 1 of the Constitution provides that the 'executive Power shall be vested in a President of the United States of America.' . . . [T]he President's power necessarily encompasses 'general administrative control of those executing the laws' throughout the Executive Branch of government, of which he is the head. . . . His faithful execution of the laws enacted by the Congress . . . ordinarily allows and frequently requires the President to provide guidance and supervision to his subordinates."[153]

Executive orders touch on issues ranging from security clearances for all government employees[154] to smoking in the workplace.[155] In the twentieth century, presidents began to use executive orders to rein in and improve the rulemaking of all executive branch agencies. As early as 1909, William Howard Taft pursuant to Executive Order No. 1142 prohibited agency officials from applying directly to Congress for funding without first obtaining consent from cabinet secretaries.[156]

Executive orders should not be considered "law" in the conventional sense. Most executive orders, at least those issued through the inherent managerial authority of the president, do not have the status of a binding rule or regulation. A violation of an executive order, therefore, cannot lead to a legal sanction such as a fine or prison sentence. Violations of executive orders can lead to repercussions in the agencies, however, for presidents may be able to discipline agency heads who ignore their terms. Moreover, because most executive orders do not have the status of "law," private parties cannot sue to force compliance with their terms. For instance, when the secretary of the interior under President Carter failed to prepare a formal economic and inflationary impact analysis as required under Exec. Order No. 11,821[157] in issuing rules regulating mining, mining companies seized upon that failure as a basis to stop the rules. The Court of Appeals for the District of Columbia held that the executive order was unenforceable in court: the executive order "was intended primarily as a managerial tool for implementing the President's personal economic policies and not as a legal framework enforceable by private civil action."[158] Most executive orders are enforceable only to the extent the president so desires. Nonetheless, through executive orders, presidents can engage in limited policymaking outside the context of a particular delegation.

No one disputes that presidents may issue many such executive orders.[159] For instance, an order that all departments celebrate the role of immigrants in contributing to our nation's success would not be problematic. President George W. Bush's creation of an Office of Homeland Security by executive order caused barely a ripple.[160] Yet, presidents through executive orders may undermine congressional policy. An executive order that flatly contradicts a congressional directive should not be enforceable. As an example, if Congress directs the EPA to preserve all endangered species, and the president directs all agencies to consider cost in promulgating rules affecting endangered species, the order constitutionally could not be applied. Similarly, presidents cannot, by executive order, prevent private parties from utilizing a seniority system that is otherwise lawful under statute.[161]

Under Executive Order No. 12,952,[162] President Clinton provided that contracting agencies of the government were not to contract with employers that permanently replace lawfully striking employees. The National Labor Relations Act,[163] however, permits employers to replace striking workers with permanent employees. Accordingly, a court of appeals invalidated the order as "pre-empted by the NLRA which guarantees the right to hire permanent replacements."[164]

Consider as well the district court's decision in *Environmental Defense Fund v. Thomas*.[165] There, an environmental organization and two individuals filed suit to force the EPA to promulgate regulations under the Resource Conservation and Recovery Act[166] covering underground tanks as required under the act. The EPA asked for an extension from a congressional deadline, in part so that OMB could conduct its internal review under the executive order. The court held that "OMB has no authority to use its regulatory review under EO 12991 to delay promulgation of EPA regulations . . . beyond the date of a statutory deadline. . . . [D]eclaratory relief is necessary to ensure compliance with the clearly expressed will of Congress."[167]

Yet, there remains a large middle range of cases in which the power of the president to influence rulemaking that Congress delegated to heads of agencies is still in dispute. For instance, Presidents Nixon and Ford created a Quality of Life review process, entitling agencies to comment on proposed rules and regulations of other agencies. In case of a conflict between two agencies, the newly created Office of Management and Budget would convene a meeting to attempt to iron out the differences. President Ford's Executive Order No. 11,821,[168] as mentioned previously, required all agencies to prepare Economic Impact Statements to submit to the Council on Wage and Price Stability. President Carter's Executive Order No. 12,044[169] repealed his predecessor's order and sought to increase public participation in the rulemaking process through advance notice, more efforts to contact known interested parties, and a requirement for public hearings. The foregoing three examples highlight ways in which presidents can influence rulemaking short of any formal role. Critics challenged the presidential initiatives, but most commentators defended the efforts to instill greater coordination within the executive branch.

The regulatory efforts of the Nixon, Ford, and Carter administrations to coordinate rulemaking efforts set the stage for President Reagan's more ambitious agenda. Under Executive Order No. 12,291[170] and then 12,498,[171] President Reagan provided for centralized controls over all major agency rulemakings. Under the orders, each agency had to ensure that the delineated benefits in all rules exceeded their costs. The orders targeted rules with a financial impact exceeding a particular monetary threshold, such as those addressing workplace safety, environmental protection, and health care. Agencies prepared a Regulatory Impact Analysis and submitted proposed rules to OMB for its independent study and comment prior to publication. After study, OMB would then present the agency head with comments and suggestions for revision, and the order purported to give OMB the power to stop publication of any rule until the agency conducted an appropriate study of the regulatory impact. During President Reagan's tenure, roughly eighty-five rules a year were either withdrawn by agencies during the review process or returned for more analysis by OMB.

Under Executive Order No. 12,498, agencies prior to the formal rulemaking process shared with OMB a draft regulatory program each year sketching the planned significant regulatory steps contemplated. This "early warning" requirement permitted OMB additional time within which to study proposed rules. The orders, taken together, conferred substantial authority on OMB, an arm of the presidency, to shape the content of rules passed. Each agency, however, retained its statutory authority to issue the final regulation. Neither President Reagan nor his successor President Bush ever applied the order to major rules of independent agencies.

Nevertheless, the impact of the executive orders was considerable. First, compliance with the orders necessitated delay.[172] To the extent that dispatch was critical to the agency agenda, adhering to the orders undermined that objective. Indeed, on several occasions, agencies failed to meet statutory deadlines for issuing rules in part because of their efforts to comply with the orders.[173] Second, the threat of OMB review and the concomitant delay forced agencies, and was intended to force agencies, to change the way they issued rules. The Department of Labor, for instance, changed its proposed rule regulating emissions of cotton dust because of intense lobbying by OMB.[174] OMB persuaded the Federal Aviation Agency (FAA) to become more efficient in allocating landing slots at airports.[175] Agencies mimicked the OMB review process within their own organizations, affording greater priority to cost-benefit analysis of the type favored by OMB overseers. OMB review therefore had a considerable impact on the ultimate rules promulgated by an agency. Third, OMB participation complicated judicial review. Because OMB declined to release summaries of oral contacts with the agencies, judges could not isolate political influence. At least one court ordered OMB to release a list of all *ex parte* contacts despite the argument that forcing disclosure of the contacts would undermine the president's ability to manage the executive branch.[176]

President Clinton, perhaps surprisingly, not only left the controversial order intact but in fact increased its scope under Executive Order No. 12,866,[177] covering for the first time independent agencies within its ambit. The order mandated that regulations with a projected impact of $100 million on the economy[178] be forwarded to OMB for analysis prior to promulgation.[179] The order counseled agencies to identify the problems that they intended to address, consider alternative ways to meet their regulatory goals, assess the costs and benefits of the intended regulation, and base their ultimate decision on "the best reasonably obtainable scientific, technical, economic, and other information concerning the need for, and consequences of, the intended regulation."[180] The order softened the cost-benefit imperative of its predecessors. Moreover, the order required agencies at the beginning of the year to forward a regulatory plan to OMB to summarize each planned significant regulatory action, including alternatives considered and projected costs and benefits.[181] All significant regulations, in other words, were to be justified on a cost-benefit basis, but other values could have been taken into account in defending the need for regulation.

Upon receipt of agency plans, OMB was to "provide meaningful guidance and oversight so that each agency's regulatory actions are consistent with applicable law, the President's priorities, and the principles set forth in this Executive Order."[182] The order further provided that review generally must be completed within ninety days to avoid the delay that arguably had plagued OMB review under the prior schemes.[183] OMB also provided written explanation if it returned any rule for greater analysis to the agency.[184] The order also directed that any continuing dispute between OMB and the agency be resolved pursuant to a White House review process.[185] The order in addition contemplated a review process under which agencies must review existing regulations as well as ensure that regulations on the books remain cost effective.[186]

The Clinton order tightened presidential control over agencies in two respects. First, with respect to the so-termed executive agencies, the order set up a formal process to resolve disputes between agencies and OMB with the president as final arbiter.[187] Although President Clinton did not exercise this prerogative significantly, the provision stands as a testament to his view of the president's control over rulemaking and the importance of executive initiative in law administration. Second, for the first time, the order placed independent agencies within the framework of regulatory review. Although the order exempted independent agencies from the dispute-resolution aspects of the order, it directed independent agencies to comply with the planning aspects of the order; such agencies had to submit their regulatory agendas to the president for comment. The rules promulgated by independent agencies may conflict with rules of the executive agencies, and independent agencies as well can learn from OMB of the successes and failures of prior agency efforts in related contexts.[188] President George W. Bush has followed his predecessor's lead.[189]

It remains unclear, however, whether the president could discharge the head of an independent agency for failing to comply with an executive order. Such a refusal might not constitute the cause needed to justify the removal, given Congress's Article I power to channel a president's exercise of management authority in many ways.[190] Congress's creation of independent agencies sends a strong signal that presidents should steer clear of interfering too much in those agencies' implementation of the laws. Congress's power to determine the identity of the delegate exercising specific powers trumps the president's inherent authority. The president should not be able to change the priorities or timetable under which the Securities and Exchange Commission (SEC) issues rules. Neither should the president be able to disturb the Federal Reserve Board's decisions setting monetary policy. Under current doctrine, therefore, presidents likely cannot discharge the head of an independent agency for refusing to adhere to an executive order.

The same inference, however, cannot be drawn from delegation of the authority to the Department of Treasury or other executive agencies. Congress has never forbidden the president to influence the rulemaking of executive agencies. Absent a specific congressional directive prohibiting the president from coordinating the Treasury's functions with other agencies, presidential initiative in the area should be preserved. Viewed from that perspective, Executive Order Nos. 12,291 and 12,866 are only problematic as applied to independent agencies, and even then they should be permitted as strong advice. Indeed, Article II vests in the president the right to demand opinions from the departments—"[H]e may require the Opinion, in writing, of the principal Officer in each of the executive Departments, upon any Subject relating to the Duties of their respective Offices"[191]—so any reporting requirements should be beyond constitutional reproach. Only when Congress orders the President not to interfere in any way with an agency's priorities or timetables would there be a clash, and Congress certainly cannot forbid a president from giving friendly advice.

Presidents, at times, however, have attempted to leverage an advisory into a more authoritative role over rulemaking. President Clinton, for instance, directed agency heads to issue particular rules, despite the lack of any statutory authorization. As one example, he directed the secretary of labor to issue a proposed regulation on the use of unemployment insurance for paid family leave. Through such commands, presidents can shape agency rulemaking directly even though it remains the agency head's formal responsibility to issue the rule. Agency heads can ignore the direction but at their political peril. Presidents can dismiss heads of executive agencies at will, and they can retaliate in other ways against the heads of independent agencies.[192] President Bush has followed his predecessor's aggressive management style.[193]

In sum, presidents enjoy the discretion under Article II—at least in the absence of congressional indication to the contrary—to mold the rulemaking of executive agencies as long as agency heads retain the formal right to issue the final rule. Presidents similarly can advise independent agencies, but more extensive pressure might violate explicit or implicit congressional direction to preserve agency independence. As in the case of the president's exercise of formal powers to control administration of the law, presidential initiative and the interest in public accountability must be accommodated with congressional prerogatives to shape delegations of authority.

b. Presidential Credit for Rulemaking Short of controlling rulemaking through executive orders, presidents have attempted to exert authority by taking credit in the public eye for specific rules. For instance, President Clinton in 1995 announced publication of a proposed rule to reduce youth smoking: "Today I am announcing broad executive action to protect the young people of the United States from the awful dangers of tobacco. . . . Therefore, by executive authority, I will restrict sharply the advertising, promotion, distribution, and marketing of cigarettes to teenagers. I do this on the basis of the best available scientific evidence."[194] President Clinton in effect substituted his authority for that of the commissioner of the Food and Drug Administration, who had been delegated authority by Congress to regulate (in part) the marketing and promotion of cigarettes. Similarly, President Clinton announced on May 23, 1999, that he would "use [his] executive authority as President" to "direct[] the Secretary of Labor to issue a rule to allow States to offer paid leave to new mothers and fathers."[195]

There are at least two facets to this development. First, President Clinton unquestionably endeavored to place his stamp on agency rulemaking in the public eye. At times, he not only announced a proposed agency rule but then the issuance of a final rule as well, after the comment period ended. Clinton's motives in part stemmed from public relations. But, in addition, he was willing to stand accountable for the exercise of delegated authority by agency heads. Although agency heads as a formal matter remained responsible for the rules, the electorate could voice any displeasure more directly. The president's statements forged a clearer link between bureaucratic action and electoral accountability.

On the other hand, President Clinton also took responsibility for those rules in order to shape the content of the rules themselves. As an empirical matter, the extent of the influence is unknown, but a constitutional problem arises if the agency head no longer can exercise judgment in fashioning the policy delegated by Congress. Congress has selected particular agencies, not the president, to address particular problems. In *United State ex rel. Accardi v. Shaughnessy,* for instance, the Supreme Court held that the attorney general, even though he appointed members of the Board of Immigration Appeals and could remove them at will, could not substitute his decision for that of the board.[196] The president should be able to mold the ultimate policy, but it is important that agency heads as a formal matter retain control of the rulemaking process. Presidential advice raises no constitutional problems; presidential commands do.

Moreover, limiting presidential intervention may ensure that agencies not focus in rulemaking on general questions of administration priorities at the expense of the more limited issues that Congress wants addressed.[197] As the Supreme Court once noted in dictum, "Of course there may be duties so peculiarly and specifically committed to the discretion of a particular officer as to raise a question whether the President may overrule or revise the officer's interpretation of his statutory duty in a particular instance."[198]

In short, centralizing and coordinating rules can bring many benefits to the public. Redundancy can be minimized, efficiencies gained, and interest-group control loosened. Yet, Congress may wish to prevent centralization when it deems a more important value is at stake, such as the independence of agency judgments. Creation of independent agencies should insulate these agencies from all coordination efforts except advice. In the absence of a clear statement from Congress, however, presidents should be able to use inherent managerial authority under Article II to coordinate efforts of federal executive agencies to fashion rules and thereby enhance executive initiatives in law administration and accountability to the public.

2. LITIGATION AUTHORITY

The tension between congressional control over the specifics of delegation and executive centralization of agency authority also plays out in the context of litigation authority. One key aspect of agency autonomy lies in an agency's authority in both the civil and criminal contexts to control its own litigation and to represent itself in court. If the agency cannot control its own attorneys, then much of the agency's authority would be sub-ordinated to the entity that can direct the counsel. The power to decide what arguments to raise shapes the rules that govern all of us. If Congress itself directed agency attorneys, the separation of powers violation would be clear: Congress cannot exercise such direct control over execution of the laws and deprive the president of his Article II powers to enforce the law. Similarly, if Congress directed agencies to use particular private attorneys whom they did not control, that limitation as well likely would violate Article II by depriving the executive branch of counsel on whom it can rely.

Consider that presidents have refused to defend the constitutionality of particular acts of Congress. For instance, the Department of Justice under George W. Bush refused to defend the constitutionality of a 1968 law that Congress had passed to overrule the famous *Miranda* decision; his father's administration refused to defend the constitutionality of a statute mandating regulatory preferences for minority-owned broadcast stations; President Reagan refused to defend the legislative veto in *Chadha*.[199] Although the executive branch *should* almost always defend statutes when challenged, there are rare cases when the administration determines that it cannot plausibly argue that a particular statute comports with constitutional dictates, particularly when its own interests are at stake, as in *Chadha*. Presidents could not perform this function if they had no control over litigation.

Even when Congress permits agencies to hire and fire their own attorneys, the problem of government-wide coordination exists. Such disputes can arise in one of two ways: first, and more commonly, the agency's strategy may conflict with that preferred by the Department of Justice (headed by the attorney general) or the president; and second, two agencies within the government may disagree and then some third entity—either the Department of Justice or the courts—must resolve the dispute. The centralization question turns both on Congress's policy decisions as to whether such conduct is preferred and on the president's ability under Article II to ensure that agency positions reflect, to the extent possible, those of his administration.

Currently, Congress has vested most agencies with the power to initiate suit and defend against suit without any oversight from the Department of Justice. Congress's delegation of power to the agencies over substantive matters has included the ancillary authority to determine when and whom to sue, and what arguments to use in response. Undeniably, the power to select cases and then mold them through litigation strategy can profoundly affect the legal landscape.

But, Congress itself has chosen to limit severely that independence. The Department of Justice currently has wide control over when agencies can appeal adverse decisions, when they can seek certiorari, and the arguments that can be made in litigation. Even with respect to the so-termed independent agencies, the DOJ controls Supreme Court litigation; Congress has funneled all representation before the Supreme Court through DOJ's Office of the Solicitor General. In short, Congress generally has authorized the agencies to use their subject-matter expertise at the trial level in crafting and pursuing litigation but has entrusted litigation at the appellate level to the generalists in the DOJ.

This section first examines the extent to which presidents as a matter of history have been able to centralize control over litigation. Next, it examines the policy issues underlying Congress's determination as to which attorneys should represent agencies. Finally, it asks whether there is a constitutional dimension to the clash between Congress's efforts to ensure agency independence and presidential efforts to centralize executive branch policy.

History

From an early period, Congress limited the executive's control over criminal and civil law enforcement by dispersing litigation responsibility among various executive officials. Congress vested limited supervisory authority in the attorney general, declining to provide him with the means to coordinate an effective federal policy to combat crime and conduct civil litigation. To pursue litigation, the executive had to rely on private citizens and state officials both to file civil actions in customs and revenue cases and to aid in apprehending and holding criminals.[200] The appearance of a relatively centralized litigation authority in the executive branch is of comparatively recent origin.

Although Congress created the office of attorney general in the 1789 Judiciary Act, it invested that office with only limited power.[201] Congress directed the attorney general "to prosecute and conduct all suits in the Supreme Court in which the United States shall be concerned, and to give his advice and opinion upon questions of law when required by the President of the United States, or when requested by the heads of any of the departments."[202] When Congress established the attorney general as the nation's principal legal officer, however, it provided the attorney general with no mechanism for supervising the district attorneys, who are now known as United States attorneys.[203] The attorney general might not learn of prosecutions progressing in the newly created trial courts; had virtually no say in the positions taken by the district attorneys in such suits; had little opportunity to coordinate the positions taken by the district attorneys; and thus could not shape the record in cases winding their way to the Supreme Court.[204] Indeed, the attorney general occupied only a part-time position, given that Congress appropriated $1500 a year for that position as opposed to $3500 a year for the secretary of state and the secretary of the Treasury. Attorneys general often conducted their own legal practices outside Washington, D.C.

Attorney General Randolph soon complained that:
* * * it may frequently arise that the United States may be deeply affected by various proceedings in the inferior courts, which no appeal can rectify. The peculiar duty of the Attorney General calls upon him to watch over these cases; and being, in the eye of the world, responsible for the final issue, to offer his advice at the earliest stage of any business; and indeed, until repeated adjudications shall have settled a clear line of partition between the federal and State courts, his best exertions cannot be too often repeated to oppose the danger of a schism. For this purpose the attorneys of the districts ought, I conceive, to be under an obligation to transmit to him a state of every case in which the harmony of the two judiciaries may be hazarded, and to communicate to him those topics on which the subjects of foreign nations may complain in the administration of justice.

Perhaps, too, in the review which the President takes of the affairs of the Union at the opening of each session of Congress, the judicial department will be comprehended. But the Attorney General, who ought to be able to represent the true situation of it, must be forever incompetent to the task, until he may officially, and with the right of expecting an answer, propound his inquiries to the district attorneys.[205]

Congress, however, failed to respond.[206]

During Washington's administration, the secretary of state assumed titular responsibility for supervising the district attorneys' litigation, although that supervision was evidently lax.[207] Moreover, the district attorneys did not even have control over all legal proceedings in their districts, for Congress vested the comptroller of the Treasury with the power and discretion to institute legal proceedings in cases of delinquent revenue officers.[208] In 1820, Madison complained to Congress of the lack of overall coordination of the nation's legal affairs, and recommended augmenting the attorney general's supervisory authority over litigation. Congress, however, reacted not by vesting the attorney general with greater power[209] but by transferring the comptroller's power to a new agent of the Treasury and vesting that agent with the authority to supervise the district attorneys' litigation.[210] By 1828, the Treasury Department had directed more than three thousand lawsuits.

Similarly, when President Jackson later protested to Congress that this bifurcated authority resulted in inefficient and insufficient litigation, Congress chose not to centralize authority in the attorney general, as Jackson had sought, but instead created a new office of solicitor of the Treasury with powers comparable to those formerly enjoyed by the agent of the Treasury.[211] Some in Congress agreed with the president that unifying control over litigation under the attorney general would enhance the executive's authority to enforce the law effectively;[212] others were suspicious of adding duties to the office.[213] Jackson signed the bill but lamented that

> I am convinced that the public interest would be greatly promoted by giving to that officer [the attorney general] the general superintendance of the various law agents of the Government, and of all law proceedings, whether civil or criminal, in which the United States may be interested.[214]

With the succeeding years, new executive efforts to centralize responsibility and control of litigation were unsuccessful.[215] Indeed, even the solicitor of the Treasury had reason to complain, importuning Congress that

> [i]t is respectfully suggested that criminal cases be reported to the solicitor in the same manner as those of a civil nature. * * * A general supervisory power over these cases would enable the solicitor to give such instructions to marshals and district attorneys as would secure the apprehension of many dangerous criminals who might otherwise escape by fleeing from one district to another.[216]

Several other departments, such as the War Department, State Department, and Post Office, had requested and received from Congress authorization to staff their own legal needs, and appointed solicitors to represent them in court. Department officials often secured legal advice from private practitioners. It was not until the centripetal pressures of the Civil War that Congress agreed to begin centralizing law enforcement authority.[217]

For almost a century, Congress thus withheld the means necessary to enable the executive to coordinate effective control over litigation. By refusing to appropriate funds, and by diffusing supervisory responsibility,[218] Congress circumscribed the executive's authority.

With the avalanche of legal claims arising from the Civil War, Congress created the Department of Justice in 1870.[219] The backlog of controversial cases relating to treason, confiscation, and revenue collection demanded that efficiency and uniformity take center stage. Congress placed both the United States attorneys and legal officers of governmental departments under the supervision and control of the attorney general. It prohibited departments from hiring outside counsel without special congressional authorization. Congress, however, did not transfer or abrogate the position of solicitor that had been created in the various departments. Conflicts continued.

Creation of additional administrative agencies, moreover, challenged the unitary control of the Department of Justice. As administrative agencies developed their own expertise, they lobbied Congress for greater control over litigation. For instance, Congress granted the Interstate Commerce Commission independent litigating authority in 1920, the United States Shipping Board in 1921, and the Veterans Board in the same year.[220] On the eve of the New Deal, Attorney General John Sargent reported to Congress that only 115 of 900 federally employed attorneys acted under his supervision.[221]

President Franklin Roosevelt attempted to regain control over agency litigation. In 1933, he signed Executive Order No. 6166,[222] which confined "the responsibility of prosecuting and defending court action to which the United States is a party" to the DOJ. The department's authority included "the decision whether and in what matter to prosecute, or to defend, or to compromise, or to appeal, or to abandon prosecution or defense, now exercised by any agency or officer."[223] With the exception of specific pockets of independent litigating authority, Executive Order No. 6166 empowered the DOJ to conduct all litigation in which the United States is a party. As in the rulemaking context, presidents sought to garner more control through promulgation of executive orders.

FDR's initiative, however, did not end congressional sanction of independent litigating authority. Indeed, Congress conferred some independent litigating authority on the Securities and Exchange Commission in 1934 and the National Labor Relations Board in 1935.[224] Continued congressional exceptions to centralized litigating authority have not followed any coherent pattern. The Federal Election Commission, the former independent counsels, and the Senate's Office of Legal Counsel enjoy independent litigating authority throughout the court hierarchy. The need for independence in this group is quite clear: entrusting litigation to the Department of Justice, given the apparent conflicts of interest that may face the executive branch, may be unwise. Other congressional judgments are more difficult to explain. Many agencies, for instance, have partial independent litigating authority, depending upon both subject matter and court. The Federal Trade Commission has full litigating authority but only on some matters; the Securities and Exchange Commission and the EEOC have independent litigating authority only in some courts.[225] The independent litigating authority granted to other agencies may be more the product of lobbying or logrolling than rational design.

Policy Issues

As a matter of policy, not all administrations have believed that centralization was critical. President Carter's attorney general, for example, emphasized that Justice Department lawyers "must take care not to interfere with the policy prerogatives of our agency clients. An agency's views should be presented to a court unless they were inconsistent with overall governmental interests, or cannot fairly be argued."[226] President Carter recognized that centralization could elevate presidential policy over expertise of the various departments. In his view, true independence necessitated the ability to communicate to a court without the need first to persuade the Department of Justice of the correctness of the agency's position. Centralization would blunt part of Congress's very purpose in creating independent agencies. For instance, the Carter administration agreed with Congress that the newly created Federal Energy Regulatory Commission should enjoy independent litigating authority, and President Carter signed memoranda recognizing such authority in other executive branch departments.[227]

In contrast, the succeeding Bush and Reagan administrations made numerous efforts to centralize litigating authority. For instance, President Reagan vetoed the Whistleblower Protection Act of 1988[228] because it authorized a special counsel to obtain judicial review of Merit Systems Protection Board decisions, and the administration tussled with the Environmental Protection Agency (EPA) over whether it could pursue enforcement actions against federal agencies without attorney general approval. In turn, the Bush administration objected to a proposed Office of Federal Housing Enterprise Oversight because it was to exercise independent litigating authority.[229]

Conflicts do not arise between only the DOJ and individual agencies. When two agencies' views differ, then either the Department of Justice or the courts must resolve the clash. Agencies frequently advocate different positions. For instance, the EPA's arguments in enforcing environmental protection often place it at odds with the Department of Defense and Department of Energy, frequent defendants in such suits. Or, the Department of the Army may disagree with an initiative by the Department of Health and Human Services (HHS) to ensure employment priority for disabled citizens at the expense of veterans. The entity that calls the shots in court sets, or at least influences, policy for the entire government.

Presidents have attempted to resolve such conflicts by asking the Office of Legal Counsel (OLC), within the Department of Justice, to rule on jurisdictional disputes between agency litigators. Under Executive Order No. 12,146, the president directed agency heads serving at the pleasure of the president to submit any legal disputes to the attorney general for resolution.[230] Presidents, however, may not be able to force independent agencies to comply with OLC's rulings. Congress has neither countermanded nor sanctioned such role for OLC.

Even when Congress has centralized litigating authority in the solicitor general, the solicitor general may invite the participation of other agencies in a litigation because of a conflict of interest.[231] A president's decision not to defend the constitutionality of a statute or regulation, for example, does not preclude representation for opposing views. One of the most famous and unusual instances arose during the early Reagan administration. The IRS had long denied tax breaks to racially discriminatory private schools, but Attorney General William French Smith ordered a reversal of policy under which private schools that discriminated were entitled to the tax breaks. As the case wound its way to the Supreme Court, the solicitor general requested the Court to appoint a private individual to represent the former IRS position. In its resulting decision, the Court rejected the administration's volte-face and upheld the earlier IRS position.[232]

Overall, Department of Justice control can bring with it four principal benefits. First, although agencies possess subject matter expertise, Department of Justice attorneys arguably gain specialized litigation expertise in the Supreme Court and, to a lesser extent, in the courts of appeals. Questions of appellate procedure can be best handled by attorneys with the greatest familiarity with the frequently arcane issues that arise. Second, only centralized control over litigation can ensure that one agency is not arguing at cross-purposes with another. HHS, for instance, might take a position on fee shifting that would harm the interests of the Equal Employment Opportunity Commission (EEOC), or the Department of Energy might take a far more crabbed view of the duty to clean up toxic waste than would the EPA. Third, resolving government splits before they reach the Court enhances the respect afforded the executive branch. If the EPA and Department of Energy urged courts to adopt different views of standing or different interpretations of statutes on the same day, then the executive branch as a whole would lose respect and influence in the Court. Appellate judges gain familiarity and often respect for government attorneys who appear before them frequently, and if such attorneys cannot explain away divergences in agencies' approaches, their ability to represent the government in all cases might diminish. Nearly one-half of the cases heard by the Supreme Court in the 1990s involved the Department of Justice in some capacity. Fourth, centralization ensures that there is a buffer between agency decisionmaking and the ultimate position taken by the executive branch in court. Judges recognize that the arguments have emerged through a filter, and therefore may accord them more deference.

Nonetheless, there is another side to the policy arguments. Department of Justice attorneys inappropriately may supplant the expert policy views of agencies, which receive the delegated authority from Congress. Consider *Local 28, Sheet Metal Workers' International Ass'n v. EEOC*.[233] There, EEOC lawyers successfully defended the authority of federal courts to order affirmative action hiring in an employment discrimination lawsuit. However, before the Supreme Court, the solicitor general asserted control. Because the Reagan White House opposed affirmative action, the solicitor general rejected the EEOC's position in a brief filed on the EEOC's behalf. Although unusual, the *Local 28* case is not unique.

Moreover, some agency attorneys are as expert as those in the Department of Justice, and the less responsibility they have, the more difficulty agencies will have in retaining them. Furthermore, the Court may learn more from specialized agency attorneys as opposed to hearing only the filtered views of DOJ attorneys. Conflicts between agency positions may exist, but perhaps it is for the Court to sort those out, and Congress may wish for courts to become more involved. In allocating litigation authority, Congress must therefore determine, on a case-by-case basis, whether the need for independence outweighs the benefits of coordination and centralization.

The remaining question is to what extent presidents can shape Congress's policy choice as to the best way to structure litigation authority. The president's supervisory power under Article II to coordinate administration includes the power to influence litigation authority through executive orders and other nonbinding mechanisms such as OLC advice. But, can the president rely on more formal means to ensure that his policies are represented in litigation involving the government?

The fight over postal rates at the end of the first President Bush's administration illustrates the stakes. Under a byzantine legislative scheme, the U.S. Postal Service's Board of Governors, a nine-member body whose members are appointed by the president and can be removed only for cause, submits proposed rate hikes to the Postal Rate Commission, a five-member body that is also independent of the president's plenary removal authority. The commission holds hearings and then determines whether to accept or modify the Service's proposals. The commission recommendation returns to the service, which then can modify the plan only by unanimous vote. In addition, the service can accept a commission recommendation under protest and allow a court of appeals to resolve the dispute. It can decide whether to sue the commission directly over the disputed rate, or whether to allow dissatisfied private mailers to sue the service, the entity implementing the commission's policies. The very structure of the scheme contemplates one arm of government suing another.

In early 1991, the service elected to sue the commission directly on certain bar code discounts that the commission proposed, and to allow the injured private mailers to sue the service on certain other changes proposed by the commission. The service sought permission to represent itself in court on the challenges while the commission urged the DOJ to withhold permission. President Bush's Justice Department attempted to resolve this dispute within the government, reasoning that a unitary executive should not litigate its differences in court. As in the rulemaking context, presidents can use suasion to influence the litigation position of particular agencies.

The constitutional issue, though, is whether presidents under Article II can take more formal action to ensure that agency litigation positions conform to presidential policy. When DOJ's conciliatory efforts failed, the DOJ denied the Service permission to represent itself and ordered it to withdraw from the suit even though the department had authorized the service to represent itself on countless past occasions. As his tenure in office waned, President Bush sent a directive to the Postal Service and each governor, threatening to remove the governors if the service did not withdraw from the proceeding. President Bush viewed control over litigation as an indispensable aspect of his Article II power. The service refused to withdraw and then filed suit against the president, seeking a preliminary injunction to enjoin its governors' ouster. The district court granted the requested relief, and the president appealed.

In *Mail Order Ass'n v. United States Postal Serv.*, the Court of Appeals for the District of Columbia enjoined President Bush from removing members of the Postal Service's Board of Governors and validated the Postal Service's independent litigation authority.[234] It held that the statutory scheme presupposed that courts at times would hear disputes between the commission and the Postal Service. According to the court, the president could not supplant Congress's choice of entity for litigating particular suits. The president, therefore, could not remove any of the governors for merely affirming their statutory right to participate in the litigation: "[W]here Congress has specifically authorized judicial review of such disputes, respect for the Department's role in litigation does not require that we permit it unilaterally to repeal the statutory authority [to the agency]."[235] To the court, the president had no right to remove an official for failing to adhere to a presidential order. Upon entering office, President Clinton saw no need to further the litigation. The president can use political but not formal means to coordinate the litigation positions of independent agencies such as the Postal Service.

For executive agencies, in contrast, the president should be able to remove the head of an executive agency for maintaining positions in litigation contrary to presidential initiatives. Although the president cannot take over the litigation efforts of even executive agencies if Congress provides for independent litigating authority, the president remains free to exercise plenary removal authority.[236]

As it stands, Congress has wide latitude in determining which executive branch agency is to represent which government interests in court. The president can resort to political means in attempting to ensure that litigation strategy is coordinated among government agencies. And, the president can threaten to discharge officials subject to his plenary removal authority if certain positions are not adopted in litigation. But, the president likely can only cajole, threaten, or importune those officers whom Congress has shielded from his at-will removal authority.

Presidential control over agency policymaking, therefore, is incomplete. The president—in addition to the power to appoint and remove officers—may try to coordinate policy through executive orders, prestige of the office, threats, and calling in personal favors. Article II vests the president with some inherent authority to manage officials within the executive branch. The president can use such means as long as there is no direct conflict with congressional direction, and even then, Congress can never prevent the president from recommending or beseeching agency officials to adopt particular policies. Congress, however, remains free to insulate such policymaking from formal presidential control by lodging authority within an independent agency and specifying which lawyers, as long as they are subject to agency supervision, are to represent the agency in court.

F. Delegations outside the Executive Branch

To this point, the discussion has assumed that Congress has delegated authority to officers within the government. What, however, if Congress instead delegates authority outside the federal government? Must the president still be able to exercise appointment and removal power or at least supervisory authority to ensure that he can exercise initiative to "take care" to ensure that the laws are enforced faithfully? Or, can Congress by dint of choosing a delegate outside the executive branch preclude presidential involvement in governmental policymaking?

The exercise of public power by entities outside the federal government may undermine the president's capacity to exert initiative in enforcing the law and blur the lines of constitutional responsibility. If, for example, Congress created a private commission to establish binding safety standards for mining, or just adopted whatever standards would be formulated by the United Mine Workers, the president's appointment and removal authority would obviously be circumvented. Private parties would be exercising significant authority under the laws of the United States in creating binding regulations, backed by the coercive force of the government. The standards adopted could not be traced to the president. The executive could well lose its ability under Article II to coordinate national policy if Congress delegated the power to set such standards outside the federal government.

Moreover, delegating authority outside the federal government may permit Congress to exercise both a de facto appointment and removal authority. With respect to appointment, Congress, and not the president, decides the identity of the delegate. In functional terms, Congress both creates the office and designates the officeholder. Congress thus can accomplish, albeit indirectly, the very combination of powers withheld from it under the Constitution.

With respect to removal, Congress may "remove" a delegate outside the federal government merely by passing a new law changing the identity of the delegate. Although such a law would need a two-thirds vote in each House if vetoed by the president, the prospect of congressional removal exists, and the private delegate would be aware of that power. The Supreme Court, in the analogous context of *Bowsher,* determined that "in constitutional terms, the removal powers over the Comptroller General's office dictate that he will be subservient to Congress."[237] The absence of executive branch controls increases the possibility that the delegate outside the federal government will heed Congress's will. To the extent there is supervision of the private enforcement of federal laws, the supervision would more likely come from Congress than from the executive.

The Supreme Court invalidated a delegation to a private party during the New Deal. In *Carter v. Carter Coal Co.,*[238] the Court reviewed the Bituminous Coal Act of 1935,[239] under which Congress authorized coal producers and miners to set maximum hours and minimum wages for the entire industry. Producers not accepting the regulatory provisions would have incurred a prohibitive tax.[240] The Court observed, "This is legislative delegation in its most obnoxious form; for it is not even delegation to an official or an official body, presumptively disinterested, but to private persons whose interests may be and often are adverse to the interests of others in the same business."[241] Delegations to private parties enable Congress to bypass Article II and its protections for the public.

Consider also a hypothetical statute delegating authority to the head of the Brookings Institution to perform the budget-cutting duties assigned by Congress in the Gramm-Rudman-Hollings Act. If the head of Brookings exercised such power, Congress could participate in the execution of the laws even more effectively than it could by vesting those same responsibilities in the comptroller general. Although the comptroller general is appointed by the president, the head of Brookings would be beholden only to Congress, and would presumably more directly reflect Congress's views. Congress could exercise a de facto removal authority merely by reassigning the same power to the head of the Cato Institute instead (subject to presidential veto and the need for two-thirds override). The delegate would know that it owed its authority to Congress, and would likely conform its actions in light of that knowledge. Thus, delegations of governmental authority outside the federal government may permit Congress to participate in executing the laws, undermining the president's overall enforcement role under Article II.

Despite *Carter Coal,* however, Congress over the years has delegated authority to state officials, to private individuals serving in government agencies, to private "experts," to private groups targeted by federal regulation, to private attorneys general, and increasingly to international tribunals. Although the examples illustrate that Congress generally has permitted the executive to superintend the delegated authority, which was not the case in *Carter Coal,* the examples also highlight that close control on occasion has been removed from the executive branch. Courts have not applied *Carter Coal* rigorously.

The most visible and pervasive examples of congressional delegations outside the federal government lie in joint federal-state programs. Congress has long fashioned partnerships with states to implement federal programs and to enforce federal law. In all, the congressional delegations of authority to state governments and officials are quite considerable. Congress has approved state compacts (as in the *Washington Airports* case), shared responsibility with states in implementing federal programs, and authorized state officials directly to enforce federal law. States qua states and state officials enjoy wide-ranging authority to implement and enforce federal statutory provisions. Indeed, it is hard today to conceive of a federal welfare program that does not depend substantially upon state discretion. In choosing to vest in states the authority to implement federal programs, Congress has placed significant segments of federal law enforcement and implementation outside the federal government and frequently outside the executive branch's practical control.

The Constitution offers some justification for the delegations to states and state officials. Article I provides that Congress can consent to state decisions to levy "Duty of Tonnage, [to] keep Troops, or Ships of War in time of Peace, [or to] enter into any agreement or Compact with another State, or with a foreign Power or engage in War. . . ."[242] This constitutional provision has been only rarely invoked (with the exception of the compact clause), yet the possibility of delegating authority outside the federal government exists within the constitutional framework. Congress apparently can, under the Constitution, consent or direct states to act in capacities that we associate today exclusively with the executive branch.

Delegations to the states, however, extend considerably beyond those directly encompassed by the constitutional text. Indeed, in *Holmes v. Jennison* the Supreme Court confronted the question whether Vermont could agree with Canadian authorities to extradite fugitives.[243] Although there were five separate opinions for the Court, a majority of the justices participating suggested that the Vermont action was illegal but would be validated by congressional consent.[244] No concern for *executive* power was expressed. Delegations to states can rather be understood—if at all—as furthering the federalism values implicit in our constitutional framework[245] and more explicit in our nation's history. Such delegations suggest that interests in federalism can override the Article II interest in exclusive executive control of administrative authority delegated by Congress.

At some point, however, delegation of certain core powers to state officials—such as conduct of foreign relations (despite *Holmes v. Jennison*)—would prevent the president from discharging his constitutionally assigned functions. Congressional delegation of the power to conduct national intelligence gathering, for instance, presumably would violate the Article II interest in executive superintendence of administrative authority. Yet, almost all of the congressional delegation to states has left the president a role in overseeing the exercise of administrative authority. Under the joint federal-state programs, federal officials either approve state plans or set the framework under which states can act. When state officials enforce federal laws, appeals are available through the court system. Thus, much (but not all) of the delegations to states leave the president a supervisory role even if the president formally cannot exercise the appointment and removal authority.

Congressional delegations of administrative authority to private groups and individuals are more unexpected. Private individuals and groups have exercised such power both in the federal government and outside it. There may be various advantages to placing private parties in positions of power: Congress may try to ensure that a particular viewpoint is represented; to tap the expertise of private individuals who would otherwise not agree to serve as government officials; to remove barriers to operation of the private market; or to generate greater respect for a particular regulatory program by including representatives of those regulated. Although some executive controls generally remain, the private individuals—who are neither appointed nor removable by the president—unquestionably have exercised governmental authority in helping to administer laws passed by Congress.

Private individuals exercise power by serving in a number of governmental agencies. For instance, Congress provided for private representation on the Federal Open Market Committee (FOMC), which operates as part of the Federal Reserve System.[246] The private members are elected annually by the boards of directors of the twelve regional Federal Reserve Banks, which are privately owned. Although the private members of the FOMC are a minority of the committee, they discharge an immensely important policymaking role. Congress charged the FOMC with complete control over the purchase and sale of government securities in the open market, and thus with decisive influence over interest rates. Yet the private individuals on the FOMC are not immediately accountable to any public official for their exercise of statutory authority. They owe loyalty instead to the private Federal Reserve Banks. As in the context of delegation to state officials, however, most of the delegations permit the president effective oversight. The president, or a subordinate executive branch official, may not be able to influence every decision of the private parties, but they can and do shape overall policy on financial matters, thus preserving the capacity for initiative and ensuring some accountability to the public on financial policy issues.

Congress has also authorized private groups outside the federal government to exercise administrative authority. Just as with delegations to private individuals serving in government agencies, such delegations reflect congressional efforts to rely on expertise developed in the private sector. For example, private health organizations have played an important role in various social security programs. Under the Medicaid statute, Congress delegated to the Joint Committee on Accreditation of Hospitals (JCAH), a not-for-profit corporation formed to create professional standards and evaluate hospital performance, at least some responsibility for determining whether to accredit hospitals and thereby permit patients in such hospitals to receive Medicare, Medicaid, and Social Security benefits.[247] JCAH determinations were not subject to revision by the Department of Health and Human Services. This delegation represents just one instance in which Congress has determined that private individuals would be more "expert" than executive branch officials in carrying out legislative objectives. Again, however, executive branch officials remain responsible for formulating broader health policy, with the private parties contributing in more discrete contexts.

Some congressional delegations permit groups targeted by a particular set of regulations to participate in formulating the content of the regulations. Although no private individual exercises substantial authority, the group as a whole—through either a referendum or some other representative process—helps determine both the applicability and substance of federal regulation. In turn, the group's actions are binding on dissenters within the groups as well as on some outsiders.

The Agricultural Marketing Agreement Act of 1937 presents a paradigm.[248] With respect to milk, Congress authorized the secretary of agriculture under the act to issue marketing orders setting minimum prices that handlers, who process dairy products, must pay to dairy farmers for milk products. Prior to setting the prices, the secretary must conduct rulemaking and elicit public comment. But before any order can go into effect, it must be approved by the handlers of at least 50 percent of the milk covered by the proposed order and at least two-thirds of the producers in the covered area.[249] If the handlers withhold their consent, the secretary may still promulgate the order if two-thirds of the affected dairy farmers concur.[250] Dairy farmers and, to some extent, handlers, can in effect veto any proposed milk marketing order, and the threat of a veto affords those groups some say in the formulation of the order.

Producer groups for other commodities help determine not only production quotas but also standards of quality, unfair trade practices, and research and development agendas. In turn, Congress has specified that marketing orders and implementation regulations, which cannot go into force without producer initiative and assent, automatically apply to imports.[251] Thus, producer groups bind not only themselves (through referenda) with cartel-type agreements but outsiders as well. Executive officials, however, determine the substance of proposed regulations.

Congress at times has vested in private groups more direct power to shape the content of the orders. In the mid-nineteenth century, Congress— in one of the earliest examples of congressional delegation to groups of private citizens—delegated substantial authority to miners on federal government land to govern themselves. Congress provided that public lands were free and open to mineral exploration and occupation in part "subject . . . to the local customs or rules of miners in the several mining districts, so far as the same may not be in conflict with the laws of the United States."[252] To a limited extent, Congress directed miners to participate in self-governance, and the product of that self-governance was enforceable through federal law. As another example, Congress in 1893 delegated authority directly to the American Railway Association to establish a mandatory height for drawbars on railroad cars, and failure to comply with the height requirement subjected the railroad companies to civil penalties.[253] Although such exercises of authority are the exception, they are difficult to square with contemporary views of executive authority, and would prevent the executive from exercising sufficient initiative in administering the law.

In addition, delegation to private individuals under qui tam actions has at times been extensive. Through qui tam actions, individuals sue on behalf of the government in the government's name and share any damages obtained with the government. Unlike other congressionally created causes of action, qui tam actions in no way depend upon the existence of individuated injury. Rather, injury to the government as a whole is the only prerequisite for maintaining a qui tam action.

Several courts rejected challenges by defendants asserting that only the executive branch could maintain lawsuits seeking to vindicate the federal government's interests. For instance, in *United States v. Griswold,* the defendant sought to dismiss the qui tam action on the ground that the complaint was not filed or approved by any member of the federal government.[254] The court rejected the challenge, reasoning that "although the United States is the plaintiff, [the private relator] is its authorized representative, and not the district attorney, who is not authorized or required to act or interfere in the matter, otherwise than as expressly provided by the statute."[255] Control over the theories of liability, construction of statutes, and penalties sought were vested in private hands.

Moreover, suit by a private individual, at least historically, has robbed the executive branch of some enforcement authority. Until the middle part of the twentieth century, a civil qui tam action likely precluded the government from subsequently maintaining its own criminal enforcement action against the same defendant.[256] Although the Supreme Court has since held that an individual can be subject to both a qui tam suit and criminal proceedings for the same conduct,[257] it has never intimated that the government could bring its own civil enforcement action after a private qui tam action has been completed—principles of res judicata would presumably bar any such effort. Only one civil enforcement action can be brought in the name of the United States, and pendency of a qui tam action has precluded the executive branch from settling with the defendants.[258] Congress has thus bypassed the executive branch by vesting some auxiliary law enforcement responsibilities directly in private individuals. Congress since has vested in the executive greater oversight over qui tam actions to ensure greater coordination of executive policy.[259]

Finally, Congress increasingly has delegated authority to international tribunals. For instance, under the Chemical Weapons Convention, approved by the Senate, a private international organization (Organization for the Prohibition of Chemical Weapons) enters and searches suspect sites, including those in the United States, to detect evidence of chemical weapons.[260] Weapons verification schemes all depend upon verification by private organizations unconnected to member states. The organization can conduct inspections of both private and public facilities, and refusal to accede to the inspections can result in penalties. Decisions of the private members on the international organization thus are backed by the coercive power of the federal government. Through the congressional delegation, the international organization exercises enforcement authority without any direct role for the president.[261] With globalization, Congress will likely face increased pressure to enter international agreements that cede some administrative authority to international groups.[262]

In a great variety of situations, therefore, Congress has delegated authority to private groups (and international entities) to help regulate their own conduct or participate in regulation of activities affecting themselves. Although the delegations largely have been narrow in scope, private and international entities have served, in essence, as partners with Congress and sometimes the executive branch in fashioning and implementing binding policy. Full control over administrative policy—as arguably required under Article II—has unquestionably been withheld from the executive.

Although courts have been reluctant to disturb these delegations, with the principal exception of *Carter Coal,* continued congressional delegations undoubtedly will trigger more challenges. To the extent that the private or international entities are not subject to formal executive branch oversight, courts over time are likely to invalidate such schemes as inconsistent with Article II's decision to create an executive that can implement the laws faithfully and energetically. Our Constitution presupposes that public power be exercised in a way that can be traced to a publicly accountable actor, and by blurring the lines of authority, congressional delegations outside the executive branch may leave individuals with little recourse for ineffectual or invidious governance.

G. One Final Check: Congressional Appropriations Power

Congress's power over the purse, however, may limit presidential power to enforce both criminal and civil laws and—as will be discussed—to set foreign policy. Article I, section 9 provides that "[n]o money shall be drawn from the Treasury, but in Consequence of Appropriations made by Law."[263] The Federalist Papers stated that "this power over the purse may, in fact, be regarded as the most complete and effectual weapon with which any constitution can arm the immediate representatives of the people . . . carrying into effect every just and salutary measure."[264] Justice Story explained that but for the appropriations clause,

> the executive would possess an unbounded power over the public purse of the nation; and might apply all its moneyed resources at his pleasure. The power to control and direct the appropriations constitutes a most useful and salutary check upon profusion and extravagance, as well as upon corrupt influence and public peculation.[265]

The appropriations clause ensures that Congress can check executive initiative to preserve policymaking dominance.

In interpreting the appropriations clause, the Supreme Court has long held that the president cannot expend money to take care that the laws be faithfully executed except pursuant to an appropriation from Congress: "No officer, however high, not even the President . . . is empowered to pay the debts of the United States . . . [T]he difficulty in the way is the want of any appropriation by Congress."[266] As one judge noted, "[T]he absolute control of the moneys of the United States is in Congress, and Congress is responsible for its exercise of this great power only to the people."[267] The president's authority under Article II is directly confined by the appropriations that Congress sees fit to make. In this respect, Congress's constitutional control over money tempers the president's Article II accountability to the people to superintend enforcement of the law.

Without money, presidential discretion can be curbed substantially, if not eliminated. One cannot enforce environmental laws or litigate cases about tax shelters absent funding. The president therefore must obtain Congress's agreement before undertaking any domestic (or foreign policy) initiative that expends resources.

Congresses for the most part have recognized the link between executive discretion and resources by granting lump sum appropriations and by permitting officers within the executive branch to shift monies from one category to another. For instance, the first appropriations act in 1789 authorized sums for four general categories of expenditures.[268] Congress cannot foresee every particular expenditure necessary to enforce the laws or carry out foreign relations. As a matter of efficiency, therefore, it routinely leaves wide room within which the executive branch can operate. Any other approach might too narrowly tie the hands of the chief magistrate.

Moreover, Congress has often chosen to look the other way when presidents have expended sums not previously authorized. As early as the Whiskey Rebellion, Congress ratified executive branch expenditures after the fact even when no prior appropriation had been made.[269] Congress has understood that presidents may be compelled to spend money when time is too short to obtain funds through the legislative process. Similarly, Jefferson spent unappropriated money on a number of occasions, including the Louisiana Purchase.[270]

But, Congress can also be much more specific. By 1793, Congress had fine tuned its approach to the point of earmarking $450 for office supplies to be used in the Department of the Treasury. Although Jefferson had approved the push toward itemization early, he soon acknowledged that "too minute a specification has its evil as well as a too general one."[271]

Congress on occasion has not been shy in wielding its appropriation power to influence executive enforcement of the laws. Many examples exist. For example, in Section 309 of the Energy and Water Development

Appropriations Act, Congress prohibited the Department of Energy and Department of Justice from using any funds for a period of ten months to "prosecute" or "enforce any judgment" against specified persons subject to a judgment previously entered.[272] Congress evidently objected to the Department of Energy's successful efforts to recover restitution from corporate officials who had overcharged customers in sales of oil and gas. In reaction to President Theodore Roosevelt's unwelcome appointment of a commission to study domestic affairs, Congress refused to appropriate monies to cover printing and distribution of its final report.[273] Moreover, under the Anti-Deficiency Act, Congress has prescribed criminal penalties for any executive official who spends money in excess of that appropriated by Congress."[274]

In more pedestrian situations, Congress repeatedly has attached the phrase "provided, that no funds shall be spent . . ." to numerous appropriations bills.[275] For instance, Congress legislated that no funds appropriated for wildlife protection be "expended for wildfire protection resources or personnel provided by a foreign fire organization unless the Secretary determines that no wildfire protection resources or personnel within the United States are reasonably available."[276] More controversially, Congress provided that no education funds can be "used to prevent the implementation of programs of voluntary prayer and meditation in the public schools."[277] And, Congress has legislated with even greater detail at times, providing, for example, that "no funds shall be used by the executive branch to change the employment levels determined by the Administrators of the Federal Power Marketing Administrations to be necessary to carry out their responsibilities."[278]

Three dimensions of this conflict can be stressed. First, most presidents have conceded that the scope of the appropriations power under the Constitution is plenary and can block the president's ability to take enforcement or security measures in the national interest. The appropriations power safeguards the interest in congressional policymaking. A congressional ban on the use of money for electronic eavesdropping, in other words, should be dispositive. Second, other structural constitutional provisions, however, limit Congress's appropriations power. In the rare case that Congress, through its appropriations power, threatens to infringe on more specific executive powers such as the power to appoint or remove officials, the president (and courts in a properly drawn case or controversy) need not comply with the limitation. Third, presidents generally have the discretion under Article II *not* to spend all the money authorized by Congress. Social or economic conditions may change, and Congress may presume that presidents should retain some flexibility to cut short a spending program when no longer in the public interest. But if Congress clearly sets forth a mandate, then presidents have no right to impound funds in the teeth of a specific congressional directive.[279]

1. The Constitution lodged the power of the purse in the House of Representatives, the most democratic of the branches. James Madison wrote in the Federalist No. 58 that "[t]his power over the purse may, in fact, be regarded as the most complete and effectual weapon with which any constitution can arm the immediate representatives of the people, for obtaining a redress of every grievance, and for carrying into effect every just and salutary measure."[280] The appropriations power controls expenditures in the foreign affairs and domestic sphere alike. The clash between Congress's appropriation power and other constitutional provisions, however, is of course hardly new, even if the frequency with which the appropriations power is used may have increased.

As a constitutional matter, the president cannot expend funds that Congress has not authorized. But, through transfers of discretionary money, redeploying funds already authorized for different purposes, or recruitment of third-party funds, presidents can—consistent with the Constitution—oversee expenditure of funds in the absence of congressional authorization. Such acts violate the spirit but not the letter of the Constitution. Congress is free to combat such efforts by using all political means it finds feasible, including broader prohibitions on support. Overall, however, the appropriations power blunts executive initiative and provides Congress a potent lever to force presidential changes in domestic and foreign policy.

2. The appropriations power, however, does not permit Congress to rely on the power of the purse to legislate in areas not otherwise permitted under Article I. Congress's power to place restrictions on the use of funds otherwise would provide a roundabout means to interfere with presidential prerogatives under Article II.

For instance, Congress in 1860 appeared to condition the availability of funds for a particular Army project on supervision by one Captain Montgomery Meigs. President Buchanan rightfully retorted that the statute so construed would "interfere with the clear right of the President to command the Army and to order its officers to any duty he might deem most expedient for the public interest."[281] Congress's power to condition funds can lead to unconstitutional curtailment of presidential discretion.

Similarly, Congress three years later prohibited payment of salary to any-one appointed during particular recesses of the Senate. This restriction in fact precluded payment for several government officials. The funding limit arguably violated the recess appointment clause in the Constitution.[282] Congress has also provided that no funding can be expended to put into effect particular presidential pardons.[283] The power to impose conditions on funding permits Congress to attain objectives outside the traditional legislative process. Such efforts should be cabined when they conflict with specific Article II prerogatives.[284]

Some might argue instead that the president should veto any funding restriction that violates his Article II powers, instead of failing to abide by the funding restrictions once enacted. But, Congress has the power to override a presidential veto, and even forcing the president to veto a mea-sure may be unreasonable. A veto of a continuing resolution can literally close down agencies by depriving them of needed funds. Thus, congressional restrictions on funding that infringe the president's specific Article II powers should not be enforced, irrespective of whether presidents have attempted to veto the restrictions first.

3. The final puzzle arises not from denial of funding but rather from a congressional decision to fund a particular project or program that the president subsequently deems unwise. Presidents have impounded funds throughout history, but the Article II pedigree for such impoundments has been hotly debated. Congress may have overestimated the cost of a particular project, or political conditions may change undermining the utility of the congressional plan. For instance, Jefferson refused to acquire gunboats—despite a congressional appropriation—for use on the Mississippi after the need for them waned with his Louisiana Purchase.[285] President Grant refused to spend river and harbor funds to benefit "private or local interests."[286] Congress reacted indignantly, but acquiesced.[287]

Congress may agree with impoundments when conditions change, and it has the right to make new authorizations in the face of presidential re-calcitrance. But, if presidents decline to expend funds through disagreement over principle, then a more acute clash over power arises. President Nixon, for instance, notoriously impounded as much as 20 percent of "controllable" federal expenditures in the inflationary period right after the Vietnam War. Nixon ended some public works projects completely.[288]

The Supreme Court reviewed the question *in Train v. New York*.[289] There, Congress had provided in the Federal Water Pollution Control

Act[290]—over President Nixon's veto—to fund certain municipal waste-sewage treatment plants. Nixon released only some of the monies. After Nixon's resignation, the Court issued its opinion invalidating the impoundment. At least at the allotment stage, the Court reasoned, the president had no choice but to follow the dictates of Congress. Supreme Court Justice William Rehnquist, then an official in President Nixon's Justice Department, advised the White House in 1969 that "with respect to the suggestion that the President has a constitutional power to decline to spend appropriated funds, we must conclude that the existence of such a broad power is supported by neither reason nor precedent."[291] The Court left open the question of what discretion the president should exercise in implementing the program over time. The line between impounding funds for policy reasons and because of changed conditions is quite fine.

Congress attempted to clarify the president's impoundment authority by passing the Congressional Budget and Impoundment Control Act of 1974,[292] which required presidents to submit any proposals for complete rescission of appropriations to Congress.[293] The act permitted presidents to defer spending temporarily within a fiscal year because of new contingencies, subject to a one-house legislative veto.[294] The court of appeals struck down the new act as violating *Chadha*'s proscription on congressional involvement in execution of the laws.[295]

As it stands, therefore, presidents likely have no inherent authority to impound funds due to a policy disagreement, President Grant's actions notwithstanding. Presidents, however, are entitled to presume that congressional appropriations include the discretion to defer spending to meet the inevitable contingencies that arise in administering programs.

Congress's power over appropriations limits presidential supervision over the administrative machinery of the state. Congress can direct no funds to be used for particular enforcement efforts. All such appropriation limitations are subject to the president's veto, and carry with them political cost: members of Congress generally do not want to appear in the public eye to block enforcement of the law. Yet, Congress retains a potent means to check particular enforcement or administrative initiatives that it finds problematic.

In sum, the president stands at the apex of the administrative arm of government. In order that the president can discharge constitutionally assigned tasks, he must have some supervisory authority over the tasks delegated by Congress, at least those that have binding force on individuals outside the legislative branch. Through the formal powers of appointment and removal, and through less formal means of suasion, presidents mold the actions of subordinates implementing congressional directives. That supervision ensures that the public can trace governmental acts to the executive to hold it accountable.

The Supreme Court, however, has rejected any notion that presidential supervision be close. In recognition of Congress's legislative prerogative to determine who should implement what policies in what way, the Court has tempered presidential control by limiting the president's removal and appointment authority. Congress can impose reasonable qualifications on candidates for office, and it can restrict the president's removal authority to a "good cause" standard as long as the president otherwise can enforce his constitutional responsibilities effectively. Congress can insist that particular functions be exercised by specific officers, and it can even vest some authority in individuals and groups outside the executive branch altogether, as long as the president is granted some general supervisory authority. And, Congress through its appropriations power can limit the president's supervision by withdrawing funding from particular initiatives. Thus, the Court has accommodated presidential control over the administrative machinery of the state with Congress's power to ensure that delegated authority be carried out in ways responsive to Congress's concerns. The resulting tension between Congress and the president can, in the long run, prevent either branch from assuming too much authority.

2

The Executive's Power
over Foreign Affairs

The Constitution assigns principal responsibility over foreign affairs neither to the legislative branch nor to the president.[1] Under Article I, Congress has the power to "declare war," "to regulate commerce with foreign nations," "to raise and support armies," to provide for "repel[ling] invasions," and to "make all Laws which shall be necessary and proper for carrying into Execution the foregoing Powers."[2] For his part, the president, under Article II, "shall be Commander in Chief of the Army and Navy of the United States," has the power to "appoint Ambassadors," and exercises the authority to negotiate and "make treaties,"[3] in addition to possessing whatever the "executive power" consisted of that was vested by the Framers. In turn, the Senate must give its consent both to ambassadorial appointments and to treaties.[4]

Presidential initiative is probably more important in foreign than in domestic affairs, given the need for dispatch, secrecy, and flexibility. Experience under the Articles of Confederation confirmed the need for an independent executive to address international developments. At the same time, however, the Constitution recognizes Congress's distinctive warmaking power and a fundamental role for the Senate in approving treaties.

As a consequence, Edward Corwin wrote that the Constitution's arrangement of powers over foreign affairs "is an invitation to struggle for the privilege of directing American foreign policy."[5] Not surprisingly, both Congress and the president have long played key roles in establishing foreign policy, but the twentieth century has witnessed increasing power exercised by the president. President Truman may have exaggerated only slightly when he declared: "I make foreign policy."[6]

In considering the foreign affairs field, it is helpful to break down executive authority into three categories. First, some powers can be wielded only by the president, such as the power to appoint ambassadors. Second, there are some powers that the Constitution vests in Congress exclusively, such as the power to declare war and to make appropriations for supporting international diplomacy. The third area is the largest and most contentious: where the Constitution assigns a primary role neither to the president nor to Congress. In that area, the president may act, whether in committing troops or sending envoys, subject to congressional statutes limiting or channeling such exercise of authority. The Constitution implicitly, if not explicitly, accords the president such critical initiative in the foreign affairs arena.

Indeed, in the seventeenth and eighteenth centuries, most commentators included foreign affairs within the executive power. The writings of Locke, Montesquieu, and Blackstone all assigned a prominent role to the executive in foreign affairs. Monarchs in Great Britain exercised wide discretion in pursuing foreign policy goals. Consistent with that tradition, presidents arguably can take foreign policy steps—whether negotiating executive agreements or sending envoys—as long as they respect the textual powers of Congress. The granting of executive power in Article II, therefore, may permit presidents to exercise residual authority in the foreign affairs context.[7]

Congress, however, has long staked out greater turf in directing the nation's foreign policy. The lawmaking power in conjunction with the authority to equip troops and declare war may argue for a greater formal role under the Constitution. Moreover, even if Congress is confined to its textual powers, permitting wide presidential initiative may prevent Congress from effectively exercising those very same powers. For instance, if executive agreements can replace treaties, then the Senate's power to consent to treaties amounts to very little. Similarly, if presidents can launch attacks and commit troops abroad in the absence of a declaration of war, the formal power to declare war is not of great moment. And, there are no constitutionally prescribed means to resolve conflicts among the branches—the political process of negotiation and give-and-take between the president and Congress must take its course.

Although the allocation of authority under the Constitution between the president and Congress is unclear, presidents as a pragmatic matter possess a substantial advantage due to their power to seize the initiative. Unlike Congress, the president is always in session and can act much more quickly, and usually secretly. Moreover, presidential communication with foreign heads of state provides the executive with greater information with which to formulate foreign policy, and Thomas Jefferson as secretary of state stressed that the president, "being the only channel of communication between this country and foreign nations, it is from him alone that foreign nations or their agents are to learn what is or has been the will of the nation; and whatever he communicates as such, they have a right, and are bound to consider as the expression of the nation."[8] Moreover, as Woodrow Wilson wrote,

> When foreign affairs plays a prominent part in the politics and policy of a nation, its Executive must of necessity be its guide: must utter every initial judgment, take every first step of action, supply the information upon which it is to act, suggest and in large measure control its conduct.[9]

Furthermore, by recalling ambassadors, sending envoys, or committing ground troops, presidents can set the agenda for foreign policy. Indeed, a consensus emerged early on that the president constituted the nation's voice on matters of foreign affairs, even if that voice did not lead to binding commitments. Future Chief Justice John Marshall opined as a member of Congress that "the President is the sole organ of the nation in its external relations, and its sole representative with foreign nations."[10] Although Congress shapes foreign policy through its power to declare war or by authorizing expenditure of funds, it faces the disadvantage of often reacting to presidential actions and speech as opposed to seizing the initiative.

One early example may prove helpful. Shortly after taking office, President George Washington faced the reality of continuing hostilities in Europe that threatened to embroil the young nation in war once again. Both France and England threatened our commercial interests. Some in Congress sympathized with France, which had helped the United States during the Revolutionary War. Others sympathized with England and believed that the nation's long-term strategic course best be tied to that mercantile power. In 1793, Washington determined to chart a neutral path between the warring factions in Europe, issuing his famous Neutrality Proclamation. He urged all citizens to observe the neutrality at the risk of criminal penalties. Many in Congress objected because the Neutrality Proclamation appeared to wrest control from Congress over foreign affairs.[11] Yet, Congress the next year enacted a Neutrality Act that criminalized any financial or logistical support for military expeditions against nations with whom we are at peace.[12] The presidential initiative seized the stage, and Congress soon followed.

Many other examples exist. President Monroe articulated the doctrine that now bears his name, committing the country to resist any moves made by European powers in Latin America. President Theodore Roosevelt's decision to dispatch the navy to back the Panamanian revolt against Colombia facilitated the independence of Panama and U.S. control over the canal. President Franklin Roosevelt's decision to help the Allies secure shipping routes at the beginning of World War II paved the way for our entry into the war. Presidents Lyndon Johnson and Nixon ordered steps during the Vietnam War, such as the bombing of Cambodia, that sank the nation deeper into the conflict. And, President Reagan, despite opposition from Congress, took extraordinary steps to help Nicaragua fight back the contras.

If the struggle between the president and Congress over foreign policy ever winds its way to court, however, Congress may well have the advantage. The Supreme Court from an early period recognized that Congress could channel the president's control over foreign affairs. In *Little v. Barreme (The Flying Fish),* the Court held that the president's directive to seize a ship on the high seas was unlawful because Congress, even though it had legislated in the area, had not authorized such action:

> It is by no means clear that the president of the United States whose high duty it is to "take care that the laws be faithfully executed" and who is commander in chief of the armies and navies of the United States, might not, without any special authority for that purpose . . . have empowered the officers commanding the armed vessels of the United States, to seize and send into port for adjudication [the suspect vessels]. But when it is observed that [an Act of Congress] gives a special authority to seize on the high seas, and limits that authority . . . the legislature seems to have prescribed [] the manner in which this law shall be carried into execution.[13]

Although the president as commander in chief may have enjoyed the inherent authority to order seizures of particular vessels, Congress could limit that authority by establishing guidelines. The president could seize the initiative but would ultimately be bound by any constitutional constraints.[14] Yet, few confrontations between Congress and the president result in justiciable controversies. Either no party is palpably injured, or courts avoid enmeshing themselves in controversies that they are ill equipped to resolve, given institutional limitations. Judicial decisions, accordingly, tell only a small part of the tale of control over foreign policy. The president's structural advantages of flexibility and speed afford him a clear edge in shaping foreign policy for the nation.[15]

Experience under the Continental Congress

According to most observers, internal squabbles, pressure from the states, and frequent change in personnel made coherent foreign policy under the Continental Congress impossible, impeding efforts of the new nation to conduct the War of Independence and gain acceptance among the nations of the world.[16] One of the principal difficulties rested with the tension between the need to conduct an effective war and the suspicion of a centralized executive. Leading figures in the revolution against Great Britain did not want to trade one type of autocratic rule for another. Congress thus understandably did not wish to delegate critical powers of foreign policy to an independent executive.

To assuage the difficulty, Congress assigned outside staff responsibility to help implement congressional directives. Problems of both accountability and efficiency arose, principally due to turf battles and lack of coordination. As one example, Congress appointed a committee of three on October 5, 1775, to prepare a plan for intercepting two vessels, containing weapons, on their way to Canada. Congress directed the committee to prepare an estimate of the cost and to contract with private parties to equip a ship to effectuate the capture. Congress received the report two weeks later, by which time the element of surprise had vanished. Undaunted, Congress added four more members to the committee. Over time, this committee became charged with more and more naval affairs. Congress vested in the committee no permanent functions but assigned it periodic tasks.[17]

The Continental Congress also attempted to direct George Washington's military campaigns. The difficulty of communication and need for speed led to broader delegations of authority to permit him greater flexibility in conduct of the war.[18]

With respect to foreign affairs, Congress in 1777 established the five-member Committee for Foreign Affairs to take the initiative in foreign policy. It periodically assigned special committees to do work when the group disagreed with decisions of the Committee for Foreign Affairs. Members on the foreign affairs committees also served on numerous other committees, making coordination all the more difficult. The Articles of Confederation, adopted in 1781, stressed Congress's principal role in conducting foreign affairs but at least created a permanent Department of Foreign Affairs. Congress directed the secretary of foreign affairs to "report on all cases expressly referred to him for that purpose by Congress, and all others touching his department."[19] Nonetheless, Congress as a whole continued to micromanage foreign affairs, including reading all correspondence with foreign powers. As the secretary of the department, John Jay, lamented, there were "unseasonable delays and successive obstacles in obtaining the decision and sentiments of Congress."[20] Robert Morris noted the structural problem: "[N]o Men living can attend the daily deliberations of Congress & do executive parts of business at the same time."[21]

Under the Articles of Confederation, Congress exercised exclusive authority to send and receive ambassadors, and to negotiate and conclude treaties. It lacked the authority to delegate to executive committees the power to enter into treaties and alliances. Decisions on treaties and the making of war were subject to a legislative supermajority of nine out of the thirteen states.[22] The ninth article of the Confederation provided that "[t]he United States, in Congress assembled, shall have the sole and exclusive right and power of determining on peace and war."[23] The confederation had neither an independent executive nor an independent judiciary. In short, the confederation privileged congressional policymaking at the expense of executive initiative.

States failed to adhere to the terms set in federally negotiated treaties,[24] embarrassing the federal government and undermining its negotiating position. The British and other foreign powers were quick to seize advantage wherever possible. Most have concluded that the legislature's record in managing foreign affairs under the articles was abysmal.[25]

Against this backdrop, the Framers granted significantly greater authority to the executive when drafting the Constitution. All of the plans debated at the convention vested additional powers in the chief executive, and both the Hamilton and Virginia Plans included substantial foreign affairs powers in the authority accorded to a chief executive. Although the quantum of the increase in the final compromise is debatable, all agree that the prior experience convinced the nation that the executive was to play at least a substantial role in foreign affairs.

Debates during the ratification period confirm the view that both the president and Congress were to play critical roles in foreign affairs. Speeches and pamphlets generally adverted to the functions of each. In particular, many viewed the president as an overall steward for the nation's foreign relations. Alexander Hamilton in the Federalist Papers wrote that general "management of foreign negotiations will naturally devolve"[26] on the president with senatorial checks. James Iredell in the North Carolina Convention asserted that the president was to "regulate all intercourse with foreign powers."[27] But, some stressed the Senate's dominant role as well, and others protested that the Constitution vested too much authority in the aristocratic Senate.[28] The precise boundaries between congressional policymaking and executive initiative were left to succeeding generations.

This chapter addresses first the president's treaty power and then his involvement in warmaking. Subsequently, the chapter will assess judicial responsibility to monitor presidential foreign policy acts in properly drawn cases and controversies. The Constitution fails to demarcate boundaries clearly among the powers in any of the contexts. The president's power of initiative as a matter of politics gives that officer a substantial, but by no means conclusive, advantage in shaping the nation's foreign policy. As a result, presidents generally stand accountable to the public for foreign policy initiatives, but their steps do not always have Congress's blessing.

A. *The Treaty Power*

The Constitution addressed the debilitating experience in foreign affairs under the Articles of Confederation in part by shifting the power to make treaties to the executive, which is where the power had long been lodged in Britain.[29] Article II, section 2 of the Constitution establishes that the president "shall have Power, by and with the Advice and Consent of the Senate, to make Treaties, provided two thirds of the Senators present concur."[30] As James Madison noted, the president's new role

> is an advantage which may be pronounced conclusive. At present the will of a single body can make a Treaty. If the new Government be established no treaty can be made without the joint consent of two distinct and independent wills. The president also being elected in a different

mode, and under a different influence from that of the Senate, will be the more apt and the more free to have a will of his own.[31]

The Framers anticipated that the president would enjoy distinct advantages over the legislature in negotiating treaties. As John Jay explained in the Federalist Papers, "[P]erfect *secrecy* and immediate *dispatch* are sometimes requisite" in negotiating treaties.[32] The risks of disclosure of information and delay by a large legislative body are too great. On the other hand, Jay continued that the president "will be able to manage the business of intelligence in such manner as prudence may suggest."[33] Accordingly, the Framers vested the power to forge treaties in the president, empowering the president to exercise considerable initiative.

Nonetheless, in a departure from the European tradition, the Constitution subjects the executive's treaty power to the Senate's approval. Although the Framers recognized that the check of consent would make concluding treaties more difficult, the corresponding benefit of encouraging greater dialogue between the president and the Senate outweighed any loss in efficiency. Article II, section 2 of the Constitution establishes that the president "shall have Power, by and with the Advice and Consent of the Senate, to make Treaties, provided two thirds of the Senators present concur."[34] Entrusting the consent power to the Senate alone made the dialogue more feasible, and may have reflected as well the presumption that senators would have greater maturity and perspective than members of the House of Representatives. Moreover, the supermajority requirement highlights the Framers' concern for international entanglements and caution about international agreements in general. In addition, consensus has emerged that the president's power to make treaties includes the power to decide, even after Senate concurrence, not to put the treaties into effect. Overall, the power to conclude treaties brings with it substantial discretion to shape the country's foreign policy. Through treaties, presidents can facilitate trade, provide for mutual defense, or help structure international regulation of the environment, weapons testing, or terrorism.

Under our system, treaties have equal dignity to legislation. In case of conflict, the most recently enacted prevails, and both are subject to constitutional review. As the Supreme Court summarized in *Whitney v. Robertson,* "By the Constitution a treaty is placed on the same footing, and made of like obligation, with an act of legislation. . . . When the two relate to the same subject, the courts will always endeavor to construe them so as to give effect to both, if that can be done without violating the language of either; but if the two are inconsistent, the one last in date will control the other. . . ."[35] In case of conflict, courts typically resolve the question of priority. Thus, in *Chae Chan Ping v. United States* the Court upheld a congressional effort to limit Chinese laborers from entering this country despite rights guaranteed in a prior treaty between China and the United States.[36]

The Constitution does not limit the subject matter addressed in treaties. Treaties can and have touched on concerns of domestic policy as well, including tax, environment, and labor issues. As Justice Story noted, however, even though the treaty power is "general and unrestricted, it is not to be so construed to destroy the fundamental laws of the State. A power given by the Constitution cannot be construed to authorize a destruction of other powers given in the same instrument."[37] And, in *Geofroy v. Riggs,* Justice Field wrote that the government through treaties cannot "authorize what the Constitution forbids."[38] In particular, no treaty "can confer power on the Congress, or on any other branch of Government, which is free from the restraints of the Constitution."[39]

Nonetheless, the federal government may be able to regulate subject areas through treaties—such as civil rights or family law—that Congress cannot itself reach due to federalism limits. The scope of treaties arguably is not limited by the Tenth Amendment and the Commerce Clause. Even if Congress, for instance, could not obligate state courts to entertain suits by foreign citizens, treaties could require that result.

Generally, however, treaties obligate the nation only internationally. Most treaties that have direct internal repercussions are non-self-executing, which means that the treaty will not have the force of law within the nation until Congress passes legislation so specifying. For all treaties that are not self-executing, therefore, Congress as a whole—and not just the Senate—plays a direct role in determining whether the treaty should govern the nation. The Senate at times will consent to a treaty only on the condition that its execution domestically be subject to Congress's approval as a whole.

Congress, and particularly the Senate, has shared power with the president over treaties ever since. Congress has set the policy parameters, limited presidents' discretion, and blocked presidential initiatives, while presidents have negotiated treaties with and without the Senate's consent. Although the Senate has ratified the vast majority of treaties presented before it, on two critical occasions during the twentieth century, the Senate blocked a negotiated treaty: the Treaty of Versailles in 1919 and the Nuclear Test-Ban Treaty of 1999.[40] Short of outright rejection, moreover, the Senate can influence the content of treaties in a variety of ways. No one disputes the fundamental role of the Senate in approving treaties negotiated by the president. And, although the legal issues triggered can be quite intricate, some examination is warranted to understand the ways in which Congress and the president jockey for authority in foreign affairs through the treaty power. Presidential initiative often has displaced congressional and or senatorial policymaking.

At least six sources of tension have arisen surrounding the president's treaty power. First, should the Senate have a role in negotiating as well as in approving treaties? Second, may the president enter into agreements with foreign nations without triggering the Treaty Clause and thereby restrict senatorial power? Third, may Congress limit the president's power by insisting upon reservations when approving treaties? Fourth, when does presidential interpretation or reinterpretation of a treaty provision depart so widely from the treaty text so as to in effect establish a new treaty provision requiring Senate ratification? Fifth, may the president unilaterally terminate treaties? And sixth, does the Treaty Clause implicitly preclude states from entering into any agreements with foreign powers? Answers from history and constitutional exegesis do not always agree.

1. THE ADVICE POWER OF THE SENATE

One source of tension has been whether the constitutional language vesting the Senate with the power not only to consent to treaties but also to give "advice"[41] should be read to contemplate an active role for the Senate in negotiating treaties—much as can be argued in the appointments process as well. Given the constitutional text, the president and the Senate could have joined as a type of council in setting negotiating priorities and parameters. Presidential initiative would be shaped by consultation with the Senate.

During the nation's first administration, President Washington sought the Senate's counsel in negotiating a treaty with the Creek Indians. The Senate blocked his efforts, and referred the issue to a committee. President Washington reportedly retorted, "[T]his defeats every purpose of my coming here."[42] Washington never returned for advice in concluding treaties again, and his successors have desisted as well.[43] Pragmatic considerations supported Washington's position: it would be extremely cumbersome and perhaps dangerous to confer with the Senate during each step of a delicate negotiation. Confidentiality might be compromised, and the delay might upset any prior momentum achieved. As the Senate has increased in size, the potential for inefficiency has grown commensurately. The Senate as an institution cannot easily act as a negotiating partner.

Some have argued, however, that the Constitution requires the Senate to fulfill an advisory role in negotiations.[44] Members of the Senate themselves periodically have sought to exercise a greater role in the negotiation process.[45] Moreover, until the end of Madison's administration, presidents submitted the names of treaty negotiators to the Senate for confirmation.[46] Our nation's practice, however, has confirmed that presidents in negotiating treaties retain the discretion to confide in or ignore the Senate as they deem appropriate. Indeed, the Senate has seemingly acquiesced in that understanding, declining numerous opportunities to protest being cut off from the advice stage.[47] Nonetheless, presidents have solicited advice from individual members of Congress. President Truman asked for help in negotiating treaties after World War II, and President Carter followed the same tack in negotiating the Panama Canal treaty.[48] Sound politics may lead presidents to enlist the help of key senators. The Senate retains the right to reject the product of any negotiations that it finds objectionable, irrespective of whether the president keeps it or key members informed of treaty negotiations.

Moreover, Congress may influence the treaty negotiation process through legislation intended to force the president's hand. The proposed development of an antisatellite weapon (ASAT) during the 1980s is a case in point.

The Soviets in the late 1970s tried to develop a weapon to destroy enemy satellites from earth. They abandoned the effort when the goal appeared financially and technologically infeasible.[49] No arms control agreement or treaty governed such weapons.

After the Reagan administration took office in 1981, it began a U.S. ASAT development program. Members of the Democratic-controlled House of Representatives, alarmed at the potentially destabilizing effect should such a weapon be deployed by either superpower, attempted unsuccessfully to cut off funding for the program. But in 1984, Congress passed a compromise amendment permitting limited ASAT testing only after a certification by the president that he was negotiating in good faith with the Soviets for a treaty imposing the strictest possible limits on

ASATs.[50] A similar amendment passed in 1985. Then in 1986 and 1987 (the latter year with both houses of Congress under Democratic control), Congress passed a complete moratorium on ASAT testing.[51]

The Soviets, for their part, had left their ASAT program lie fallow. Following the 1987 testing moratorium passed by Congress, the U.S. Department of Defense chose to abandon the ASAT program altogether, and it has never been revived.

Some members of Congress had sought to avert an ASAT arms race, and they had pursued two tacks, more or less successfully. The first, legislation forcing the president to negotiate in good faith toward a specific goal if the nation were to adopt an ASAT program, was an explicit incentive for the president to exercise his treaty power. The second, a flat moratorium on testing, was an implied but no less potent incentive. No treaty was ever negotiated, yet the anti-ASAT forces in Congress succeeded in their goal of averting a provocative unilateral test by the United States. In short, the constitutional language of "advise and consent" over time has been reduced to "consent," but Congress can rely on other means to influence negotiation of treaties and check presidential initiative.

2. EXECUTIVE AGREEMENTS

Presidents increasingly have entered into executive agreements with foreign powers that seemingly circumvent the Senate's constitutional responsibility under Article II to ratify all treaties.[52] Recent examples include United States' agreement to be bound by the North American Free Trade Agreement (NAFTA)[53] and the World Trade Organization (WTO).[54] President Reagan's agreement with Iran to establish a claims tribunal at the conclusion of the hostage crisis illustrates another controversial occasion in which a president never asked for Senate authorization of an agreement with a foreign power. During one thirty-year period after World War II, more than seven thousand executive agreements were concluded, ten times the number of treaties negotiated during the same period.[55]

There are two distinct types of executive agreement. First, presidents arguably enjoy the power under Article II to enter into some agreements unilaterally, as President Franklin Roosevelt did, for example, in recognizing the Soviet Union.[56] Use of executive agreements to recognize foreign governments might be seen as a special case—many believe that Article II vests implicit authority in the president to recognize foreign governments, particularly given the textual power to appoint and receive ambassadors.

But, the use of executive agreements has not been so constrained. For example, Roosevelt agreed without Congress's authorization to trade destroyers to Britain for the right to use British bases in the Atlantic and Caribbean.[57] Roosevelt's maneuverings, without congressional sanction, led the nation toward confrontation with Germany. Similarly, President Madison initiated the Rush-Bagot agreement in 1817 with Britain, agreeing to limit both nations' naval forces on the Great Lakes. Some agreements have covered terrain so quotidian, such as routine claims against foreign governments, that Congress may well have agreed, if asked, to delegate the responsibility of concluding the agreement to the president. Other agreements grew out of a need for a decisiveness that might not have afforded the Senate sufficient time within which to act. The constitutional question posed, therefore, is whether the president enjoys the authority under Article II to take such actions without congressional participation.

Second, presidents more frequently enter into agreements and seek congressional approval afterward, as with the NAFTA and WTO examples. Even when Congress as a whole approves of the agreement, however, the measure cuts out the senatorial ratification responsibility—only a simple majority vote is required. The congressional approval role makes the process more democratic,[58] but the constitutionality of such agreements—though certainly not their recent pedigree—is suspect.[59] After presenting a case study illustrating the practical need for unilateral executive agreements short of treaties, this section will discuss the more problematic area of the constitutionality of congressionally sanctioned executive agreements that have a significant impact on U.S. citizens.

a. Unilateral Executive Agreements Through executive agreements, presidents can accomplish a wide variety of aims in foreign policy without awaiting the Senate's concurrence. The advantages for executive initiative in terms of flexibility and speed are apparent. Such executive agreements, however, cannot supersede a prior treaty or congressional enactment. For instance, in *United States v. Capps,* the court of appeals held that an executive agreement with Canada covering importation of potatoes conflicted with a statute and was hence unenforceable.[60] In terms of priority, executive agreements are subordinate to both treaties and statutes.

Nonetheless, executive agreements afford presidents a powerful tool with which to shape foreign policy. A relatively recent example illustrates both the flexibility and utility of the unilateral executive agreement. Jean-Bertrand Aristide, a former Catholic priest, was elected president of Haiti in 1990, in what international observers certified as a free and fair election.[61] President Bush formally recognized the Aristide government. A year after his election, Aristide was overthrown in a military coup and replaced by a junta headed by General Raoul Cédras. Aristide went into exile in the United States, which continued to recognize his government in preference to that of Cédras's eventual figurehead, Émile Jonassaint.[62]

By September of 1994, political refugees were fleeing Haiti to the United States; the Cédras regime was committing egregious human rights violations; and the United States was faced with the specter of a brutal military regime at its doorstep. The new Clinton administration in Washington increased pressure on the Haitian military leaders to step aside and allow the return of Aristide. Cédras was intransigent. When diplomatic initiatives failed to bear fruit, the United States began to prepare for military action that would oust the generals and restore some semblance of democracy. As an invasion neared, it became clear that it would be extremely unpopular in the United States.[63] President Clinton dispatched special envoys to conduct last-ditch negotiations to obviate the need for an invasion. Representing the president were former President Carter, retired chairman of the Joint Chiefs General Colin Powell, and Sam Nunn, chairman of the Senate Armed Services Committee.[64]

When negotiations stalled, President Clinton ordered paratroopers into the air for an invasion even as his team continued to bargain with Cédras.[65] At the last minute, Cédras became aware of the imminent invasion and agreed to terms. Although he declined to proffer his signature, Cédras gave his word orally to General Powell that he would comply. The U.S. planes were ordered to turn around and return to their base. Under the agreement, the U.S. military would enter Haiti at the request of the government, and the junta would step down in favor of Aristide.[66]

President Clinton reached the agreement with the Haitian military leaders without any formal input from the Senate. The story strongly suggests, however, why this nation has accepted a category of executive agreements entirely distinct from treaties.

First, time was of the essence. The need to obtain Senate approval would have cast the entire arrangement in doubt. The Haitian junta, which had already reneged on one commitment to the United Nations to leave the government, likely would not have waited in limbo for Senate action once the immediate threat of invasion had passed.[67]

Second, Clinton reached the agreement not with the legally recognized government of Haiti (represented by Aristide) but with the military junta, so the pact essentially bound the United States and private individuals. Constitutionally, the United States cannot conclude a treaty except with sovereign nations or international organizations.[68]

Finally, treaties must be concluded by the president himself, and in writing. By long-established practice, no such limits are imposed on executive agreements, which may be concluded by anyone whom the president designates, and may take any form. The president can delegate to subordinates subsidiary policymaking authority in the foreign realm without necessarily triggering the Senate's constitutional authority to ratify treaties.

Although executive agreements in the Haiti context may provoke little controversy, unilateral agreements test the outer ambit of plenary executive authority. By virtue of the Article II power to command the armed forces and appoint ambassadors, some leeway is permitted, and an argument can be made that the Framers were aware of and approved such agreements.[69] But President Clinton arguably could not have concluded an executive agreement with Haiti that in any way significantly would have changed trading rights or the right to travel, issues with a more direct impact on U.S. citizens. Presidential flexibility in foreign policy should not supplant the constitutional role accorded to the Senate and the Congress as a whole.

b. Ex Post Ratification by Congress of Executive Agreements In contrast to the Haiti example, congressionally approved executive agreements are more common. Such agreements have had an impact on U.S. citizens, and some executive agreements functionally are indistinguishable from treaties. Presidents have concluded written agreements with acknowledged heads of state even when time would have permitted negotiation and then ratification of a treaty.

Congress at times has protested the use of executive agreements.[70] Nonetheless, it has seemingly acquiesced in the practice. At first blush, such agreements accommodate executive initiative with congressional policymaking prerogatives. Indeed, Congress implicitly recognized the tradition in 1972 in the Case Act, which merely required the secretary of state to "transmit to the Congress the text of any international agreement

... other than a treaty, to which the United States is a party" no later than sixty days after "such agreement has entered into force."[71] The notification requirement suggests that Congress, at least in most cases, is prepared to accept a presidential power under Article II to conclude such agreements.

Moreover, such agreements have been implicitly upheld by the courts. Consider, for instance, President Lyndon Johnson's agreement with the Republic of the Philippines granting preferential employment for Filipino citizens at United States military bases in the Philippines. Congress subsequently enacted a statute prohibiting employment discrimination against U.S. citizens at United States military bases overseas unless permitted by "treaties." U.S. citizens in the Philippines, who were later notified that they would lose their jobs, argued that, as a statutory matter, the exemption reached only "treaties" enacted through the formal process delineated in Article II.

In *Weinberger v. Rossi,* however, the Court held that the president's executive agreement could be considered a "treaty" within the meaning of the statute.[72] As the Court explained, "We have recognized . . . that the President may enter into certain binding agreements with foreign nations without complying with the formalities required by the Treaty Clause of the Constitution. . . . Even though such agreements are not treaties under the Treaty Clause of the Constitution, they may in appropriate circumstances have an effect similar to treaties in some areas of domestic law."[73] Executive agreements have, through tradition, become an accepted part of the governmental fabric.

President Carter's executive agreement ending the seizure of the U.S. embassy in Iran represents a good example. To resolve the hostage crisis, the United States pledged "that it is and from now on will be the policy of the United States not to intervene, directly or indirectly, politically or militarily, in Iran's internal affairs."[74] In addition, the government agreed to release billions of dollars in frozen Iranian assets in exchange for establishment of an international Iran claims tribunal, which would resolve all past and future claims against the government of Iran. At the time of the agreement, three hundred suits had already been filed, and an estimated two thousand additional claims existed. Carter declined to seek any formal approval from either the Senate or Congress as a whole.

The executive agreement posed a politically acceptable way to end the hostage crisis, free U.S. citizens, and set a means for resolving claims against the government. Time was of the essence. Carter had followed in the footsteps of President Franklin Roosevelt and others in using the agreement as a means of effectuating critical foreign policy.

On the other hand, the executive order directly affected the property rights of those pressing claims against Iran. Before Carter concluded the agreement, several firms had obtained judgments against Iran that the agreement purported to vacate, and other firms had litigation pending. By releasing the frozen assets, President Reagan also deprived litigants of a potential source from which to collect any judgment.

In *Dames & Moore v. Regan* the Supreme Court reviewed a constitutional challenge to the president's authority to settle claims with foreign nations.[75] The Court held that the congressional framework statute authorizing presidential acts in emergencies—the International Emergency Economic Powers Act[76]—authorized the nullification of judgments and release of the blocked assets. With respect to the authority to suspend claims pending in U.S. courts, however, the Court held that there was no specific authorization. Nonetheless, the Court noted that, even though many prior settlements had been reached by treaty, "there has also been a longstanding practice of settling such claims by executive agreement without the advice and consent of the Senate."[77] The Court explained that Congress had acquiesced to prior exercises of presidential authority, and it concluded that Congress had implicitly sanctioned such use of executive agreements in the Iran case. Past precedent influenced the Court's decision. The line between treaties and executive agreements is difficult to distinguish—both have addressed issues of fundamental national importance and affected individual rights directly. Viewed from the lens solely of the Constitution, however, the legitimacy of such agreements is open to serious question.

A useful analogy lies in the frequent presidential practice of appointing special envoys to negotiate over particular issues. Although the Senate has the power to approve ambassadorial appointments, the president under Article II arguably enjoys the capacity to appoint "special" envoys at will.[78] For instance, President Washington sent Gouverneur Morris to engage the British in negotiations over the future of relations between the two countries. President Wilson sent Colonel Edward House on diplomatic missions during the First World War, Franklin Roosevelt used Harry Hopkins in a similar fashion during World War II,[79] and President Clinton dispatched Jesse Jackson to negotiate among the parties during the Bosnian conflagration. Although some envoys have far more limited power than would an ambassador, the importance of others has dwarfed that of ambassadors themselves. Envoys have played a critical role in shaping foreign policy.

In both the executive agreement and envoy contexts, therefore, presidents have sought to respond to foreign policy challenges with more flexible means than those prescribed explicitly in the Constitution. Through executive agreements and envoys, presidents can act with greater dispatch and possibly secrecy. The formal constitutional objections have receded with the increased complexity and importance of international relations. Line-drawing problems remain, for the lesser steps of concluding executive agreements and sending envoys can result in circumvention of the Senate's policymaking authority.

There may be a core set of circumstances, however, for which treaties are indispensable. Congressional agreements should not be possible as a constitutional matter in contexts over which Congress lacks power to regulate under Article I of the Constitution. For instance, given that the Supreme Court has cut back congressional power over civil rights and family law issues in furthering its view of federalism, congressional executive agreements that touch on such concerns would violate the constitutional limits on congressional authority. Treaties, therefore, might be the only constitutionally permissible path to pursue.[80] Otherwise, it is for presidents to determine whether to conclude treaties or agreements with congressional backing.

3. The Senate's Power to Condition Consent

The Senate's practice of conditioning its acceptance of treaties on modifications of conduct highlights a third area in which the executive and legislature have clashed over the treaty power. With increasing frequency since World War II, the Senate through the attachment of reservations, understandings, and conditions (RUDs) during the approval process has attempted to reign in the president by shaping the scope, interpretation and enforcement of treaties.[81] For instance, in approving a general arbitration convention, the Senate attached the condition that each specific arbitral matter under the treaty had to be submitted subsequently to the Senate for its approval.[82]

Presidents by and large have acquiesced to this practice. Presumably, the greater power of rejecting a treaty includes the lesser power of conditioning consent on particular revisions. Moreover, early judicial decisions found this practice to be constitutional (*Haver v. Yaker*, 1869; *Fourteen Diamond Rings v. United States*, 1901). The president must accept and abide by RUDs if the treaty is to go into effect. The Senate participates in shaping international policy through such means. As Justice Scalia has noted, if the president disagrees with the conditions, "his only constitutionally permissible course is to decline to ratify the treaty."[83]

To illustrate further, the Senate has on a number of occasions appended language during the treaty approval process declaring a treaty to be non-self-executing. This has occurred repeatedly in the case of multilateral human rights treaties in the 1980s and 1990s.[84] Some have argued that the Senate has overstepped its bounds by attaching such condition because a treaty's substance—and not merely language—dictates whether it is self-executing. On the other hand, the Senate in approving a treaty logically is concerned whether further legislation is required before it goes into effect. The condition of non-self-execution should be no different than any other RUD.

In related vein, some treaties have required future congressional action for the United States to remain in compliance with the treaty's provisions. This would appear to offer a substantial congressional check on the president's power to make treaties. In such a case Congress could block American participation in a treaty, for example, simply by failing to appropriate funds necessary for compliance. Although Congress has often threatened to carry out such actions (or omissions), it has seldom done so in practice. Rather, the mere threat of noncompliance has proven to be a potent political tool.[85]

The payment of dues to the United Nations, for instance, is a U.S. obligation under the treaty providing for its establishment, and one that falls within Congress's purview under its appropriations powers in Article I. Congressional unhappiness in the 1990s with the UN as an institution, with various of its programs and expenditures, and with the large share of dues (more than 20 percent of the total budget) allotted to the United States, led to long delays in the payment of dues by Congress and to threats not to pay at all.[86] A treaty term contemplating further congressional acts permits Congress to control treaty execution. Presidential agreement with such conditions paves the way for a greater congressional role in treaties than otherwise might have been thought possible.

Other conditions, however, might be unenforceable even if approved by the president. One can fancifully imagine that the Senate predicate approval of a treaty on a condition that the president attend church services or fire a particular officer. Courts likely would refuse to enforce conditions that are so loosely connected to the merits of the treaty. And, if the conditions seek to deprive others of constitutional rights—such as a condition that the president must refuse to promote women in the foreign service—then they almost certainly would not be enforceable.

Moreover, reservations that purport to limit executive discretion in future international dealings should be unenforceable. Through the reservation process, the Senate should not be able to permit itself such control over future conduct. For instance, the Senate has proposed a reservation attached to a commerce treaty directing the president to take particular negotiating positions in the future. Presidents should be able to ignore any such restrictions.[87]

In short, by attaching conditions to a treaty, the Senate can achieve a powerful voice in foreign affairs, limiting presidential initiative. If the treaty is signed by the president, then the president must respect the limitations and reservations imposed by the Senate. However, the conditions must be linked to the subject matter of the treaty; otherwise, the Senate could rearrange other constitutional arrangements through its power of approving treaties.

4. PRESIDENTIAL POWER TO INTERPRET TREATIES

After a treaty has been ratified by the Senate and implemented by the president, there is no easy way to resolve disputes over treaty interpretation. At some point, a president's interpretation of a treaty can change its meaning, and the alteration circumvents the Senate's constitutionally prescribed ratification power. In other words, the president may be able to obtain indirectly through interpretation that which he could not achieve directly by modifying the treaty. On the other hand, given the inherent ambiguity of language, there is no easily ascertainable way to determine when interpretation ends and the making of a new treaty begins.

Consider President Reagan's tussle with the Senate over the "Star Wars" program. The legal question was whether Reagan's Strategic Defense Initiative (SDI) conflicted with terms of the previously negotiated anti-ballistic missile (ABM) treaty with the Soviet Union. The Reagan administration construed the ABM treaty to permit testing of the SDI by reading into the treaty an exception for testing missiles that were built using different physical concepts than then existed.[88]

President Reagan, in advocating missile defense, was faced with a choice: either renegotiate the ABM treaty so as unambiguously to permit the contemplated missile defense plan, or simply *reinterpret* the treaty in a more flexible light, to achieve the same purpose. He chose the latter path. The prospect of renegotiating would have been slow and uncertain at best.

During the last stages of the conflict over SDI, Reagan faced a Senate controlled by the opposition party. He cannot have relished the prospect of seeking two-thirds approval for a renegotiated ABM treaty from a hostile Senate. Reagan thereafter tried to justify the program in terms of the existing treaty.

Protests erupted in the Senate, leading the Foreign Relations Committee to issue a report calling the reinterpretation "the most flagrant abuse of the Constitution's treaty power in 200 years."[89] Members of the Senate charged that the president was reserving the right to amend treaties without any input from the Senate. Influential senators threatened to withhold funding for administration projects in protest, and warned that they would hold up the president's nominee for the Supreme Court. As is often the case, the entities compromised, and the administration never conducted the tests.

No doubt influenced by the conflict with the president over the ABM treaty and SDI, the Senate a year later approved the Intermediate Nuclear Forces (INF) Treaty governing land-based nuclear weapons in Europe but explicitly conditioned its approval on the understanding that the Senate's present interpretation of the treaty's meaning, and no other, should determine its application and boundaries. President Reagan, not to be outdone, accepted the RUD but deemed it "improper."[90] Thus, although most reservations must be accepted by presidents, the question of interpretation still lingers.

The potential for a difference in interpretation always exists, and the Constitution provides no means with which to reconcile differences in interpretation. The president has the advantage because he can exercise discretion in implementing treaties. His interpretation, in other words, can alter the international relations framework. But, as the SDI example shows, the Senate is not powerless and can exercise political means to force the president to adhere to its interpretation of the treaty.

In short, the president retains the initiative in treaty making. The president proposes a treaty, negotiates the framework, can withdraw the treaty from consideration at any time, and can reject any modifications imposed. Over time, the Senate has left to the president the authority of initiating contact with foreign sovereigns as well as formulating treaty strategy.

Furthermore, at times, a particular treaty interpretation may directly affect rights of private parties—unlike in the debate over missile systems testing. If the disagreement, for instance, concerns claims against foreign governments or tariffs, the courts may need to determine which interpretation to uphold. The presidential interpretation may merit deference, but courts likely will determine the meaning of the treaty provision for themselves. Thus, even though the presidential interpretation of treaties may in effect change a treaty, checks of both the political process and possible ex post monitoring by judges limits that potential.

5. THE POWER TO TERMINATE TREATIES

The Constitution does not clarify whether the president, the president in conjunction with the Senate, or Congress has the power to terminate United States participation in a treaty. Congress can, of course, override a treaty's effect on domestic law and, if the treaty is not self-executing, block its enforcement within the United States. However, it is not clear whether Congress can nullify treaties completely. Congress, for instance, purported to abrogate treaties with France in 1798 as hostilities on the seas grew,[91] but, as a matter of international obligation, the impact of Congress's action is not clear.

Nor is it settled whether the president has the power to terminate treaties without the Senate's consent. On the one hand, it is logical that the president should be able to cancel a treaty in case of another signatory's default; the president is better institutionally positioned than Congress to make that on-the-ground assessment. President Franklin Roosevelt, for instance, nullified the Treaty of Commerce, Friendship and Navigation with Japan as its aggressiveness became increasingly clear in 1939, and terminated an extradition treaty with Greece when Greece failed to turn over a fugitive to the United States.[92]

Many presidents have also believed that, in light of their role as principal policy makers in the foreign affairs field, they should be able to terminate treaties in other contexts as well. As world conditions change, they need the flexibility to act decisively. Just as presidents can determine whether to put into effect treaties ratified by the Senate, so they can decide whether to halt a treaty once implemented. Given that the treaty power is vested in Article II of the Constitution and not in Article I, it may be logical to infer that it is the president's responsibility solely to determine when treaties should be abrogated. Indeed, numerous examples exist of presidential termination.

On the other hand, if the president can terminate a treaty in light of policy changes, then the Senate's ratification role seemingly can be circumvented. Some presidents have hesitated to cancel treaty obligations until informal senatorial (or congressional) assent could be obtained.[93]

If congressional assent is needed, then a further question would be the form that assent must take. Given the Constitution's silence, two options are readily apparent. First, Congress might terminate a treaty through a statute. Because treaties have equal dignity to laws under our system, then Congress could follow the same path in terminating a treaty that it does in repealing a law. Second, two-thirds of the Senate might need to reach agreement with the president before any treaty could be nullified. The first option eschews any special role for the Senate and includes the possibility of treaty termination even when the president is opposed. The second option retains the partnership between the Senate and the president enshrined in the Constitution at the expense of Congress as a whole.

As a legal matter, the question still remains open. In *Goldwater v. Carter*, Senator Barry Goldwater and twenty-three other members of Congress challenged President Carter's right to abrogate a mutual defense treaty with the Republic of China (Taiwan) in order to meet the conditions of the People's Republic of China for full normalization of diplomatic relations.[94] The court of appeals held that Art. II, § 2 of the Constitution did not imply a requirement that the Senate's approval be sought to end U.S. participation in a treaty. It stated that the president could exercise the authority "to determine whether a treaty has terminated because of a breach, [and] to determine whether a treaty is at an end due to changed circumstances."[95] At least in cases of signatory breach, the president under Article II may possess the right to terminate our treaty obligations.

On the other hand, Congress historically has also passed statutes lifting requirements imposed by treaty.[96] For instance, in 1798, Congress passed a statute purporting to negate prior treaties with France.[97] The Supreme Court treated the statute as valid (*Chirac v. Chirac's Lessee,* 1817).[98] If Congress as a whole, however, can lift international obligations imposed by treaties on the United States, then the president and Senate's constitutionally assigned functions could be thwarted. The Constitution omits any clear way to resolve which entity can abrogate treaties. In the absence of any settled doctrine, the House, Senate, and president are left to use political levers to achieve their objectives once the attractiveness or usefulness of treaties wanes. For instance, on at least one occasion, President Wilson declined to comply with a statute directing him not to enforce particular provisions of the Merchant Marine Act of 1920.[99] Congress as a whole can decline to appropriate funds to implement the treaty. Thus, it is possible that the president and Congress enjoy the concurrent power to abrogate treaty obligations, and resolution of any conflict may turn on the outcome of the political process.

6. THE RESIDUAL ROLE OF STATES IN FOREIGN AFFAIRS

The historical record suggests that state and local governments were to play no appreciable role in foreign affairs. After the Articles of Confederation experience, consensus emerged that we needed to conduct foreign relations as an entire nation. As the Supreme Court stated in *Japan Line Ltd. v. County of Los Angeles* the Framers' overriding concern had been "that 'the Federal Government must speak with one voice when regulating commercial relations with foreign governments.'"[100] Or, as the Court maintained in *Zschernig v. Miller* "state involvement in foreign affairs and international relations [are] matters which the Constitution entrusts solely to the Federal Government."[101] In that case, the Oregon law had prohibited any non-U.S. citizen from inheriting property if his or her home nation denied U.S. citizens that right. After losing in Oregon's courts, an East German citizen successfully sought review in the U.S. Supreme Court, which reversed the Oregon decision on the ground that the state statute had impermissibly intruded "into the field of foreign affairs which the Constitution entrusts to the President and Congress."[102] Consider, also the older Supreme Court precedent in *Holmes v. Jennison*.[103] There, the Supreme Court confronted the question whether Vermont could conclude an extradition agreement with Canada in the absence of congressional authorization. There was no opinion for the Court, but a majority of the justices were of the view that Vermont had to await such authorization. Otherwise, states too easily could direct foreign policy for the nation as a whole.

The Constitution states in Article I, § 10 that

> [n]o State shall enter into any Treaty, Alliance, or Confederation; grant Letters of Marque and Reprisal. . . . No State shall, without the Consent of the Congress, lay any Imposts or Duties on Imports or Exports. . . . No state shall, without the Consent of Congress, lay any Duty of Tonnage, keep Troops, or Ships of War in time of Peace, enter into any

Agreement or Compact . . . with a foreign Power, or engage in War, unless actually invaded"[104]

But that seemingly clear language belies the inevitable impact that cities
and states have had on international relations. In addition to relatively in-
nocuous ties such as sister-city programs, local and state governments
have established offices oversees, signed multilateral agreements, and par-
ticipated in international summits. When Illinois passed a resolution providing that the language and culture of Macedonians has been Hellenic
for three thousand years, few legislators predicted the adverse diplomatic
repercussions.[105] The import of other state actions have been more pre-
dictable. The governors of New York and New Jersey attempted to deny
the Soviet foreign minister's plane the right to land during the UN's debate over the downed Korean plane incident;[106] Oregon sought to bill the
Soviet Union for costs associated with the Chernobyl incident,[107] and
California enacted its Buy American Act.[108]

For another example, Massachusetts in 1996 established a restrictive
purchasing list targeting companies doing business with Burma (Myanmar), to protest the dictatorship's policies.[109] That action placed the
United States in the awkward position of defending the Massachusetts
approach before the World Trade Organization while attempting behind
the scenes to pressure Massachusetts into changing the law.[110]

Litigation ensued, and firms doing business in Burma challenged the
law in part on the ground that it violated the constitutional commitment
of foreign commerce to the federal government. Lower courts agreed with
the firms, reasoning that the law "unconstitutionally impinge[d] on the
federal government's exclusive authority to regulate foreign affairs."[111]
Although the U.S. Supreme Court in *Crosby v. National Foreign Trade
Council* affirmed on a different ground, it, too, stressed that the state law
would impede executive flexibility in addressing the internal situation in
Burma.[112] In particular, the Court noted that, because Congress, after
Massachusetts had passed its law, had delegated authority to the president to impose sanctions on Burma, state actions would interfere with
that congressionally granted authority. States have even less authority to
impact foreign relations when Congress has conferred power over a particular international issue to the president.

More recently, California passed a law requiring any insurer in that
state to disclose information about insurance policies issued in Europe

between 1920 and 1945. Its intent was to prod such insurance companies to resolve claims arising out of Holocaust-era policies. The U.S. government protested the measure, arguing that the California statute could threaten its efforts to ensure payment to Holocaust victims. The government had helped engineer an international framework under which compensation could be gained from a consortium of insurers, backed by the governments of Germany, Austria, and France. The group of insurers challenged the California law, arguing in part that California had impermissibly interfered with the executive's conduct of foreign relations.

The United States Supreme Court agreed. It noted that "[m]aking executive agreements to settle claims of American nationals against foreign governments is a particularly longstanding practice."[113] In reliance on *Zschernig,* the Court continued that "[t]he exercise of the federal executive authority means that state law must give way where, as here, there is evidence of clear conflict between the policies adopted by the two."[114] To the Court, California's statutory scheme undercut the executive's efforts to promote resolution of claims outside litigation.

The difficulty is that, with increased globalization, almost every state act may have a ripple effect internationally. A state's decision to increase production of natural gas, for instance, may have a dramatic impact on gas prices worldwide. Similarly, a state's decision to encourage trade with sister cities abroad may affect commerce among nations. Some accommodation between state and federal authority in international relations must be made. If no direct conflict exists, leeway should be afforded the states. The federal position, however, must remain dominant, with states playing an ancillary role at best. Otherwise, state diplomacy could thwart presidential initiative as well as congressional policymaking.

In sum, the president under Article II shares the treaty power with both Congress and the Senate. Under the Constitution, the president and Senate each exercise formal power. However, the country's experience has made it plain that forceful presidential action at times is needed. Accordingly, the president has largely seized the initiative by entering into executive agreements, and less frequently by abrogating treaty obligations. The Senate for its part has agreed to treaties only after insisting upon reservations and conditions, and the House has confined presidential power by limiting the reach and funding for treaty obligations. The branches have continued to joust for authority in international relations, with the executive's institutional advantage giving it an edge.

B. War Powers

Unlike the murky constitutional allocation of authority between the president and Congress in foreign affairs generally, most academics have concluded that the Constitution vests Congress with the principal role in declaring and waging war. In their view, the Constitution's grant to Congress of the powers to declare war, equip armies, control appropriations, and to define and punish offenses against the law of nations indicates that Congress is to play the principal role in military actions. The constitutional authorization to Congress to "grant Letters of Marque and Reprisal"[115] to private individuals to carry out hostilities against foreign nations is to similar effect.[116] Indeed, given the prevailing European trend at the time of the Founding to vest such power in an executive, the Constitution's different path strongly suggests that Congress was to play the fundamental role.[117] And, in the mind of the Framers, the decision as to war or peace loomed as the preeminent determination in the foreign affairs arena. Such momentous decisions should not lie with the executive alone. As Justice Story later wrote: "[T]he power of declaring war is not only the highest sovereign prerogative; but . . . it is in its own nature and effects so critical and calamitous, that it requires the utmost deliberation, and the successive review of all the councils of the nation."[118]

David Gray Adler has written that the Constitution "makes Congress the sole and exclusive repository of the ultimate foreign relations power—the authority to initiate war."[119] John Hart Ely has noted that the Constitution requires all warmaking, whether major confrontations or light skirmishes, "to be legislatively authorized."[120] Charles Lofgren concludes that the constitutional language and structure "likely convinced contemporaries even further that the new Congress would have nearly complete authority over the commencement of war."[121]

On the other hand, the Constitution vests key responsibilities in the president as well. The president pursuant to Article II serves as commander in chief of the armed forces: "The President shall be Commander in Chief of the Army and Navy of the United States, and of the Militia of the several States, when called in to the actual Service of the United States."[122] The supreme command of the armed forces is a critical position, one with the power to influence the extent and duration of any military campaign. Moreover, the Constitution grants the president the authority to exercise the "executive powers" of the United States generally, which might include the power to protect the security of the country.[123] The authority to engage in hostilities abroad may also be traced to the aggregate of the powers explicitly granted in the Constitution, including the vesting of the executive authority and the office of commander in chief.

Alternatively, the power to conduct military actions may be inherent in the concept of sovereignty and thus implicit in the Constitution—the president must be able to exercise such powers as necessary to preserve the sovereignty of the nation. Prior to ratification of the Constitution, many thought that the executive possessed the power to initiate hostilities in response to provocations.[124] Arguments supporting such an executive role are not specious, and the power to declare war is not necessarily tantamount to the power to make war.[125] Rather, the policy decision to declare war may represent a congressional prerogative to trigger special international responsibilities such as prisoner of war conventions and thereby determine the type of hostilities in which we are engaged. Nonetheless, as a matter of language and structure, Congress's role seems paramount.

Historical precedent lends credence to the congressional primacy position. Over the first hundred fifty years of our nation's history, almost all major wars were fought either with congressional authorization or after a declaration of war. Indeed, as mentioned earlier, the Supreme Court in 1804 invalidated seizure of a foreign merchant vessel during the war with France on the ground that the presidentially authorized action was beyond the scope of authority granted by Congress.[126]

The question of what constitutes a war, however, has never been decided. In the more than two hundred years since ratification of the Constitution, Congress has declared war only five times. Declarations were used for the War of 1812 against England; the War of 1846 against Mexico; the Spanish-American War of 1898; and both world wars in the twentieth century.[127] This country has engaged in military combat, however, on more than one hundred additional occasions.[128] Declarations of war have lost their importance over time: nations have engaged in hostilities without complying with such formal niceties. Irrespective of whether a formal declaration is issued, however, the constitutional requirement of congressional authorization still should be applicable. Yet, it is not clear when the authorization requirement is triggered, for the line between war and military or other covert action is difficult to assess. Should all troop landings be considered war? What about the pursuit of pirates or robbers onto foreign land? Moreover, countries have engaged in hostilities in increasingly novel ways with the passage of time, whether through eavesdropping, use of third-party agents, or industrial sabotage.

At a minimum, most agree that the president in the absence of congressional authorization can deploy the military in defensive maneuvers. The Founders evidently contemplated that presidents without notifying Congress would immediately take action to repel foreign invasions directly threatening the nation's sovereignty. In rejecting a proposal that only Congress be empowered to "make" as opposed to declare wars, they determined that the president needed the discretion to engage in hostilities in emergency situations.

There is no consensus, however, as to when military actions can be considered "defensive" only. Presidents, from the outset of the nation, distinguished between defensive and offensive wars, as did writers of the time.[129] President Washington dispatched troops against hostile Indian forces; President Jefferson pursued actions against the Barbary pirates; President McKinley dispatched five thousand troops to help quell the Boxer Rebellion; FDR ordered troops in 1940 to occupy Greenland after the Nazis marched through Denmark.[130] At some point, almost every military action can be cast in terms of protecting U.S. lives or property. Ascertaining what is a "defensive" military operation is inherently subjective, but most would agree that some military operations—such as President Clinton's bombing of Iraq in the wake of the failed assassination of President Bush—stretch the concept of defensive too far.[131] Furthermore, what starts out as a defensive use of troops may rapidly escalate into a traditional conflict. Arguably, the Korean conflict can be so understood.

Despite the line-drawing problems, Congress unquestionably exercised the principal responsibility to oversee warmaking throughout the first one hundred fifty years of the nation's history. Wars could be pursued only with Congress's blessing, and even military actions short of full-scale war required authorization as long as they were not considered "defensive." President Tyler articulated the traditional view when he stated that "the employment of the army or navy against a foreign power, with which the United States is at peace, is not within the competency of the President."[132]

President Lincoln's energetic response to the South during the Civil War represents the first major exception. Lincoln conducted the military campaign, often leaving Congress scrambling behind. He spent money not authorized by Congress, increased the army's strength beyond congressional limits, and imposed a naval blockade on southern ports. He later justified his acts on the ground that "whether strictly legal or not, [they] were ventured upon under what appeared to be a popular demand and public necessity; trusting then . . . that Congress would readily ratify them."[133] His actions foreshadowed the style of twentieth-century presidents who faced less dire circumstances. In the midst of the Civil War, the Supreme Court only narrowly upheld his blockade of Southern ports 5–4, reasoning that Congress had in fact ratified his acts.[134] In dissent, Justice Nelson lamented that "Congress alone can determine whether war exists or should be declared; and until they have acted, no citizen of the State can be punished in his person or property, unless he has committed some offense against a law of Congress."[135] With the possible exception of the Civil War, however, presidents generally sought congressional authorization before, or at least ratification immediately after, any armed hostilities.

That all changed after the Second World War. President Truman attacked North Korea without a declaration; President Johnson took vigorous action in Southeast Asia in the absence of clear congressional authorization; the first President Bush disclaimed any need for congressional authorization in attacking Iraq (though he later obtained eleventh-hour approval); and President Clinton committed troops to Bosnia and elsewhere in advance of congressional approval. Presidents typically justified such actions on the ground that the power to commit troops flowed from their general constitutional discretion. For instance, President Clinton declared that he determined to bomb Serbia "pursuant to his constitutional authority to conduct U.S. foreign relations and as Commander-in-Chief and Chief Executive."[136] In the past fifty years, the pendulum of power has shifted to the president.

The Vietnam War presents a case in point, reflecting Congress's growing willingness to follow the executive's lead in warmaking. Presidents Truman and Eisenhower had sent U.S. troops and advisors to the embattled nation, and under the Kennedy administration the escalation grew in earnest. President Lyndon Johnson followed suit, and in response to two disputed attacks on U.S. destroyers in the Gulf of Tonkin, requested Congress for authorization to take decisive steps against communist aggression. On August 7, 1964, Congress gave its authorization, empowering the president "to take all necessary measures to repel any armed attack against the forces of the United States to prevent further aggression."[137] The resolution was set to expire only "when the President shall determine that the peace and security of the area is reasonably assured by international conditions created by action of the United Nations or otherwise, except that it may be terminated earlier by concurrent resolution of the Congress."[138] Thus, although presidents had introduced tens of thousands of troops into Vietnam without congressional authorization, the Gulf of Tonkin resolution apparently ratified executive actions and authorized continued escalation, despite subsequent denials by members of Congress.

The 1970 military incursion into Cambodia as well reflects the new dynamic of the ascendant presidential role in warmaking. Once again, a U.S. president, Nixon, introduced a major military offensive in a foreign land without specific congressional authorization. More than thirty thousand troops were dispatched. President Nixon may have consulted with one member of Congress first, Senator John Stennis, chair of the Armed Services Committee.[139] The presidential move triggered a firestorm of controversy domestically. Nonetheless, the president arguably could find support in the broad language of the Gulf of Tonkin Resolution passed five years previously: the president was taking "all necessary measures to repel any armed attack against the forces of the United States to prevent further aggression."[140] Even when Congress later rescinded the Gulf of Tonkin Resolution, it continued to pass massive appropriations to carry out the war.[141]

A number of explanations for the sea change in power exist. First, presidents began to seek authorization for military action not from congressional authorization but from international sanction. Second, the United States' emergence as the chief superpower arguably imposed on the president new obligations to defend our interests worldwide.

1. ROLE OF INTERNATIONAL SANCTION

In recent decades, presidents have justified unilateral military action based on the approval or request of an international organization, such as NATO or the United Nations, of which the United States is a member.[142] President Clinton partly justified the bombing and eventual occupation of Kosovo by U.S. forces, for instance, based on a request from NATO, as well as on claimed violations by Serbia of the UN Charter and Security Council resolutions.[143] Similarly, his justification for the bombing of Serbian forces in Bosnia in 1995, and his use of the military in Haiti in 1994, were based on requests from the Security Council.[144] Presidents, therefore, have attempted to use international authorization to circumvent the need for congressional approval.

As a matter of international law, presidential justifications for exercise of the warmaking power have been less than persuasive. First, Congress has not clearly delegated its power to declare war to the president or to international organizations. Article 55 of the UN Charter, which has been ratified as a treaty by the Senate, requires the United States and all member states to cooperate with the UN in maintaining international security. Subsequently, Congress enacted the UN Participation Act of 1945,[145] providing that armed forces by member states should be supplied to the Security Council, with minor exceptions, "in accordance with their respective constitutional processes."[146] When the Security Council, therefore, authorizes war as it did against North Korea and Iraq, it does not necessarily authorize the president to dispatch troops without waiting first for congressional authorization.

Indeed, President Truman's conclusion in the Korean conflict that he could dispense with prior congressional authorization precipitated a relatively sharp attack from influential members of Congress.[147] The Senate debated the scope of presidential warmaking authority for three months in the shadow of the ongoing Korean War.[148] Senator Robert Taft, in particular, urged members of Congress to assert congressional prerogatives, and the Senate ultimately passed a resolution approving President Truman's past decision to send troops to Europe but stating that no ground troops in addition to the four divisions should be sent "without further congressional approval."[149] In the face of presidential decisiveness, the congressional protests had little effect.

Similarly, under Article 5 of the NATO treaty, ratified in 1949, "the Parties agree that an armed attack against one or more of them in Europe or North America shall be considered an attack against them all."[150] In addition, the treaty provides that the member nations may use armed force to pursue matters of collective self-defense, as required under Article 51 of the UN Charter. But, as under the UN Participation Act, provisions of the act are to be "carried out by the Parties in accordance with their respective constitutional processes."[151] The NATO agreements did not cut off Congress's constitutional role.

Nor is it clear that international treaties, as a constitutional matter, can authorize the president to declare war and thereby supplant the congressional prerogatives. In other words, the power to declare war may be nondelegable, irrespective of the wording of any treaty or statute.[152]

Congress has protested, if tepidly. For instance, in the Haiti context, the Senate passed a nonbinding resolution that the Security Council resolution "does not constitute authorization for the deployment of United States Armed Forces in Haiti under the Constitution of the United States or pursuant to the War Powers Resolution."[153] Congressman Ron Dellums previously had challenged President Bush's reliance on Security Council authorization for the military initiative against Iraq. The court rejected the challenge, in part because Congress had not sufficiently challenged the president's actions (*Dellums v. Bush,* 1990). Overall, presidential reliance on international treaties to justify warmaking efforts circumvents the constitutionally prescribed scheme.

2. THE POTENTIAL IMMEDIACY OF CONFLICT

Some have argued that the nation today faces far more diverse and potentially devastating attacks than in the early years. The emergence of terrorist states and the reality of the nuclear bomb, the argument goes, require vigilant, swift action by a chief executive. The president must be ready to strike out decisively whenever the national interests are compromised.

In confronting the perceived menace in Vietnam, for example, LBJ's legal advisors acknowledged that the Framers likely intended the president to wage only a defensive war in the absence of congressional authorization. But, in 1789, they argued, "[T]he world was a far larger place,"[154] and thus the president would have had time to react and consult with Congress prior to a direct attack. Given the greater interconnection of nation states centuries later, "[A]n attack on a country far from our shores can impinge directly on the nation's security."[155] Therefore, they concluded, "The Constitution leaves to the President the judgment to determine whether the circumstances of an armed attack are so urgent and the potential consequences so threatening to the security of the United States that he should act without formally consulting the Congress."[156] President Nixon reportedly never even asked his lawyers to prepare a legal case for the invasion of Cambodia until four days into the campaign.[157]

As a historical matter, the change in political realities argument is not fully persuasive. At the founding of the country, we faced direct threats from both England and France, two of the leading superpowers in the world. Our very existence was at stake. Moreover, we had yet to establish peaceful relations with the native inhabitants of the continent who, at that time, constituted a formidable fighting force. In addition, given that Congress was often not in session and communication poor, one would have thought that the need for executive discretion in warmaking was greater then than later.

Although war can lead to swifter conflagration and calamity now than in years past, that consequence seemingly militates for more deliberation and caution before initiating hostilities, not less. At least whenever feasible Congress arguably should have a greater say before launching such a potentially ruinous course of action. To be sure, the need for decisive defensive action might be more pressing now than before, but presidents historically have great leeway in ordering defensive actions, even recognizing the blurred lines between defensive and offensive actions. The argument of changed global political realities, therefore, does not convincingly make the case for the increased presidential control over warmaking.

In short, the balance of power in the warmaking realm has shifted markedly to the president in the past fifty years. Presidents have seized the initiative in dispatching U.S. troops and in engaging hostile troops to a degree that perhaps would have shocked the Framers. To many, the ascendant executive powers are antidemocratic, exactly opposite to the purposes of the Framers, who wished that wars be difficult to wage and possible only with the approval of the body politic, as represented by both houses of Congress.[158]

The chief congressional countermeasure—the War Powers Resolution—has little bite. In the wake of the Vietnam War, Congress passed the War Powers Resolution over the veto of President Nixon in a seeming effort to assert more congressional influence over the commitment of U.S. troops.[159] The core requirement in Section 4(a) of the act is that the president must report to Congress within forty-eight hours of introducing U.S. forces (1) "into hostilities or into situations where imminent involvement in hostilities is clearly indicated by the circumstances"; or (2) into foreign nations for the purpose of supplying or training foreign forces; or (3) to expand U.S. forces already stationed overseas. Pursuant to Section 5(b), the president must thereafter terminate the use of troops within sixty days (which the president can extend to ninety days for military necessity) unless (1) Congress has declared war or specifically authorized the use of troops; (2) Congress has extended the sixty-day period; or (3) there has been an armed attack against the United States. The resolution, in Section 2, also includes a provision mandating, whenever possible, broad consultation with members of Congress before such steps are pursued.

The resolution is remarkable in part in that it recognizes unbridled presidential power to commit U.S. troops anywhere for a period between sixty and ninety days prior to needing congressional authorization. Despite the historical understanding to the contrary, Congress therefore sanctioned in the resolution presidential use of troops without Congress's authorization.

We can all imagine scenarios in which secrecy and dispatch are absolutely critical. If the president learns of a planned nuclear strike against the United States or an invasion of a close ally, he might not have the luxury of consulting with Congress as a whole or even congressional committees beforehand. As soon as the need for dispatch wanes, however, then the president should be required to obtain congressional authorization to continue the hostilities. The sixty-to-ninety day period under the War Powers Resolution affords more than ample time within which to notify Congress, for it is difficult to imagine any pressing needs for secrecy and dispatch that would last longer. After all, our opponents will likely learn of our intent far earlier.

The resolution also permits Congress to use its concurrent resolution power—a determination reached by a majority of both houses of Congress—to require the president to bring troops home. After *Chadha*, however, this part of the resolution is almost assuredly unconstitutional. Congress can alter the rights of those outside its branch only by acting in the constitutionally prescribed manner, which includes presentment to the president. Thus, Congress must pass a law and risk presidential veto, as it did in rescinding the Gulf of Tonkin Resolution, if it wishes to bring U.S. troops home.

Presidents at times have reported to Congress with respect to their deployment of military forces as required under the War Powers Resolution. For instance, President Ford complied with the resolution's timing provisions when he reported the use of troops in the *Mayaguez* crisis; President Carter notified Congress of the failed rescue efforts to capture the hostages in Iran; and the second President Bush obtained congressional authorization for the invasion of Iraq.

Despite the examples mentioned above, presidents for the most part have consistently refused to acknowledge that they are bound by the resolution, or to behave as if they were, and Congress has been unable or unwilling to take action to give the resolution teeth. Although the resolution has the force of law, having been enacted by both houses over President Nixon's veto, the resolution is now widely viewed as moribund.[160]

Indeed, Congress, itself, has not insisted upon compliance with the resolution. When President Reagan, for instance, ordered troops to Lebanon in 1982, he failed to comply with the resolution, announcing only that he deployed the troops pursuant to his "constitutional authority with respect to the conduct of foreign relations and as Commander-in-Chief of the United States Armed Forces."[161] Congress responded not by mandating compliance with the resolution but by providing that it would deem the trigger period under the resolution to commence on August 29, 1983, and that it would authorize military action for eighteen months thereafter, well beyond the sixty- to ninety-day period under the resolution.[162] Reagan signed the bill but stated, "I do not and cannot cede any of the authority vested in me under the Constitution as President and as Commander-in-Chief of the United States Armed Forces. Nor should my signing be viewed as any acknowledgment that the President's constitutional authority can be impermissibly infringed by statute."[163]

Similarly, the first President Bush invaded Panama with eleven thousand troops, declining to seek congressional authorization. He justified the operation on a number of grounds, including defending American lives and restoring democracy to Panama.[164] The first President Bush prepared for the Gulf War without seeking congressional authorization, and requested congressional support only later.[165]

Congress has also established a framework within which presidents are to undertake covert actions against hostile powers. Such actions increased in magnitude and complexity during the second half of the twentieth century. The CIA has been implicated in assassination attempts both in Cuba and the Congo; the agency sponsored guerilla wars in Laos, Afghanistan, and Angola, among others; and it has tried to destabilize other governments around the world.

Although the War Powers Resolution largely leaves covert operations untouched due to its focus on military personnel, Congress in the Intelligence Authorization Act of 1991[166] created a structure to cabin covert activities. Covert acts must be based on a presidential finding that they are important to the national security and must be, absent extraordinary circumstances, reported to the Senate and House Intelligence Committees. If the president finds that such extraordinary circumstances exist, then he must report the activities to chairs and ranking minority members of the two committees, the Speaker and minority leader of the House, and the majority and minority leaders of the Senate. No congressional authorization is required.

With respect to covert aid, as opposed to military operations, Congress should be able to structure, though not administer, the extent and nature of our covert activities. Congress has created the Central Intelligence Agency, the Defense Intelligence Agency, and the National Security Agency, and should be able to dismantle such organizations as it sees fit. To the extent that Congress wishes to outlaw particular techniques, whether using journalists as spies or deploying sensitive eavesdrop technology, that, too, should fall within Congress's prerogative. Congress clearly can require executive spy agencies to report on the scope and success of their activities. The president under Article II retains the discretion to direct and alter the nation's covert activities, but subject to congressional policy direction.

As one example, consider the Ford administration's covert efforts to supply and train Angolan rebels in the early to mid 1970s. At the end of 1974, Portugal prepared to grant independence to its former colony after years of combat with Angolan insurgents. The CIA had been funding one of the non-Marxist groups vying for power. Congress called hearings to monitor the extent of CIA activity in Angola. At a hearing before the Senate Foreign Relations Committee, the CIA deputy director of operations acknowledged that the CIA had sent arms to the insurgents. That same day, the deputy assistant secretary of state for African affairs testified that no arms had been sent. When confronted with the earlier testimony, the deputy assistant secretary of state changed his story. To exert closer control over the situation, Congress then passed a statute providing that no assistance "of any kind may be provided for the purpose, or which would have the effect, of promoting or augmenting, directly or indirectly, the capacity of any nation, group, organization, movement, or individual to conduct military or paramilitary operations in Angola unless and until the Congress expressly authorizes such assistance by law."[167] Congress determined that all such assistance should be debated in the open. Through its power of inquiry, Congress can probe the extent of the nation's covert operations, and then through legislation can change its determinants.

Finally, the power of the purse—as previously discussed—remains a weapon with which Congress can influence all aspects of foreign relations. Congress long has exercised its appropriations power as a tool of congressional foreign policy, prohibiting, for instance, the deployment of aid to Angolan[168] and Nicaraguan insurgents.[169] Congress has used the appropriations power to limit executive discretion.[170]

To take another illustration, the 1987 authorization bill to finance operations of the State Department included eighty-six amendments.[171] As one commentator summarized, the amendments permitted members of Congress to express "outrage, support, concern and frustration" about various aspects of U.S. foreign relations.[172] One amendment purported to direct the president to seek reimbursement from NATO allies whose ships were being protected by the U.S. Navy. Another amendment excoriated Chinese persecution of Tibetan nationalists. Yet another amendment created an exception from the U.S. trade boycott of Nicaragua for anticommunist newspapers. And the bill included a clause requiring the president to close the Palestine Liberation Organization (PLO) offices in both the District of Columbia and New York.[173] This one bill amply reveals Congress's ability to influence foreign policy by means of the appropriations process.[174]

The power to appropriate or not appropriate gives Congress a potent tool to affect domestic and foreign policy. In response to the president's request for additional FBI positions or particular weapons procurement programs, Congress can just say no, or Congress can grant the money subject to conditions. In funding the reconstruction of Iraq after the second Persian Gulf War, for example, Congress provided $87 billion in assistance tied to establishment of a new position of inspector general for the Baghdad-based Coalition Provisional Authority.[175]

At the same time, presidents on notable occasions have sought to evade the reach of the congressional appropriations power. President Jefferson arguably expended unauthorized funds in making the Louisiana Purchase. President Lincoln after Fort Sumter committed funds to defend the Union when Congress was not in session. In both contexts, the president shortly thereafter requested Congress to approve the expenditures retroactively.

President Reagan's covert funding of the Nicaraguan contras during the 1980s provides a more controversial example. The CIA and the Defense Department had been channeling funds to aid the insurgent contras against the Sandinista government. When news of the aid came to light, Congress responded by prohibiting assistance "to any group or individual, not part of a country's armed forces, for the purpose of overthrowing the Government of Nicaragua or provoking a military exchange between Nicaragua and Honduras."[176] Then, with news that aid continued, Congress attempted in 1984 to close more loopholes in the so-termed Boland amendment. There, Congress provided that "no funds . . . may be obligated or expended for the purpose or which would have the effect of supporting, directly or indirectly, military or paramilitary operations in Nicaragua by any nation, group, organization, movement, or individual."[177] The administration, however, did an end run around the restrictions by soliciting money for the contras from private citizens and foreign governments. Reports that the government had sold weapons to Iran and diverted the proceeds to the contras grabbed the public spotlight. The Iran-Contra scandal led to criminal indictments against some of President Reagan's closest allies, including Defense Secretary Caspar Weinberger, National Security Advisor Robert McFarlane, CIA Deputy Director Clair George, and Assistant Secretary of State Elliott Abrams.

Despite occasional presidential efforts to circumvent Congress's appropriations authority, Congress's control of the purse strings provides a powerful weapon that it can wield to shape foreign policy. Congress has the means to assert more force in the foreign relations arena if it so chooses.

Congress has also taken more comprehensive steps to maintain control of covert operations. For instance, in the Hughes-Ryan Amendment of 1974, Congress prohibited expenditure of funds

> by or on behalf of the Central Intelligence Agency for operations in foreign countries, other than activities intended solely for obtaining necessary intelligence, unless, and until the President finds that each such operation is important to the national security of the United States and reports, in a timely fashion, a description and scope of such operation to the appropriate committees.[178]

Indeed, although Congress currently does not disclose the amounts it appropriates to certain intelligence agencies such as the CIA, it could reverse course and insist upon a public accounting. Congress can, consistent with the Constitution, shape the nature of our covert operations abroad.[179] The president's Article II responsibility over foreign affairs does not preclude congressional determinations as to the nature, extent, and duration of covert activities; presidential initiative should be checked by congressional direction and oversight.

C. *The Role of Judicial Oversight*

Courts have reviewed myriad aspects of presidential administration of the law. The vesting of executive power under Article II has not immunized the president from judicial oversight. The president's appointment and removal powers have been examined in court, as has his ability to issue executive orders and his authority to impound funds. Individuals and firms have utilized courts in an effort to ensure that presidential acts conform to constitutional dictates.

In contrast, judges have long been loath to become involved in disputes over foreign affairs. Whether the issue concerns the president's treaty interpretation or presidential authority to carry out military exercises, courts by and large have tried to duck the issues to preserve presidential initiative under Article II. Even when asserting jurisdiction, they have deferred even more than usual to acts of presidents, refusing to compel presidents to be more accountable to Congress and the public. Through these decisions, judges have acquiesced in and indeed furthered the shift in power in foreign affairs from Congress to the president. Although nothing in the Constitution directly precludes review of presidential acts in the foreign policy arena, pragmatic concerns fully support the courts' skittishness.

Article III, section 2 grants the federal courts a special role in resolving foreign affairs disputes. That section provides that "[t]he judicial Power shall extend to all Cases, in Law and Equity, arising under this Constitution, the Laws of the United States, and Treaties made" and "to all Cases affecting Ambassadors, other public Ministers and Consuls."[180] In addition, "[i]n all Cases affecting Ambassadors, other public Ministers and Consuls . . . the supreme Court shall have original Jurisdiction."[181] The Constitution contemplates review of issues touching on foreign affairs, given the explicit recognition that the Supreme Court is to resolve cases and controversies involving treaties. In addition, to ensure that sensitive matters not be resolved by local courts, the Constitution grants the Supreme Court exclusive jurisdiction over "Cases affecting Ambassadors, other public Ministers and Consuls."

Litigants challenging executive implementation of a treaty or rights under international law, however, first must demonstrate a live case or controversy. Litigants must show a cognizable injury to their property, liberty, or other socially sanctioned interest. When the government seizes property of a U.S. citizen in a foreign land or imposes restrictions on U.S.

residents because of a dispute with a foreign nation, standing should be easily demonstrated.[182] Similarly, when presidential interpretations of treaties affect the livelihood of firms, traditional standing principles are satisfied.

Nonetheless, some disputes over our relations with foreign countries cannot fit readily into that framework. Disagreements over our deployment of troops in the Balkans or our periodic forays into Iraq may involve questions of the president's Article II power and congressional authorization for the incursions,[183] but individuals have rarely been harmed in a way that gives rise to an Article III injury. Thus, courts will not have occasion to be drawn into some of the more ticklish questions of presidential power in the foreign affairs arena.

As one example, consider an individual's challenge to the CIA's failure to provide a public accounting of its expenditures. The plaintiff alleged that the CIA Act of 1949,[184] which permits the CIA to keep its expenditures secret, violated provisions of Article I, section 9 mandating "a regular Statement and Account of the Receipts and Expenditures of all public Money."[185] As a taxpayer, the plaintiff alleged that the wasteful spending harmed him directly. In *Richardson v. United States,* however, the Supreme Court rejected the claim, holding that the plaintiff had not suffered cognizable injury.[186] Rather, he merely asserted a "generalized grievance" about the conduct of government and, as such, did not satisfy the constitutional requirement of a case or controversy.[187] The Court acknowledged that there was a class of claims for which no one would have standing to sue. Such claims would ultimately be committed to the political process.

Moreover, even when Article III injury can be asserted, courts have declared that certain types of cases are off-limits. The political question doctrine, though lambasted by academic critics,[188] has long recognized that some executive branch acts should not be second-guessed in court. In a wide variety of contexts, the Court has stayed its hand from interfering with the actions of the more politically accountable branches. Although the political question doctrine, at its core, sensibly reflects the judiciary's limited institutional power, it can be overused to the point of wide-scale abdication to Article II presidential power.

As early as *Marbury v. Madison,* the Court stated that "[b]y the Constitution of the United States, the President is invested with certain important political powers, in the exercise of which he is to use his own discretion, and is accountable only to his country in his political character and to his own conscience. . . . [B]eing entrusted to the executive, the decision of the executive is conclusive. . . . Questions, in their nature political, or which are by the constitution and laws, submitted to the executive, can never be made in this court."[189] More recently, the Court in *Baker v. Carr* articulated several categories of cases in which courts should not interfere:

> Prominent on the surface of any case held to involve a political question is found a textually demonstrable constitutional commitment of the issue to a coordinate political department; or a lack of judicially discoverable and manageable standards for resolving it; or the impossibility of deciding without an initial policy determination of a kind clearly for nonjudicial discretion; or the impossibility of a court's undertaking independent resolution without expressing lack of the respect due coordinate branches of government; or an unusual need for unquestioning adherence to a political question already made; or the potentiality of embarrassment from multifarious pronouncements by various departments on one question.[190]

Of the three principal strands presented in *Baker v. Carr*—textual commitment; manageable standards, and need for uniform voice—all have relevance in the foreign affairs arena. With respect to textual commitment, consider the Supreme Court's relatively recent decision in *Nixon v. United States*.[191] There, the Court rejected on political-question grounds claims arising out of Judge Walter Nixon's impeachment. Judge Nixon challenged the Senate's process for trying him after being impeached by the House. Nixon had been convicted at trial for making false statements to a grand jury while serving on the bench. Nixon asserted that the Senate violated the constitutional command in Article I, § 3 that it "shall have the sole power to try all Impeachments"[192] by delegating the Senate's authority to a special committee. The Court found the claim nonjusticiable, reasoning that Article I, § 3 demonstrates a textual commitment of impeachment to the Senate.[193] Moreover, the Court explained that judicial review would undermine the importance of impeachment as a legislative check upon judicial officers. As the Court stated, "impeachment was designed to be the *only* check on the Judicial Branch by the Legislature . . . judicial involvement in impeachment proceedings . . . is counterintuitive because it would eviscerate" that important check.[194]

Similarly, when the Constitution provides that the president "shall from time to time give to the Congress information of the State of the Union,"[195] the Constitution may be read to vest in the president the power to determine what "time to time" means. And, the Constitution likely commits to the president the power to determine that particular agreements with foreign powers are "treaties" appropriate for ratification by the Senate. Courts should refuse to rule in the relatively infrequent situation when the Constitution vests Congress or the president with the power to be the final interpreter of a particular constitutional provision. As in *Nixon,* courts may reject on political question grounds challenges to some executive determinations in the foreign affairs realm.[196] Indeed, the Supreme Court's refusal to entertain the merits in *Goldwater v. Carter,* the treaty nullification case, stemmed in part from a similar conviction that the Constitution implicitly vested in the political branches the power to determine whether a treaty should continue in effect.[197] As Justice Rehnquist noted in an opinion for four justices, judges should stay their hand in "a dispute between coequal branches of our Government, each of which has resources available to protect and assert its interests."[198] And, in *Chicago & Southern Air Lines v. Waterman S.S. Corp.* the Supreme Court justified nonintervention in even more sweeping terms.[199] The Court noted that determinations like the landing rights issue under consideration "are wholly confided by our Constitution to the political departments of the government, Executive and Legislative. They are delicate, complex, and involve large elements of prophecy. . . . They are decisions of a kind for which the Judiciary has neither aptitude, facilities nor responsibility and which have long been held to belong in the domain of political power."[200]

With respect to the manageable standards prong, consider a class action that was brought by a class purporting to represent those missing in action in the aftermath of the Vietnam War. Plaintiffs sought a declaration that they enjoyed the protections of the Hostage Act,[201] which requires presidents to exercise diligent responsibility on behalf of citizens detained unlawfully by foreign governments. In order to provide relief, however, the court would first have had to determine whether such a class of plaintiffs in fact existed. It would have been difficult, indeed, for the trial court to amass sufficient facts to ascertain whether service personnel were being held against their will in Laos, Vietnam, or Cambodia. The court, in other words, lacked manageable standards to hear and resolve the lawsuit. Although the district court—despite the obstacles—would have made that effort, the court of appeals dismissed the case, explaining,

> The courts also lack the powers for the task which plaintiffs would have them undertake. The political branches have worked for years, since the end of American involvement in hostilities in southeast Asia, to obtain a full accounting of missing Americans from foreign governments. The courts, which lack even the limited tools of diplomatic leverage, are unlikely to be more successful in obtaining information from those governments. Further, the courts lack the expertise to evaluate what information would be laid before them. . . .[202]

Although courts often strain to find manageable standards when there is a case or controversy, occasions may arise when the task is too daunting or sensitive. Remedial problems frequently defy judicial resolution when unscrambling the egg is impractical such as when the property at stake is in foreign hands. But the missing in action case also reveals that, in a rare case, courts lack the tools to permit a case to proceed.[203]

With respect to the need for a uniform voice, consider the same case. The Reagan administration, and before that the Carter and Ford administrations, had worked assiduously behind the scenes after hostilities in Vietnam ceased to ascertain whether any U.S. service personnel remained behind. The official position was that the administration assumed the existence of service personnel there, and that it was doing all within its power to ascertain the truth. The court remarked that

> [i]t is important that this country speak with a single, clear voice in these negotiations. Pronouncements by the federal courts may differ sharply from those of the executive, and might themselves not be consistent. . . . The resulting cacophony would necessarily hamper United States negotiators. It might prove a significant hindrance to diplomatic efforts to effectuate the release of any Americans who may still be in captivity.[204]

Accordingly, the court concluded that the challenge presented a nonjusticiable political question not only because of the lack of manageable standards but also because of the need of a uniform voice in negotiations.[205]

During the Vietnam War, many cases were filed challenging the legality of the administration's conduct of hostilities in the absence of a declaration of war. For a mixture of reasons, generally involving the need for a uniform voice and a lack of manageable standards, the courts declined to entertain the merits of such cases.[206] As Judge Kaufman noted in *Da Costa v. Laird*: "Judges, deficient in military knowledge, lacking vital information upon which to assess the nature of battlefield decisions, and sitting thousands of miles from the field of action, cannot reasonably or appropriately determine whether a specific military operation" falls within Congress's guidelines.[207] The political question doctrine provided the courts with a convenient hook on which to rest their desire not to get involved in the war.

On one occasion, a district court judge held President Nixon's bombing of Cambodia unconstitutional. He determined that, in light of Congress's stated opposition to the bombing, the president's persistence flew in the face of constitutional restraints.[208] Accordingly, the court issued an injunction ordering a halt to the bombing.

The Court of Appeals for the Second Circuit thereupon ordered a stay of the injunction pending review, prompting plaintiffs to request the United States Supreme Court to lift the stay. Although Justice Thurgood Marshall stated that the Court on full review "might well conclude on the merits that continued American operations in Cambodia are unconstitutional," he determined that the stay should not be lifted pending review.[209] By a procedural quirk, plaintiffs persuaded Justice Douglas to vacate the stay, reinstating the injunction against continued bombing.[210] The remaining members of the Supreme Court overruled Justice Douglas by phone, sending the case back to the Second Circuit for resolution.[211] That court ultimately determined that the original challenge presented a nonjusticiable political question: "While we may as men well agonize and bewail the horror of this or any war, the sharing of Presidential and Congressional responsibility particularly at this juncture is a bluntly political and not a judicial question."[212] Courts did not wish to hamstring presidential initiative.

The need for a uniform voice should not be overemphasized. Congress often has disagreed with the president over particular foreign policy initiatives, and Congress itself has been internally split. Although there is always an advantage in foreign affairs if the nation appears to back a position unanimously, much of our nation's foreign policy has been successful despite detractors at home, from World War II through the Cold War to the military intervention in the Balkans in the 1990s. Such divisions, therefore, should not persuade the courts to reject the lawsuit. Nor, can the political question doctrine be predicated on a concern for showing proper respect to the coordinate branches. As the Court explained in *United States v. Munoz-Flores,* "[D]isrespect, in the sense the Government uses the term, cannot be sufficient to create a political question. If it were, *every* judicial resolution of a constitutional challenge to a congressional enactment would be impermissible."[213] The missing-in-action case presents one of the most compelling, if rare, instances in which the need for a uniform voice during presidential negotiations logically calls for application of the political question doctrine. For the most part, however, the need for a uniform voice in foreign affairs should not persuade a court to stay its hand.

Not all foreign affairs cases by any stretch of the imagination, however, should be considered nonjusticiable. Most involve treaty interpretation or individual rights claims, subjects that lie at the core of judicial competence. The Court in *Dames & Moore,* for example, did not hesitate to address the merits of the constitutional claim presented. Similarly, when a U.S. ship bombarded Greytown and destroyed the dwelling of a U.S. citizen, the court entertained the claim, even though rejecting it on the merits.[214] And, in *Hamdi v. Rumsfeld,* the Supreme Court considered a challenge to the executive branch's authority to detain terrorist suspects indefinitely, finding "that a citizen held in the United States as an enemy combatant be given a meaningful opportunity to contest the factual basis for that determination before a neutral decisionmaker."[215] The Court explained: "It is during our most challenging and uncertain moments that our Nation's commitment to due process is more severely tested; and it is in those times that we must preserve our commitment at home to the principles for which we fight abroad."

In general, courts should be more reluctant to use the political question doctrine in cases involving individual rights than in those addressing the allocation of power between the executive and Congress, which affect individual rights more obliquely. Congress can rely upon an arsenal of weapons, including the appropriation power, to preserve its own prerogatives. Cases challenging the legitimacy of the Vietnam War can be seen in the same light. In cases such as *Dames & Moore,* however, only courts can demand that the executive stand accountable to the public to some degree for its actions. Presidential initiative should be accommodated, where possible, with claims of individual right.

The Supreme Court, even when entertaining the merits of cases, however, has afforded considerable deference to executive decisions. For instance, in *Harisiades v. Shaughnessy* the Court in an immigration case explained that

[i]t is pertinent to observe that any policy towards aliens is vitally and intricately interwoven with contemporaneous policies in regard to the conduct of foreign relations, the war power, and the maintenance of a republican form of government. Such matters are so exclusively entrusted to the political branches of government as to be largely immune from judicial inquiry or interference.[216]

In *Hamdi,* the Court stressed the great deference owed to the executive branch in determining the steps necessary to combat terrorism.[217]

The language of deference to executive discretion is even more clear in *United States v. Curtiss-Wright Export Corp.*[218] There, Congress had delegated to the president the power to forbid the sale of munitions by American manufacturers in the Chaco region in South America over which Bolivia and Paraguay were fighting. The conflagration eventually claimed more than 100,000 lives. Federal prosecutors indicted the Curtiss-Wright Export Corporation for funneling weapons to Bolivia through an intermediary. In defense, the company challenged the legitimacy of the president's exercise of delegated authority from Congress to interdict the shipment of weapons. The Court upheld the president's exercise of power, stating that "[t]he President is the constitutional representative of the United States with regard to foreign nations. He manages our concerns with foreign nations and must necessarily be most competent to determine when, how, and upon what subjects negotiation may be urged with the greatest prospect of success."[219] The Court consciously embraced a larger role for the executive in international than in domestic policy: "congressional legislation which is to be made effective through negotiation and inquiry within the international field must often accord to the President a degree of discretion and freedom from statutory restriction which would not be admissible were domestic affairs alone involved."[220]

Consensus has emerged that presidents exercise greater authority in the international as opposed to domestic arena. Considerations of efficiency and flexibility support enhanced executive initiative. Yet, no language in Article II plainly supports that result. Although the president is commander in chief of the army, can appoint ambassadors, and negotiate treaties, the Constitution vests Congress with the power to declare war and to control commerce amongst the nations, and grants the Senate the power to approve treaties. The Constitution permits substantial executive initiative in foreign affairs but provides both courts and Congress the means to ensure that the president remain accountable for his actions both to Congress and the public. Over the generations, presidents have gained dramatic power in the foreign affairs arena—pragmatic need has overtaken the constitutional design.

3

The Protective Power
of the President

Our constitutional system fundamentally limits executive power by granting the president only such authority as vested directly under the Constitution or pursuant to explicit or implicit delegation from Congress. But crises have confronted presidents throughout our nation's history that defy easy categorization and yet seemingly call for decisive action. When faced with foreign threats, as discussed, many presidents have initiated vigorous action that did not comfortably fit within the constitutional scheme. In domestic contexts, are presidents under Article II free to seize the initiative to combat threats to the public weal? Must presidents in such contexts instead await congressional action at the risk that the domestic crisis might deepen into a national emergency? Should the need for accountability to Congress remain paramount?

In writing about executive power, John Locke described what he termed the prerogative power of the chief magistrate, which recognized that executives could pursue actions for the public good where law did not exist to block that course of action.[1] In emergencies, law must give way "to the executive power, or rather to this fundamental law of nature and government . . . that, as much as may be, all the members of society are to be preserved."[2] Such conception of executive power apparently would allow steps to defend the nation when Congress is silent, but not if Congress has addressed either the scope of the president's emergency powers generally or the particular emergency in question. The Lockean notion of prerogative includes the law of self-preservation. Some type of prerogative may have been included in the Framer's decision to vest the "executive power" in the president.[3]

Even if Locke's view influenced the Framers, many questions remain unanswered. For example, if the president can exercise extrastatutory powers only in an emergency, who defines emergency? Can the presidential initiative to determine the appropriate steps to take in an emergency brush aside concerns for accountability to Congress? What consequences should result if either Congress or the people disagree with the presidential determination of emergency or the steps needed to confront it?

The question of the president's exercise of nonstatutory powers in a domestic crisis has perplexed presidents from the outset of our history. The Framers certainly understood that emergencies might arise yet inserted no special provision recognizing a right of self-preservation in the Constitution. They determined only that habeas corpus could be suspended in an emergency, but nothing more.[4] Representative Alexander White defended the decision to leave any language about emergency powers out of the Constitution, arguing that it would be better for the president "to extend his power on some extraordinary occasion, even when he is not strictly justified by the constitution, than [that] the Legislature [or Constitution] should grant him an improper power to be exercised at all times."[5] A constitutional system, in other words, may be able to survive only by tolerating limited exceptions.

Presidents may well have adhered to some notion of a Lockean prerogative. Jefferson gambled and completed the Louisiana Purchase despite the lack of clear authority.[6] Lincoln later commented in 1854 that "Jefferson saw the necessity of our government possessing the whole valley of the Mississippi, and though he acknowledged that our Constitution made no provision for the purchasing of territory, yet he thought that the exigency of the case would justify the measure, and the purchase was made."[7] Lincoln seemingly played out that theory and imposed the blockade on the South and expended funds during the Civil War without waiting for congressional authorization. Truman took steps both internationally (Korea) and domestically (seizure of the steel mills) to protect his vision of the United States role in the international sphere, prior to obtaining congressional approval.

In recognition of such executive actions, the political scientist Edward Corwin wrote of "a broadly discretionary residual power [which is] available when other governmental powers fail."[8] The existence of broad discretionary powers and their bounds, however, defy easy elaboration.

Presidents long have asserted such a residuum of inherent power to act in an emergency. Theodore Roosevelt's stewardship theory is a prominent but by no means aberrant example.[9] The question of emergency powers brings into sharp tension two of the overriding determinants of presidential power: the desiderata of accountability to Congress and initiative. In the context of emergency powers, the two goals seem hopelessly opposed: the greater the ambit of presidential power to pursue steps in the public interest, the less the accountability to the legislative branch.

The tension often plays out in conflicts between the president and Congress as to how to address a national crisis. Congress, at times, may welcome presidential initiative. Emergency measures in the face of the British invasion in 1812, for instance, were not particularly controversial.[10] On other occasions, however, Congress may strenuously object to the president's unilateral actions. There may not even be an agreement as to whether a crisis exists. Presidential initiative reallocates the burden of overcoming inertia: Congress must exert sufficient political will to counteract the president's action, and the costs of generating a coalition to block the president can be exorbitant, particularly given the riskiness of opposing presidential power in the time of a perceived emergency. Moreover, Congress must gather support from two-thirds of each house to ensure that any congressional response is veto proof. In lieu of passing legislation, influential members of Congress may convene hearings to ply pressure, or Congress can try to retaliate in other ways, by withholding funds or confirmation of key officials. Congress, however, clearly faces an uphill battle because the exercise of presidential initiative can be so difficult to overcome.

In light of the structural barriers facing Congress when considering a response to presidential initiative, the president may well gain power in excess of that contemplated in the Constitution. The critical constitutional check on presidential action—the need for ex ante congressional authorization—is missing. Presidents can justify that gain in power only on the theory that their ultimate responsibility under Article II to the public as a whole trumps the constitutional mandate of circumscribed executive powers and accountability to Congress. Accountability, in other words, is a double-edged sword: presidents' duty in extraordinary times to the people can outweigh their constitutional obligations to Congress.

Presidential invocation of extrastatutory powers, however, may also affect individual rights. Presidential action may infringe on property or individual rights protected by the Constitution or positive law, such as statutes and regulations. In such contexts, the individuals harmed can resort to the courts to test the limits of the president's authority. The

Supreme Court, therefore, in myriad contexts, has confronted the executive's claims of nonstatutory powers. The president's record before the Court is mixed, and no clear doctrinal analysis emerges from the cases.

Although the Court has not delineated the scope of emergency powers directly, it has carved out areas in which presidents may act beyond the authority granted to them explicitly by the Constitution and Congress. For instance, the Court held that the president has the right to use military force to quell domestic disturbances.[11] Moreover, the Court has determined that presidents have the right to take emergency steps, not authorized by Congress, to protect special federal interests, including public property, federal officials, and natural resources located on federal lands.[12] In addition, the president at times may seek relief in litigation even when Congress has not authorized such participation.[13]

Courts, however, have imposed limitations. In *Youngstown Steel,* the most famous case addressing the scope of presidential emergency power, the Court held that the president could not seize steel mills in order to ensure production and fuel the Korean War effort.[14] In other cases, courts have held that the government cannot sue to protect rights if Congress has chosen an alternative path to enforce such rights.

Taken together, a number of factors emerge. The degree of congressional authorization or prohibition is critical. Presidential emergency powers are at their greatest when Congress has explicitly or at least implicitly delegated such authority to the president. Courts may also ask the counterfactual question whether Congress, if asked, would have agreed that the situation justified an emergency response. Conversely, presidential powers are at their most suspect when Congress has prohibited such actions directly. Moreover, the Court may be swayed by the nature and extent of the interests affected: individual rights may be protected more than property or procedural rights. The Court may also be persuaded by the magnitude and imminence of the emergency. Finally, courts might inquire whether Congress, irrespective of the lack of prior authorization can, after the fact, undo whatever steps the president has taken. If the only issue is money, Congress can reverse the presidential initiative, but when other interests are at stake, Congress may not be able to unscramble the egg.

At the end of the day, the Court's articulation of these principles has not been sufficient. No clear doctrine has emerged. The Court has not instructed us how to assess presidential initiative under Article II in the face of congressional silence. Nor has it illuminated how specific each congressional approval or disapproval must be. The Court's rulings have prompted a cacophony of scholarship but no consensus. Constitutional exegesis, in fact, may miss the point: the president should use emergency powers and stand accountable both to Congress and the people for the chosen course of action. Even if not authorized by the Constitution, presidents should take emergency measures when the country's welfare is jeopardized and be willing to pay the political price afterward. As a constitutional matter, we must insist on accountability but, as a political matter, accept on rare occasions the presidential exercise of initiative outside the constitutional structure.

A. Exercise of War-Type Power in the Face of Domestic Disturbances

Presidential use of military force domestically has long generated controversy. Commentators have debated whether presidents can rely on inherent power to take war-type measures within the country in the face of an emergency. On occasion, presidents have tried to rely on the Commander-in-Chief Clause as a foundation for expansive executive power: "The President shall be Commander in Chief of the Army and Navy of the United States, and of the militia of the several States, when called in to the actual Services of the United States."[15] However, most believe that the clause does not permit presidents to use war-type measures domestically whenever they determine it appropriate. After all, it is Congress, not the president, that has the right to create and regulate the armed forces, pay for them, and declare war. Consensus has emerged that the Commander-in-Chief Clause confers authority on the president only to respond to foreign as opposed to domestic threats, at least in the absence of authorization from Congress.[16]

As a matter of history, George Washington hesitated whether to send troops in response to the Whiskey Rebellion. Once he was convinced of a need, he dispatched troops irrespective of any lingering constitutional concern. His initiative drew little criticism, although some wondered about the precedent of relying on federal troops. Subsequent presidents considered the range of war-type options available when confronted by domestic disturbances, whether arising from tension with foreign powers or slavery. However, it was not until the Civil War that the question of exercising war-type measures domestically rose to the forefront.

President Lincoln blockaded four Southern ports in the early 1860s. Owners of ships belonging to foreign nationals seized by Northern vessels sued for return of the property. In addition, Northern shippers seized ships operated by Southern interests and claimed the property as prizes of war. Owners of the seized vessels used the courts to challenge not only the legality of the seizures but also the propriety of Lincoln's emergency measures.

As one example, Massachusetts shippers captured the *Amy Warwick,* flying under the U.S. flag, as it traveled from Rio de Janeiro back to Virginia with supplies of coffee. At the time, the crew had not even learned of the outbreak of war. The United States defended the power of private shippers to seize the ships as enemy property—a prize of war—given that the owners lived in Richmond.

Because the United States was not officially at war, the government could not rely solely on the president's constitutional powers as commander in chief of the army and navy to justify the capture of the civilian vessel.[17] Lincoln refused to call the secession of the Southern states a war, for fear that other nations would establish relations with the breakaway states.[18] Lincoln argued instead that he enjoyed the inherent power to order and enforce the blockade due to a combination of his authority as chief executive and as commander in chief.[19] Lincoln further argued that no prior congressional authorization for the blockade was necessary because the nation faced an emergency.[20] The de facto state of war sufficed to justify the extraordinary measure. As he asked Congress in special session, "[A]re all the laws but one to go unexecuted, and the government itself go to pieces, lest that one be violated?"[21] Lincoln later rationalized that "certain proceedings are constitutional . . . when, in cases of rebellion or invasion, the public safety requires them, which will not be constitutional when, in the absence of a rebellion or invasion, the public safety does not require them."[22]

Congress had passed statutes in 1795 and 1807 authorizing the president to call out the militia and to use the armed forces to repel invasions, but Congress was silent as to the rights of neutral shipping and property rights of insurrectionists. Arguably, Congress had considered the emergency context given the nation's experience with the Whiskey Rebellion and withheld authority from the president to impose a blockade and seize property owned by insurrectionists and their sympathizers.

Most lower courts upheld the legality of the seizures, and thus validated Lincoln's view of his emergency powers. And, in the *Amy Warwick* case, the lower court similarly sanctioned the capture. Union supporters nervously awaited the Supreme Court's view, however, for as one newspaper reported, "How deeply these questions touch the powers of our Government, at this interesting period, can at once be seen; and the decision of the Supreme Court upon them cannot fail to be one of the most grave duties of their session."[23]

After a delay of one term, the Court in the so termed *Prize Cases* concluded that the president alone had the power to determine (1) the existence of an emergency that necessitated war-type measures, (2) which measures were needed to meet the emergency, including in the *Amy Warwick* context the blockade and seizure of civilian property; and (3) when the measures should be terminated.[24] The decision recognized that the president could exercise extrastatutory powers in an emergency, and no one could doubt that the Civil War constituted such an emergency.

In dissent, Justice Nelson wrote for four justices that the power to use military force against civilians expanded the presidency beyond what the Constitution and the laws allowed.[25] The dissent believed that even an ex post ratification by Congress would not give the president the authority to seize the ships because Congress had not declared war: "[B]efore this insurrection against the established Government can be dealt with on the footing of a civil war, within the meaning of the law of nations and the Constitution of the United States . . . it must be recognized or declared by the warmaking power of the Government."[26] Justice Nelson also relied on the prior congressional framework statutes delineating presidential power in case of insurrections. The president was authorized, under those statutes, to use military might to quell the insurrection but not to confiscate the property of civilians living in enemy territory. Justice Nelson concluded "that the President does not possess the power under the Constitution to declare war or recognize its existence within the meaning of the law of nations, which carries with it belligerent rights. . . . This power belongs exclusively to the Congress."[27]

The Court's result should not be surprising. The Civil War was a fact that hardly could be ignored. In that light, the president's decisive actions at the outset of hostilities must have seemed necessary. Furthermore, Congress's ratification of the presidential steps must have reaffirmed the propriety of the presidential actions in some justices' view. Indeed, that the decision was as close as it was during wartime—5–4—was remarkable, and the tally cannot be explained away merely by the split between Union and Southern sympathies.

The majority, however, may have confused politics with law. President Lincoln's energetic defense of union may have been admirable but nonetheless have violated the Constitution. Indeed, Lincoln's acts at times starkly violated other constitutional limits on executive power; the president had no right under the Constitution to spend money in excess of that appropriated by Congress or to suspend individual liberties—both hallmarks of Lincoln's administration during the war. It may be no contradiction to praise Lincoln while acknowledging that he violated the constitutional restraints that originally had been set with an imperfect eye to the type of emergencies that could befall the nation.

Congress in part reacted to the Civil War experience by enacting additional restrictions on the use of military force in the 1878 Posse Comitatus Act.[28] The act, as later amended, states: "Whoever, except in cases and under circumstances expressly authorized by the Constitution or Act of Congress, willfully uses any part of the army or the Air Force as a posse comitatus or otherwise to execute the laws shall be fined under this title or imprisoned not more than two years, or both."[29] By making it illegal to use the military to enforce general laws except in times *expressly authorized by Congress,* the act seemed to tie the hands of the president.

The Posse Comitatus statute drew the nation's attention in the midst of the civil rights tensions of the 1950s. In 1955, the governor of Arkansas refused to abide by a plan to permit desegregation of Little Rock high schools as mandated under the second U.S. Supreme Court decision in *Brown v. Board of Education.*[30] A state court supported the governor on the ground that the integration plan could spark violence, but the federal district court ordered the plan to proceed. Despite the federal court order, Governor Faubus directed the Arkansas National Guard to prevent desegregation. After the federal court again ordered that desegregation proceed, the mayor of Little Rock wired the president requesting deployment of federal troops. The president, relying on an opinion from the attorney general, stepped in and used the National Guard to enforce the desegregation of local schools. The attorney general had counseled that

> [t]he Governor did not use his powers to support the local authorities. I thereupon advised you [the president] that you then had the undoubted power, under the Constitution and the laws of the United States, to call the National Guard into service and to use those forces, together with

such of the Armed Forces as you considered necessary, to suppress the domestic violence, obstruction and resistance of law then and there existing. I further advised you, and do again advise you, that your power so to act rested upon both your powers as president under the Constitution and the powers vested in you by the Congress under Federal law, particularly as reflected by sections 332 and 333 of title 10 of the United States Code.[31]

Under 10 U.S.C. § 332, Congress gave the president the power to stop obstructions or rebellions against the authority of the United States.[32] Under the companion provision, § 333, Congress recognized that, in an emergency, it could direct the president to suppress an insurrection, domestic violence, or conspiracy, which hinders the execution of the laws of the United States and where the state refuses, is unwilling, or fails to act.[33] Certainly, the argument can be made that Congress implicitly gave the president the power to enforce school desegregation in an appropriate context with military forces.[34] But the terms of the Posse Comitatus statute require express authorization. If Section 333 is read broadly, the Posse Comitatus statute would become a nullity. In any event, the attorney general opinion recognized a distinct constitutional source for the president's intervention.

President Eisenhower seized the initiative to send troops without first receiving Congress's blessing. As a matter of politics, Eisenhower's decision was exemplary. But as a matter of constitutional law, Eisenhower's decision—like that of Lincoln's—perhaps showed insufficient regard for Congress's role in determining the measures to be used in an emergency. Presidential initiative cannot readily be accommodated with the constitutional imperative of accountability to Congress, but as a political matter, President Eisenhower's decision seems warranted.

B. Curtailment of Rights Domestically during Time of War

In addition to the use of military force domestically, presidents pursuant to Article II have curtailed the rights of citizens and noncitizens alike in emergencies. Civil liberties may be a luxury that few can afford in time of war.[35] And, although many presidents have been careful to tread lightly when civil liberties are at stake, some presidents have pursued vigorous action during time of war irrespective of the impact on civil liberties.

1. Of perhaps greatest note, history has not been kind to President Franklin Roosevelt's domestic measures relocating approximately one hundred thousand residents of Japanese descent who lived on the West Coast. Roosevelt wrote that "the successful prosecution of the war requires every possible protection against espionage and against sabotage."[36] FDR relied on no specific authority in the Constitution to justify the emergency measures, which resulted in a draconian loss of liberties for citizens and noncitizens alike. Congress soon thereafter ratified FDR's order, and the Supreme Court later upheld the wartime measures in *Hirabayashi v. United States*.[37] The Court reasoned that "[l]ike every military control of the population of a dangerous zone in war time, [FDR's order] necessarily involves some infringement of individual liberty, just as does the police establishment of fire lines during a fire."[38] The Court required little executive justification for FDR's claim of a domestic emergency.

With words that could have been used in the Civil War blockade case as well, Justice Jackson later commented that "a judicial construction of the due process clause that will sustain this order is a far more subtle blow to liberty than the promulgation of the order itself. A military order, however unconstitutional, is not apt to last longer than the military emergency. . . . But once a judicial opinion rationalizes such an order to show that it conforms to the Constitution . . . [t]he principle then lies about like a loaded weapon."[39] Judicial validation of executive actions pursued in an emergency can have a long-range debilitating impact on constitutional liberties.

2. Perhaps in light of second thoughts about the relocation of Japanese-Americans, the Supreme Court rebuffed President Truman's exercise of nonstatutory powers during the Korean War. The Court's decision in *Youngstown Sheet and Tube Co. v. Sawyer* remains the leading case exploring limits on the president's extrastatutory powers.[40] In response to a threatened nationwide steel strike, President Truman issued an executive order on April 8, 1952, directing the secretary of commerce to seize and operate most steel plants. President Truman based the order not on any statute but on his constitutional authority to "take care that the laws be faithfully executed" and to act as commander in chief of the Armed Forces. President Truman feared a strike would shut down the steel mills and hurt our war efforts on the Korean Peninsula.[41] The steel companies immediately sought injunctive relief.

The president argued that he had the right to take the plant, in part, because of the Executive Power clause in the Constitution.

> The Court: And is it . . . your view that the powers of the Government are limited by and enumerated in the Constitution of the United States? Mr. Baldridge: That is true, Your Honor, with respect to legislative powers. The Court: But it is not true, you say, as to the Executive? Mr. Baldridge: No. The Court: So, when the sovereign people adopted the Constitution, it enumerated the powers set up in the Constitution but limited the powers of the Congress and of the judiciary, but it did not limit the powers of the Executive. Is that what you say? Mr. Baldridge: That is the way we read Article II of the Constitution.[42]

Indeed, President Truman apparently had sought and received Chief Justice Vinson's sanction prior to the seizure. He read Article II to include a broad protective power analogous to the prerogative power championed by Locke. Truman, however, agreed to abide by any legislative determination to block his executive order.[43]

Although the Court was unable to agree on any one line of analysis, it disavowed President Truman's position, largely on the basis that his action impermissibly departed from the path previously set by Congress. Justice Black, in the opinion for the Court, stressed that

> [i]n the framework of our Constitution, the President's power to see that the laws are faithfully executed refutes the idea that he is to be a lawmaker. The Constitution limits his functions in the lawmaking process to the recommending of laws that he thinks wise and the vetoing of laws he thinks bad. . . .
>
> The President's order does not direct that a congressional policy be executed in a manner prescribed by Congress—it directs that a presidential policy be executed in a manner prescribed by the President.[44]

According to Justice Black, presidential power must stem from either an act of Congress or the Constitution.[45] In this case, no act of Congress authorized Truman's seizure.[46] In fact, as the Court noted, Congress had specifically rejected seizure as a method of solving labor disputes when it voted against a seizure amendment during the debate on the Taft-Hartley Act, which became law in 1947.[47] Justice Burton similarly stated in an opinion concurring in the judgment that the president's action "invaded the jurisdiction of Congress" because Congress had previously qualified the president's authority to determine when and where to authorize the seizure of property in meeting such emergencies.[48] And, Justice Frankfurter stated that "'[t]he duty of the President to see that the laws be executed is a duty that does not go beyond the laws or require him to achieve more than Congress sees fit to leave within his power.'"[49] Congress's articulation of policy objectives and its specification of the means for implementing those policies directly constrain presidential power. Once Congress considers the need for emergency action, then its specifications limit the options that a president can take.

In the most famous opinion of the *Youngstown* case, Justice Jackson concurred in the result based on a type of balancing test. Unlike the other justices, he acknowledged a realm of inherent executive authority. Even when Congress had acted to channel executive authority, he suggested that presidents *might* be able to exercise extrastatutory powers. He reasoned that presidential powers are not fixed, but fluctuate depending on congressional action or inaction.[50] He continued that the authority of the chief executive is at its height when he acts in accordance with an order from Congress or an implied command from Congress.[51]

In the middle is a "Zone of Twilight," within which both the president and Congress can act concurrently.[52] The president may use this middle ground when Congress has been silent on an issue, or when there has been congressional inaction.[53] The third, and weakest point for a president to act is when the president takes measures incompatible with the expressed or the implied will of Congress.[54]

Jackson thought that Truman had acted in the third category.[55] Congress had set out ways to deal with a strike in an economic emergency, particularly in the Taft-Hartley Act.[56] The executive did not follow Congress's express intent; therefore he had to rely only on his power as chief executive, which did not authorize him to legislate even in an economic crisis.[57]

Chief Justice Vinson, not surprisingly, dissented. He stated that the president's constitutional responsibility to "take care" that the laws be faithfully executed included the power to seize the mills,[58] and therefore he would have upheld President Truman's emergency measure.[59]

Youngstown reflects the limits of presidential power to act in a domestic emergency. The most critical factor articulated in the various opinions lies in Congress's prior determination to channel the president's authorities in a different direction. Congress's articulation of policy objectives and its specification of the means for implementing those policies directly constrain presidential power. In the face of a congressional determination addressing the particular issue at hand, the president has only limited power to act extrastatutorily.

That same understanding of presidential powers emerges by comparing *Youngstown Steel* to a similar case, *Montgomery Ward,* decided a decade earlier.[60] There, the president seized properties affected by strikes in Montgomery Ward plants and facilities.[61] At the time of the dispute, the United States was at war with Germany and Japan. However, Montgomery Ward was not producing bombs or tanks or even steel but, rather, domestic products.[62] The president, pursuant to his authority as chief executive and as commander in chief, took over the Montgomery Ward facilities in order to facilitate the flow of products domestically.[63]

The president justified the takeover on the ground that domestic goods were as vital to the war effort as any piece of armor.[64] In order to accomplish a victory abroad, the United States must be running smoothly at home, and any domestic disturbance could hamper that effort.[65] The justification, in other words, was identical to that which would be raised in *Youngstown Steel.*

Yet, one critical distinction exists. Unlike in *Youngstown,* the President seized the Montgomery Ward facilities *before* the Taft-Hartley Act became law. Even then, the district court in *Montgomery Ward* was unimpressed and determined that the Constitution did not confer any inherent authority upon the president to take such steps in an emergency, at least given that Congress had provided a mechanism for resolving labor strife.[66] And, the court held that the War Labor Disputes Act[67] did not authorize the president to seize plants such as the one owned by Montgomery Ward, which were engaged solely in distribution as opposed to production.[68]

A divided court of appeals, however, disagreed on statutory grounds, upholding the seizure.[69] The court determined that the statute contemplated that all matters of distribution were closely enough connected to production to fall within the purview of the act.[70] In the court's view, Congress clearly articulated its design that the president assume the responsibility for ensuring that there be no crippling work stoppage.[71] Thus, the pivotal difference in the two cases lies in the fact that Congress had yet to enact the Taft Hartley framework statute that more greatly limited when the president could intervene in labor management relations.

Youngstown Steel demarcates some limits to presidential actions domestically during war: the president cannot take steps at odds with Congress's fundamental policymaking.

3. Some presidents during war not only have relocated citizens and attempted to seize property but have limited individuals' access to our court system. Availability of the writ of habeas corpus may be critical to ensure that the rights of citizens and noncitizens alike be respected.

The Constitution authorizes the suspension of the privilege of habeas corpus but does not direct whether it is the president or Congress that can suspend the privilege. Some think it significant that the Habeas Corpus Clause appears in Article I, not II, and some rely upon the British tradition, under which only Parliament could suspend the right.[72] Indeed, Justice Story in his commentaries assumed that the power belonged to Congress alone: the power to determine whether to suspend "the great bulwark of personal liberty . . . must exclusively belong to [Congress]."[73]

President Lincoln considered suspending the privilege in 1861. He hoped to prevent judicial challenges to military arrest and suit before military tribunals. Particularly in the border states, threats to the Union were grave: the loyalties of Missouri and Maryland were uncertain, at best. Lincoln requested congressional support for his decision, but none was forthcoming.

After hostilities broke out in Baltimore, President Lincoln unilaterally directed Commanding General Winfield Scott to suspend the writ as necessary to suppress the rebellion. When John Merryman, a state legislator, was arrested for secessionist activities and placed in prison, he filed a writ of habeas corpus. Counsel for Merryman submitted the petition to Chief Justice Taney, sitting as a circuit judge. Without argument, Taney ordered the prisoner brought before him, but the government refused. Taney then released the statement that "[t]he President, under the Constitution and laws of the United States, cannot suspend the privilege of habeas corpus, nor authorize any military officer to do so."[74] The statement caused a sensation and constituted a direct rebuke to Lincoln's early conduct of the war. In fact, Taney thought it likely that he would be imprisoned for taking that stand. Taney subsequently issued a more formal opinion, reiterating that the president lacked authority to suspend the great writ absent congressional authorization.[75] The president, however, continued to ignore petitions for habeas corpus relief wherever possible. The military transferred Merryman to civil authorities to moot the conflict.[76]

When Congress suspended the privilege of habeas corpus in 1863, it did not clarify whether it was approving the actions of the president or acting within its own discretion to suspend the right. Challenge to suspension of the writ continued. Northern citizens committed to prison protested and filed suit to contest the lawfulness of their continuing incarceration. Ultimately, in *Ex parte milligan,* the Court confronted a challenge to the presidential action.[77] Lambdin P. Milligan, a citizen of Indiana, helped lead a military wing of the Peace Democrats, who by 1864 had plotted military action on behalf of the South, including liberating Confederate prisoners of war, seizing Union weapons, and kidnaping the governor of Indiana. Upon arrest by a military officer, Milligan was tried and convicted in a military court for treason to the Northern cause. Subsequently, he filed a writ of habeas corpus to contest the legality of his conviction by the military court.

Although the Supreme Court did not disturb Congress's suspension of habeas corpus, it held that the suspension did not carry with it the power to close the civil courts of the country when they were open. In a powerful message for restraint at the outset of the Reconstruction Era, the Court pinned its analysis on a conception of necessity: "As necessity creates the rule, so it limits its duration; for, if this government is continued *after* the courts are reinstated, it is a gross usurpation of power. Martial rule can never exist where the courts are open, and in the proper and unobstructed exercise of their jurisdiction. It is also confined to the locality of actual war."[78] The necessity must be actual and present; and the crisis must effectively close the courts. According to the Court, the president "is to execute, not [] make, the laws"[79] and thus cannot unilaterally determine the extent to which the writ be suspended, "no matter how great an offender the individual may be, or how much his crimes have shocked the sense of justice of the community, or endangered its safety."[80] Even when a writ of habeas corpus can be denied, the Court continued that the Constitution could have, but does not state that the citizen "shall be tried otherwise than by the course of the common law."[81] In a broad plea for limited emergency powers, the Court stated that the Constitution was "law for rulers and people, equally in war and in peace, and covers with the shield of its protection all classes of men, at all times, and under all circumstances. No doctrine, involving more pernicious consequences, was ever invented by the wit of man than that any of its provisions can be suspending during any of the great exigencies of government."[82] In short, the Court sanctioned the prior suspension of the privilege but narrowed the duration and ramifications. Editorial writers manifested outrage, such as the *New York Times* quip that "in the conflict of principle thus evoked, the States which sustained the cause of the Union will recognize an old foe with a new face."[83]

In wartime, however, the pendulum clearly swings to presidential initiative. Despite the *Milligan* precedent, President Franklin Roosevelt did not hesitate in authorizing use of military courts during the Second World War to try German infiltrators. After the FBI stumbled upon Nazi saboteurs, FDR issued a proclamation establishing military courts for those "subjects, citizens, or residents of any nation at war with the United States . . . and who during time of war enter or attempt to enter the United States . . . and are charged with committing or attempting . . . to commit sabotage, espionage, hostile or warlike acts, or violations of the law of war."[84]

In upholding the use of special courts in *Ex parte Quirin*, the Supreme Court held that *Milligan* did not apply to enemy belligerents, even those who may have been United States citizens:[85] "[T]hose who during time of war pass surreptitiously from enemy territory into our own . . . have the status of unlawful combatants punishable as such by military commission."[86] And, in *In re Yamashita*, the Supreme Court upheld the use of military commissions after World War II to try Japanese servicemen charged with crimes against humanity.[87]

Similar issues arose in the wake of the September 11, 2001, terrorist attacks. President Bush issued an emergency directive authorizing trial of terrorists and sympathizers by an administrative tribunal, without affording access to Article III courts.[88] President Bush's move echoed those of Presidents Lincoln and FDR but with even greater scope. The order included prosecutions for war crimes or violations of other applicable laws arising out of any act of international terrorism that has "adverse effects on the U.S., its citizens, national security, foreign policy, or economy."[89] If the president unilaterally determined that a noncitizen has committed, aided, or abetted an act that the president decides is an act of international terrorism, the jurisdiction of the special tribunal could have been triggered. The breadth of the order was alarming, and in comparison to criminal cases before Article III courts, evidentiary requirements were relaxed and new rules of procedure created.[90] President Bush could find even less congressional authorization to justify the tribunal than could FDR or Lincoln before him.[91]

Moreover, the order purported to depart from the *Milligan* Court's stress that the government must proceed through Article III courts when available. The order stated that the tribunals shall have "exclusive jurisdiction" and that individuals tried before them "should not be privileged to seek any remedy or maintain any proceeding . . . in any court of the United States."[92] Military tribunals in Afghanistan may be one thing, but tribunals in the United States for individuals within this country are something else. By the same token, the order's seeming evisceration of habeas corpus undermined the Civil War judicial precedents. Despite the scope of the order, President Bush chose to proceed against most terrorist suspects in the United States within the framework of the federal courts.[93] The Supreme Court in *Hamdi* guaranteed that at least some access to Article III courts be afforded to citizens charged as enemy combatants, but permitted forestalling full criminal trials until after the hostilities with the terrorists ceased.

The habeas cases, in conjunction with the *Prize Cases,* suggest that courts will defer to presidential assessment of emergencies. Courts will not directly confront presidential measures in the face of threats to the nation's integrity. The desire for accountability takes a back seat to the pressing imperative of presidential initiative. But, the precedents also suggest that, to the extent cases and controversies are present, courts may attempt to narrow the reach of presidential initiatives to protect civil liberties, at least at the margin.

C. Emergency Measures to Protect Governmental Personnel and Property

The Lincoln and Eisenhower illustrations focus on use of military force domestically to quell in one case civil insurrection and in the other massive resistance to federal court orders. The Roosevelt and Truman examples involve the extent to which presidents can curb rights during time of war. Presidential authority to exercise nonstatutory powers in emergency contexts is not confined to periods of actual hostilities. The power to protect, as reflected in those decisions, arguably extends more broadly. Many presidents believe that a principal duty of government is to protect citizens as fully as possible.

A key Supreme Court case arose from a presidential decision to assign marshals to federal officials while they were on duty.[94] Because of threats on the life of Justice Field, the president assigned a marshal to protect him. No statute authorized use of federal marshals for such purpose.

While traveling by train, the marshal intervened to thwart an attack on Justice Field, and killed the assailant. The state of California subsequently imprisoned the marshal for the killing. Neagle then filed a petition for habeas corpus, arguing that he should be let go under a federal statute authorizing release of anyone committing an act "in pursuance of a law of the United States."[95] Neagle reasoned that his act was authorized by presidential decree and that the authorization shielded him from prosecution.

The Supreme Court in *In re Neagle* struggled to justify the president's decision to assign the marshal to protect Justice Field.[96] No specific law authorized deployment of the marshal. The Court asked whether the duty to protect federal officials was "limited to the enforcement of acts of Congress or of treaties of the United States according to their express terms, or does it include the rights, duties, and obligations growing out of the Constitution itself, our international relations, and all the protection implied by the nature of the government under the Constitution?"[97] The Court concluded that the president could exercise this power arising out of the Article II duty to "take care that the laws be faithfully executed."[98] According to the Court, although its reasoning was not entirely clear, the structure of the Constitution assigned the power to the executive branch not only to execute the laws but also to protect those individuals who are executing the laws.[99]

The dissent's analysis was less flexible. It acknowledged the importance of the presidential decision but would have awaited authorization from Congress:

> The President is sworn to "preserve, protect and defend the Constitution." That oath has great significance. The sections which follow that prescribing the oath (sections 2 and 3 of article 2) prescribe the duties and fix the powers of the President. But one very prominent feature of the Constitution, which he is sworn to preserve, and which the whole body of the judiciary are bound to enforce, is the closing paragraph of sec. 8, Art, 1, in which it is declared that "the Congress shall have power . . . to make all laws which shall be necessary and proper for *carrying into execution the foregoing powers,* and all other powers vested by this Constitution in the government of the United States, or in any department or officer thereof."[100]

The "take care" clause empowers no presidential action beyond that authorized in the delegations from Congress.

The same tension between accountability and initiative emerges as in the emergency contexts discussed previously. Few presidents faced with threats to the life of a Supreme Court justice would tolerate the delay of seeking congressional authorization prior to sending a marshal to protect his life. Moreover, Congress had never forbidden the president to take such action, arguably leaving more room for executive discretion. On the other hand, if presidents feel free to take measures not authorized by Congress whenever they perceive the need to protect the country, the shift in power might become striking. Accordingly, courts have temporized, resolving each challenged instance based on the particular facts of the case—no enduring legal principles have been articulated.

The Supreme Court's near-contemporaneous decision in *In re Debs* is quite similar.[101] There, a Pullman railroad strike in 1894 threatened to interrupt interstate commerce and mail delivery across the nation.[102] The Socialist Party strongly supported the strike, and the economic action garnered the support of much of the surrounding populace. The railroad companies' efforts to use strikebreakers had only minimal success. In the face of the continuing success of the strike, President Cleveland sought to enlist the courts in the effort to break the strike. The government filed suit to enjoin the strike on the ground that the action interfered with the distribution of the U.S. mail and, more broadly, the flow of interstate commerce. The president relied upon inherent authority to protect interstate commerce and the congressionally authorized mail system. No statute authorized suit, and no statute criminalized the offending conduct.

Nonetheless, a unanimous Court supported the president. As in *In re Neagle,* the Court's reasoning was far from clear. It noted that "[a]s, under the Constitution, power over interstate commerce and the transportation of the mails is vested in the national government, and Congress, by virtue of such grant, has assumed actual and direct control, it follows that the national government may prevent any unlawful and forcible interference therewith."[103] The Court continued that the Constitution permitted the president to use "[t]he entire strength of the nation" to remove the obstruction to interstate commerce."[104] It explained that

whenever the wrongs complained of are such as affect the public at large, and are in respect of matters which by the Constitution are entrusted to the care of the Nation and concerning which the Nation owes the duty to all the citizens of securing to them their common rights, then the mere fact that the Government has no pecuniary interest in the controversy is not sufficient to exclude it from the courts.[105]

The Court, therefore, seemed to imply some protective power in Article II to permit the president to protect not only federal officials but also federal property and the instrumentality of interstate commerce itself. As in *Neagle,* there was no evidence that Congress previously had intended to limit the ambit of executive discretion.

Courts have been wary about any extension of the *Debs* principle, which by its terms seems quite expansive. The emergency was far more attenuated than in the *Prize Cases,* and the need for federal intervention less clear even than in *In re Neagle.* Congress had not chosen to vest the president with the authority to take such protective measures. Read broadly, *Debs* may authorize the executive to obtain injunctive relief in any case in which a broadly defined public interest is at stake: the only limit in the Court's decision is that the scope of presidential protective power must affect interstate commerce, which poses hardly a restraint at all.

The Court would have been on firmer ground if it had restricted its ruling to permit the government to bring suit—in the absence of congressional authorization—to vindicate a property interest. Earlier in the nation's history, the Court had recognized the president's common-law right to sue on a bill of exchange endorsed by the secretary of the Treasury.[106] The government should enjoy the rights of other property holders to protect its property, including the right to go to court. *Debs* represents only a limited extension once one conceptualizes mail as the property of the country. Although the question of the authority of the United States to seek injunctive relief to abate threats to the public welfare has arisen only rarely, courts have declined to extend *Debs*'s reasoning much further.

The issue came to the fore once again in the Pentagon Papers case. After the *New York Times* started publishing classified government documents about the Vietnam War, the government sought an emergency restraining order against publication based in part on the president's inherent authority to protect government secrets and national security. Government attorneys analogized to the *Debs* and *Neagle* line of cases. The trial court granted the requested relief, but the Supreme Court shortly thereafter lifted the ban. The *New York Times* promptly continued printing the papers, to the dismay of government officials.

The Supreme Court later issued an opinion explaining its refusal to block publication, with no opinion commanding a majority.[107] Justice

Marshall wrote separately to explain why he thought that the attorney general lacked the power to seek injunctive relief to protect the public. He wrote that, although "Congress has on several occasions given extensive consideration to the problem of protecting the military and strategic secrets of the United States," it had declined to approve an injunctive remedy.[108] Justice Marshall continued that "[w]hen Congress specifically declines to make conduct unlawful it is not for this Court to redecide those issues—to overrule Congress."[109] The "extensive consideration," however, was never explicit, and it is difficult to infer congressional intent from a failure to act. In dissent, Justice Harlan also queried whether the attorney general was even authorized to seek the injunctive remedy, given that the government could assert only inherent authority to justify filing the suit.[110]

Subsequently, President Carter directed that suit be brought against the Philadelphia police department to enjoin continued practices of police brutality targeted primarily at African Americans.[111] Philadelphia police had been notorious in harassing, beating, and occasionally even shooting African American citizens, and state law enforcement agencies had either been unwilling or unable to halt the egregious conduct. The federal government predicated suit directly under the Fourteenth Amendment, arguing a deprivation of the equal protection of the laws. The government relied on the *Debs* precedent, reasoning that the federal government, as a matter of constitutional law, should be empowered to protect the rights of citizens as well as interstate commerce. Indeed, protection of the individual has long been thought one of the first duties of government.[112] No claim of emergency, however, was made.

In *United States v. Philadelphia,* the Court of Appeals for the Third Circuit rejected the federal government's suit. The court echoed the view expressed in Justice Marshall's concurrence in the Pentagon Papers case, distinguishing *Debs* on the ground that Congress, unlike in the former case, had carefully limited the contexts in which the government could seek redress for civil rights violations. Under 18 U.S.C. §§ 241 and 242, Congress authorized criminal actions against state and local officials for unconstitutional conduct. At the same time, Congress had rejected amendments to confer injunctive authority upon the United States. According to the Court, "There certainly is no evidence of congressional intent to create an additional remedy with the incredible breadth and scope of this one."[113] Moreover, "examination of three express refusals of modern Congresses to grant the Executive general injunctive powers in this field . . . reveals an understanding . . . that no such power existed."[114] Al-though the Court acknowledged that the federal government had a duty to protect federal rights, it concluded that it was Congress's province to determine what power the executive should wield.

In dissenting from a petition for rehearing, Judge Gibbons, joined by three others, would have followed the *Neagle* and *Debs* precedents. The opinion states that "the Executive has the inherent constitutional power and duty to enforce constitutional and statutory rights by resort to the courts."[115] Furthermore, Judge Gibbons clarified that

> [w]hile the potential of unbridled executive initiation of suits in the "national interest" understandably may evoke visceral fears of executive power run rampant . . . [w]hen, as here, the Attorney General can substantiate the "national interest" and "public welfare" by reference to clearly articulated legislative policies or judicial precedent, the danger of untoward exercise of executive power is fanciful.[116]

There is some question currently, therefore, as to how far *Debs* can extend to confer nonstatutory authority upon the executive to enforce conduct deemed contrary to the public interest. Litigation can be a tool of presidential authority to protect property and lives, no less than troops. But, permitting the president to define conduct contrary to the public interest would intrude upon Congress's realm. It is for Congress, not the president, to define and determine how to combat conduct that threatens the public weal. Otherwise, presidents in conjunction with judges could bypass the principal policymaking arm of the nation. At a minimum, courts will limit presidential discretion to take protective measures when evidence that Congress would object exists. Perhaps not surprisingly, the few court cases do not spell out the precise extent of the president's power to seek injunctive relief. No consensus exists as to whether there must be an emergency to warrant such efforts to obtain relief or to what extent congressional consideration of whether the executive should wield such litigation authority precludes the president from maintaining the suit.

The *Debs* and *Neagle* line of cases, however, found flower in a nonlitigation context. For much of the nation's history, Congress has declared particular federal lands containing oil and other natural resources free and open to the public for exploration and purchase by American citizens.[117] In the interests of conservation, President Theodore Roosevelt in the beginning of the twentieth century exercised the discretion to withdraw many parcels of land for forest and bird reserves, among other reasons. He departed from the congressional framework, which permitted him to withdraw land only on which "mineral deposits" had been found.[118] President Roosevelt evidently theorized that Congress could always have reversed his action and permitted public access. Still, the Roosevelt initiatives placed the burden upon Congress of overcoming inertia, and Congress did not respond.

President Taft subsequently followed Roosevelt's lead. His administration deemed oil critical to the nation's economic health, for it faced the need to acquire oil for military and domestic purposes. The government feared that most federal lands would soon be depleted of oil, and that the United States would then have to buy the very same oil on the market that it was giving away at below market prices. In reaction, President Taft withdrew some of the federal lands eligible for private acquisition *in aid of legislation that would be proposed later.*[119] An oil company sued to contest the legality of Taft's action.

To resolve the issue, the Court stated that it "need not consider whether, as an original question, the President could have withdrawn from private acquisition what Congress had made free and open to occupation and purchase."[120] Rather, the Court looked to historical precedents in which presidents had removed lands from public purchase for various reasons. Those precedents suggested that Congress had not written on a blank slate but had allowed access to the public lands in question in light of "a long continued practice to make orders like the one here involved."[121] Congress's silence in the face of past presidential exercises of nondelegated authority seemingly was a reason to sanction the current act. Although the historical practice lessened the accountability problem in light of Congress's tacit acquiescence, the historical exercise of power seemingly expanded the president's constitutional power.

The decision in *Midwest Oil* might stem from the president's special responsibility as the administrator of public lands. Viewed in this vein, the Court merely acknowledged the powers of the president to take steps to preserve public property even when Congress has not directly authorized such action.

More broadly, *Midwest Oil* recognizes that presidents at times may take emergency action unauthorized (and perhaps contradicted) by Congress to protect the government's property, at least as long as Congress has the ability ex post to block the president's action. *Neagle* and *Debs* support this view of *Midwest Oil,* for in these situations as well, Congress (for the most part) could have reversed the presidential initiative, barring use of marshals or the injunctive remedy. As the government argued in its brief, "As we understand the doctrine of the Neagle case, . . . it is clearly this: The Executive is authorized to exert the power of the United States when he finds this necessary for the protection of the agencies, the instrumentalities, or the property of the Government."[122]

The government's theory privileges presidential initiative at the expense of accountability to Congress. The president can act outside Congress's authorization whenever the *president* finds it necessary to do so. Nor need the president first turn to Congress for support even if ample time is available, Indeed, no true emergency existed in *Midwest Oil*: the president withdrew access to the lands in order to prevent the need to pay market rates to fill the nation's oil needs. Congress would have had time to make the cost-benefit decision whether to permit continued access and incur greater cost or whether to withdraw the lands, as President Taft decided. *Midwest Oil* supports expanded executive power, but its ruling must be tempered by *United States v. Philadelphia,* the Pentagon Papers cases, and other subsequent developments.

The limits of the president's nonstatutory powers to protect government property, personnel, and the public are unclear. There is no easy way to determine what is an emergency, and no way to ascertain how direct a threat must be before justifying invocation of nonstatutory authority. Courts have permitted presidents considerable leeway in fashioning emergency measures to protect the public weal. The greater the emergency, the more that courts will uphold presidential initiative at the expense of accountability to Congress.[123] Where the Court will apply brakes is anyone's guess, and the mixed precedents provide support for a variety of positions.

The Constitution could not and did not definitively circumscribe the scope of executive power. Nor, could the Framers have anticipated the many financial and political crises that would arise. Congress can, of course, delegate to the president sufficient power to address emergency situations. Congress, for instance, enacted the Trading with the Enemy Act (TWEA)[124] in 1917 to permit the president broad powers over international trade during war. In times of emergency, presidents could halt exports or imports, seize enemy property, prohibit financial transactions, and the like. Congress, however, did not define national emergency, and FDR cited the TWEA in ordering a bank holiday in 1933, and President

Nixon relied on the TWEA in combating a postal strike in 1970. Internationally, presidents imposed controls on China, Cuba, Vietnam and other nations pursuant to the TWEA. Presidents have not been quick to end previously declared emergencies. Passage of the National Emergencies Act of 1976[125] terminated all authorities previously exercised by presidents by virtue of findings of national emergency under the TWEA, but the next year permitted grandfathering of existing declarations of emergency, as with Vietnam and Cuba. The TWEA still applies in time of war.

All new assertions of national emergency in peacetime must follow the broad guidelines set out in International Emergency Economic Powers Act (IEEPA).[126] In framing that statute, Congress sought to cabin the president's exercise of emergency authority outside war, authorizing emergency powers only in the event of an "unusual and extraordinary threat, which has its source in whole or in substantial part outside the United States, to the national security, foreign policy, or economy of the United States."[127] In addition, unlike in the TWEA, the president now can declare states of national emergency only if he specifies the provisions of existing law supporting the proposed action and publishes the declaration of emergency in the Federal Register. The president must consult with Congress where possible and immediately report to Congress all actions taken pursuant to the emergency. Once a declaration is made, the president can block imports and exports, freeze foreign owned assets, and prohibit new financial transactions such as loans, although the president cannot take title of any foreign-owned property, as he can under the TWEA. Nonetheless, the president can effectively block trade and travel to a foreign nation by utilizing such emergency authority.[128] President Carter invoked IEEPA in the Iran hostage crisis, and Reagan later declared national emergencies with respect to nations such as Libya and Nicaragua. Moreover, IEEPA does not circumscribe the president's discretion to determine the length of the emergency. The president annually can renew the national emergency declaration. Congress first in the TWEA and then in IEEPA, therefore, delegated a host of powers that presidents can pursue in an emergency, and it can limit those authorities further if it should so choose.[129]

But Congress cannot foresee every circumstance in which the nation may find itself, and cannot predict what tools will be needed to meet the challenge. Passage of IEEPA does not foreclose the possibility that future presidents will confront emergencies and deem the congressionally authorized steps inadequate. The events of September 11, 2001, demonstrate that any congressionally sanctioned steps cannot preclude the future need for extrastatutory measures. As Representative Bruce Barton quipped during FDR's regime, however, "Any national administration is entitled to one or two emergencies in a term of six years. But an emergency every six weeks means plain bad management."[130]

In dire circumstances, the constitutional pressure to spin a theory defending the president's exercise of nonstatutory powers can be powerful. Courts as well as academics have rationalized a reservoir of inherent authority to protect the nation in an emergency. Cases such as *In re Neagle* and *In re Debs* sketch a view of a flexible, dynamic president who can come to the nation's defense under Article II irrespective of congressional inaction. Currently, therefore, presidents can exercise a limited range of nonstatutory powers to act in an emergency contingent upon the nature of the emergency and prior congressional action in channeling or reacting to presidential authority in similar circumstances.

Courts have been willing to find space for presidential exercises of initiative in emergency contexts within the constitutional framework. Each instance, however, creates a precedent and provides cover for future presidential steps. Moreover, emergency restrictions on the rights of terrorists or foreign nationals may soon expand to limit the rights of "ordinary" criminals and suspects. As a consequence, presidential power has expanded at the expense both of congressional prerogatives and individual rights.

In responding to the perceived need, courts have missed the cleanest and perhaps safest course. The Constitution may not recognize any inherent authority to act in an emergency. The principal and most fundamental check on presidential authority is that, before presidents can act, Congress (subject to presidential veto) must set the governing policy. The executive must abide by statutes as written. The president can exercise a great range of explicit and implicit powers, but each exercise should be traced to a congressional delegation with the limited exceptions for acts closely tied to the president's power as commander in chief, his power to receive ambassadors, or his power to appoint officers, as previously discussed.

This is not to suggest that a president should do nothing while the country implodes. As a matter of politics, presidential initiative in such contexts is absolutely essential. President Franklin Roosevelt, for instance, insisted that Congress in 1942 repeal a provision of the Emergency Price Control Act that he believed had a dangerous inflationary impact and might hamper the fight against Japan and Germany. He argued, "The President has the power, under the Constitution and under Congressional acts to take measures necessary to avert a disaster which would interfere with the winning of the war."[131] He threatened that "[i]n the event that the Congress should fail to act and act adequately, I shall accept the responsibility, and I will act."[132] Congress acquiesced the next day.

To President Roosevelt, as to President Lincoln before him, the Constitution seemingly authorized expanded executive power in times of national emergency. But, as a matter of political science, it might be safer to say that effective presidential leadership requires risk taking, and one of the risks to bear is violation of the Constitution. Congress and the people ultimately can respond to any perceived departure from the Constitution through impeachment and the ballot box.[133] Politics and constitutional law should remain at least somewhat distinct: reading a set of emergency powers into the Constitution might embolden adventurous presidents to pursue too many otherwise illegitimate actions under the guise of responding to or preventing domestic emergencies.

In short, despite the pressure to articulate a range of extrastatutory powers that presidents can exercise in an emergency, upholding such presidential initiatives may sacrifice the accountability to Congress and to the public that are woven into the constitutional framework. We may want presidents to take risks, but there is no reason to cloak that political exercise of power in constitutional garb.

4

Presidential Immunities
and Priviledges

Any view of presidential power stressing accountability of the president both to Congress and the people includes an important role for judges. A democratic republic cannot easily thrive if its leader is perceived to be above the law. We do not wish to exempt presidents from the same rules governing the behavior of the rest of us.

As has been discussed, judicial review of presidential action can ensure that presidents conform to law both in the domestic and foreign affairs arenas. Courts at times may invoke the political question doctrine to insulate the president's actions from review, and they may extend a considerable amount of deference to the president even when reviewing the president's actions. Despite the courts' general reluctance to second-guess the president, presidential acts, from discharge of subordinate officials to executive orders, have been overturned. Judicial review therefore can make presidents more responsive to Congress and the public. The legacy of *Marbury v. Madison* demands as much.

Judges also play a role in umpiring others' demands for information in the executive's possession. Both Congress and private litigants at times need information from the executive branch. Without information, Congress may not know whether to continue or revise a particular program. Litigants may not be able to represent themselves adequately if relevant information remains concealed by the executive branch. Both courts and Congress, therefore, depend upon information to effectuate their role under the constitutional scheme.

Nonetheless, lawsuits seeking direct relief from the president—as opposed to merely challenging presidential acts—and requests for information in the president's control may undermine the executive's ability under Article II to carry out constitutional functions and exercise initiative. Suits filed against a president in his individual or private capacity seeking monetary relief, suits filed against a president in his official capacity seeking some mandatory action, and disclosure of presidential documents may threaten presidential control over law administration in both domestic and foreign contexts. Presidents' fear of personal liability may make them too passive in office, and presidential disclosure of confidential and otherwise sensitive documents may harm private interests as well as impede presidents' ability to obtain candid advice in the future, thereby placing an obstacle in the way of the president's exercise of Article II responsibilities. The continuing fights over the president's amenability to judicial process and control over information thus reveal a basic recurring tension in our jurisprudence: the president as an individual should not be above the law, but the office itself should retain sufficient prestige and power to ensure that the country can be governed effectively and energetically. The desire for accountability to Congress and the public may, in rare occasions, be subordinated to the need to preserve the dignity of the office of the presidency, and the capacity of presidents to exert initiative. Courts have vacillated in assessing the trade-offs among the three goals and, as a consequence, no coherent framework for assessing disputes has arisen.

This chapter illustrates the tension in several different contexts. First, it addresses the president's Article II immunity from suit in his individual capacity for both his official and private acts; then it explores whether judges can impose mandatory relief on presidents even when acting in their official capacities. Finally, the chapter focuses on the president's duty to respond to congressional and judicial requests for information. Congress and the judiciary may have compelling needs for materials within the president's control, but disclosure may undermine the president's ability in the future to discharge his constitutional responsibilities.

A. Immunity from Suit

Although government acts routinely have been scrutinized in court, government officials themselves long have enjoyed some immunity from suit: officials in all three branches have been shielded to some extent. They have been protected from facing the same individual liability as the rest of us. The level of immunity enjoyed has both a policy and constitutional dimension.

Courts, and at times legislatures, have determined that the costs of suit in some contexts outweigh the benefits to the judicial system. For instance, judges have long enjoyed individual immunity for any private suit against them for acts within their judicial function. Although judges unquestionably may injure parties through their rulings—defaming litigants or depriving parties of constitutionally protected rights—permitting suit could significantly skew judging by introducing another consideration in the judicial calculus, namely, the potential for a ruinous lawsuit. Judges might resolve issues in a way that would minimize their own exposure, which is not likely to further justice in the specific case.[1] Courts have held judges absolutely immune from suits challenging their judicial pronouncements and decisions, without specifying whether the absolute immunity is constitutionally required under Article III.

Similarly, legislators might decline to enact measures if they feared that they, too, could be subject to individual suit because of the impact of their enactments. Legislators through legislation may deprive parties of constitutional rights or rights protected at common law, but one cannot sue legislators individually to redress any financial harm. Conscientious legislating arguably demands that the legislators be free from the concerns that a particular measure will expose them individually to suit.[2] We have made a commitment that judicial and legislative harms should go unredressed to serve the overall public goods of vigorous judging and legislation. Article I's Speech and Debate Clause bolsters the argument for absolute immunity at least in part, but whether Article I requires absolute immunity for acts falling outside the ambit of "speech and debate" is unclear.[3]

The question of presidents' immunity from suit extends to both cases seeking individual liability from presidents for civil wrongs (including unconstitutional acts harming private parties) and cases challenging presidents acting in their official as opposed to private capacity. Authorizing suit against the president in either capacity is not cost free. There are at least four related dangers. First, permitting suit may affect the president's conduct in office—the president may reach decisions with an eye toward avoiding litigation, irrespective of whether he individually faces liability. Second, the more that the president is involved in litigation during his presidency, the less time can be devoted to governance. Third, opponents can use the litigation process to achieve political ends. Finally, enmeshing the president in litigation-related activities might tarnish the prestige of the office itself.

The Constitution, however, nowhere in Article II directly protects the president from suit. From a textual perspective, therefore, the case for immunity appears suspect. Indeed, not only does Article I provide that members of Congress are immune from civil or criminal liability due to any "Speech or Debate in either House,"[4] but it also states, "The Senators and Representatives . . . shall in all Cases, except Treason, Felony and Breach of the Peace, be privileged from Arrest during their Attendance at the Session of their respective Houses."[5] Thus, one can argue that the Founders' failure to insert comparable protections in Article II was not inadvertent, and that no immunity therefore should be recognized.

Despite the plausible interpretive inference, courts have implicitly read into Article II substantial, though far from total, protection for the president. Functional concerns for protecting the president seemingly have triumphed. In the absence of some immunity, the president's ability to accomplish his constitutionally assigned tasks would be impaired. But line-drawing problems remain, and the extent of the immunity to afford the president has been hotly contested.

Immunity from suit has both a constitutional and common-law dimension. Judicial recognition of presidential immunity at times may stem from courts' common-law powers. Congress, in addition, may step in to expand or contract the scope of individual immunities conferred.[6] But there likely remains a core or floor of immunity for the president that Congress cannot take away in light of the overarching constitutional structure. Congress has never addressed presidential immunity,[7] and courts therefore have never faced the question of the extent to which Congress may modify or refine their immunity decisions.

1. Individual Immunity for Acts within the Outer Perimeter of the Presidency

Courts have conferred less protection on executive branch officials than on officials in the coordinate branches. Unlike judges and legislators, who are absolutely immune from suit for carrying out their legislative and judicial functions, the Supreme Court has shielded senior executive branch officials only with a cloak of qualified immunity when confronted with constitutional claims arising out of the officers' official duties.[8] Qualified immunity—as formulated currently—shields officials from constitutional claims but not if the constitutional right was clearly established at the time of the act in question and the official should have known of the right.[9]

Although the prospect of suit can chill the exercise of executive functions as well as judicial and legislative acts, greater restraints arguably already channel the conduct of executive branch officials, minimizing the prospect that the fear of suit will chill such officials from effectively carrying out their jobs. Moreover, the sheer number of executive branch officials—in comparison to the number of officials in the legislative and judicial branches—makes monitoring through litigation all the more important. Furthermore, there may be less concern for overdeterring low-level executive officials than for legislators or judges who engage in broader judicial and legislative policymaking. In general, therefore, executive officials face individual liability far more than do their counterparts in the coordinate branches.

In *Nixon v. Fitzgerald,* the Supreme Court considered whether the president should enjoy absolute immunity for acts taken within the scope of his official duties.[10] Ernest Fitzgerald, who lost his job as a management analyst with the Air Force, sued President Nixon for damages arising from the discharge.[11] Fitzgerald alleged that his discharge stemmed from his exercise of the right to free speech, for he had roundly condemned the administration's profligate procurement policies. Fitzgerald gained fame in the early 1970s as a whistle-blower, exposing waste in the military. He asserted that President Nixon retaliated against him by arranging for his dismissal. Indeed, one of the tapes released from Nixon's office revealed that Nixon had ordered his subordinates to "get rid of that son of a bitch."[12]

The Court in *Nixon v. Fitzgerald,* however, held that Article II implicitly protected the president with greater protection than other executive branch officials, namely, the same absolute immunity enjoyed by judges and legislators. The Court explained that "[w]e consider this immunity a functionally mandated incident of the President's unique office, rooted in the constitutional tradition of the separation of powers and supported by our history."[13] The Court quoted with approval from Justice Story's *Commentaries,* "There are . . . incidental powers, belonging to the executive department, which are necessarily implied from the nature of the functions, which are confided to it. . . . The president . . . must be deemed, in civil cases at least, to possess an official inviolability."[14]

The Court provided a functional explanation as well. Even though Nixon had long since resigned from office, the Court reasoned that, in light "of the singular importance of the President's duties, diversion of his energies by concern with private lawsuits would raise unique risks to the effective functioning of government."[15] The Court continued that "[i]n view of the visibility of his office and the effect of his actions on countless people, the President would be an easily identifiable target for suits for civil damages."[16] Thomas Jefferson had warned of the threat to the executive branch if subpoenas keep the president "constantly trudging from north and south and east and west to withdraw him entirely from his constitutional duties."[17] The president's sweeping responsibilities under Article II of the Constitution "distinguishes him from other executive officials."[18] Consistent with that reasoning, the Court plainly included within that immunity both common-law actions such as those grounded in contract and tort and constitutional suits as long as they arose out of acts "within the 'outer perimeter' of his duties of office."[19] Fitzgerald's case could proceed against other officials in Nixon's White House—subject to qualified immunity—but not against Nixon himself.

Thus, current Supreme Court doctrine protects the president completely from suits based upon his official acts in office—his acts can be examined but no personal liability can be imposed. Article II shields the president from suit. The interests in protecting the office of the president and presidential initiative outweigh the need to ensure that the president is accountable to Congress and the public. Although the Court has not precluded Congress from limiting that immunity, Congress has never tried, and the Court is unlikely in any event to permit Congress to chip away the absolute immunity it has recognized.

2. IMMUNITY FROM SUIT BASED ON PRIVATE ACTIONS OF THE PRESIDENT

In *Fitzgerald* the Court omitted any discussion of whether the president could be sued for acts outside the outer perimeter of his duties while in office. On the one hand, Article II does not seem to prescribe an "official inviolability" for acts unconnected to the exercise of presidential authority. On the other hand, authorizing suits to proceed during a president's term might, as a functional matter, interfere with the president's exercise of constitutionally assigned duties. Permitting suit might also offend the dignity of the office.

Several historical precedents exist but provide little illumination. Complaints against Theodore Roosevelt and Harry Truman for conduct unrelated to administration of the nation had been dismissed before their inaugurations, and courts affirmed dismissals during their respective presidencies.[20] A tort claim against President Kennedy arising out of a car crash during his campaign was settled.[21] There is no constitutional bar preventing private suits against any other governmental official—whether in Congress, the judiciary, or the executive branch—so the question is whether the president is somehow different.

The issue resurfaced in the midst of the independent counsel investigation of President Clinton. In *Clinton v. Jones,* the Court considered whether Paula Corbin Jones could maintain her suit against President Clinton while he was in office, based on alleged acts of sexual assault and harassment prior to his inauguration.[22] Unlike in *Fitzgerald,* President Clinton argued only that the suit should be delayed until after he left office. Staying a lawsuit can at times cause plaintiffs serious hardship not only by delaying the date of any ultimate recovery and vindication but also by weakening the evidentiary bases of plaintiffs' claims. Memory fades and documentary evidence may disappear. Thus, the *Jones* case asked the question that had been avoided in the prior examples: whether the president should be immune from responding to a lawsuit unrelated to his official duties to protect against "diversion of his energies by concern with private lawsuits," as the Court had suggested in *Fitzgerald.*[23] Given the president's wide-ranging responsibilities and round-the-clock duties, a temporary immunity from private suits might be warranted.

The Supreme Court rejected the *Fitzgerald* Court's functionalist reasoning. The Court explained that, despite the language in that case, its central concern had been "to avoid rendering the President 'unduly cautious in the discharge of his official duties.'"[24] To the Court, the key rested on "the nature of the function performed," not the identity of the actor who performed it."[25] The Court recognized the president's "unique position in the constitutional scheme" and that "[i]n drama, magnitude and finality his decisions so far overshadow any others that almost alone he fills the public eye and ear."[26] But the Court was skeptical that a rash of suits would impair the chief executive's discharge of constitutionally assigned functions: "If the past is any indicator, it seems unlikely that a deluge of such litigation will ever engulf the Presidency."[27]

Even if the president's focus on national affairs could be diverted, the Court continued that the obligation to comply with judicial process was paramount. The Court noted that judges routinely consider whether a wide variety of presidential acts conform to law, and that presidents had been required to testify or produce materials in lawsuits in which they were not directly involved.[28] Thus, "[t]he burden on the President's time and energy that is a mere byproduct of [the civil lawsuit] surely cannot be considered as onerous as the direct burden imposed by judicial review and the occasional invalidation of his official actions."[29] Subsequent history has not treated the Court's analysis kindly.[30]

In reaching its conclusion, the Court elevated one formalist concern over another. The Court stressed the value of ensuring that no one be above the law at the expense of the dignity of the president's office. And, the functionalist concern with diverting the president's energies did not outweigh—in the Court's view—the importance of mandating that the president be subject to the same rule of law as the rest of us.

In short, one can currently sue the president for acts outside the perimeter of his official duties, as one can sue a member of Congress or a judge. The suit need not be stayed, depending upon the sensitivity of the issues raised, the plaintiff's need for expeditious resolution of the suit, and the likely impact on the president's performance of his official duties. The president remains accountable to the people for his actions. But, by virtue of Article II, the president is immune from any challenges that seek redress for common law or constitutional wrongs committed within the scope of his office. The interference with presidential initiative in that context is too great; presidents, like judges and members of Congress, should not choose among policy options with an eye to their own liability in court. Concerns for preserving presidential initiative and ensuring that the president carry out statutory responsibilities as vigorously as possible outweigh concerns that private individuals receive complete redress for any injury suffered from presidential acts.

3. SUING THE PRESIDENT IN HIS OFFICIAL CAPACITY

As discussed, presidential acts harming individuals and firms can be examined by a court for conformance with law. A court may be able to require a president to change a policy when that policy violates the terms of a congressional delegation or clashes with the Constitution. Such has been the practice throughout our nation's history. Judicial review serves as a critical check on presidential action to ensure that presidents remain accountable both to congressional directives and to the public at large.

To be sure, the doctrine of sovereign immunity protects the government (just as immunity doctrine protects the president in his individual capacity) from paying damages for presidential acts absent a waiver of congressional immunity. The underlying concern is to protect policymaking from the potentially distorting impact of damages assessment.[31] The prospect of damages—even if payable by the government and not the president personally—might deter presidents from pursuing initiatives that they believe are in the public interest. Allowing judges to impose damages also may afford them excessive influence over presidential policy.

Concerns over skewing governmental incentives and expanding judicial policymaking, however, do not prevent judicial scrutiny when injunctive or declaratory relief is sought. The rule of law presupposes some review of the propriety of presidential actions, and judicial review is arguably more important to prevent ongoing harm than to redress wrongs committed in the past. But, interestingly, the form of the lawsuit may matter.

There has long been debate over the extent to which presidents can themselves—given their status under Article II—be defendants in suits challenging their official conduct in office. Although courts have used a variety of devices to ensure that presidential conduct be subject to review, they by and large have rejected the option of permitting suit against the president directly. In contrast to the debates over suing the president in his private capacity, the issue hinges on whether the president formally should be included as a party in litigation over government policies.

Consider the challenge to the Reconstruction Acts passed by Congress in the wake of the Civil War. Under the acts, Congress divided ten Southern states into military districts to be controlled by an army officer. The army officer enjoyed full control and responsibility to ensure the peace in those districts. The state of Mississippi challenged what in essence was the imposition of military rule, arguing that the acts violated the Constitution by depriving citizens in Mississippi of trial by jury and other constitutional protections. The state sought an injunction restraining the president from appointing General Ord and otherwise carrying out the act. President Johnson, through his attorney general, argued in part that no injunction could be issued against the president because there is no "less dignity belonging to the office of President than to the office of King of Great Britain. . . . He represents the majesty of the law and of the people as fully and as essentially, and with the same dignity, as does any . . . head of any independent government in the world."[32] Article II, in other words, blocked at least some suits directed against the president.

In *Mississippi v. Johnson* the Supreme Court dismissed the suit, holding that no injunction could lie against the president "in the performance of his official duties."[33] Although the Court noted that it might be able to compel the president to take a ministerial or nondiscretionary action, it could not enjoin the performance of an executive or discretionary act. Given the discretion inherent in the Reconstruction Acts—the power to appoint officers in the military districts, assign personnel to the districts, and issue controlling regulations—the challenge could not go forward. The Court evoked *Marbury v. Madison* in which Chief Justice Marshall had stated that "in cases in which the executive possesses a constitutional or legal discretion, nothing can be more perfectly clear than that their acts are only politically examinable."[34] Moreover, the Court continued that an injunction would be inappropriate because, if the president refused to obey it, then the Court would be "without power to enforce its process."[35] The Court did not want to face the constitutional crisis that could arise by holding the president in contempt, or by ordering him imprisoned.[36]

On one level the Court's reasoning in *Mississippi v. Johnson* is quite unsatisfactory. Courts second-guess the discretionary exercise of authority by executive branch officials all the time, including in *Marbury v. Madison*, when the Court asserted the power to review President Jefferson's refusal to deliver the judicial commissions. Review of executive action for conformance to statutory and constitutional dictate is a common feature of our constitutional system. Moreover, there are many ways of enforcing judicial rulings short of ordering the president incarcerated: declaratory judgments or injunctive relief against subordinate executive branch officials are alternatives. There are few functional reasons to justify a refusal to impose prospective relief directly on the president to prevent unlawful action. The charged political atmosphere of the Reconstruction era may explain the Court's decision: it wished to avoid tackling the constitutionality of the military districts at all costs.[37]

Yet, the Court's decision in *Mississippi v. Johnson* might be understood to rest instead on the unique position of the president in our constitutional structure. Although the distinction between the categories of executive and ministerial discretion may fall apart if subject to scrutiny, there is something jarring about judges confronting the president so directly. It may be unseemly to enjoin the president, particularly when indirect coercive measures are available. As the Supreme Court more recently stated, an order directed formally at the president "raise[s] judicial eyebrows."[38]

Litigants usually can gain comparable relief by suing agency heads directly. In *Kendall v. United States ex rel. Stokes*, a dispute arose out of a disagreement between the postmaster general and some contractors over past amounts due.[39] Even after Congress directed the postmaster general to pay the amount awarded under an arbitral process, the postmaster declined, whereupon the contractors sued the postmaster in mandamus. The Court found no obstacle to awarding relief. Had the contractors sued the president individually, however, the result may have been different.

Judges should be able to monitor executive action without the need to stare down the president.[40] Or, as Justice Scalia has commented, it is "incompatible with [the president's] constitutional position that he be compelled personally to defend his executive actions before a court."[41] Whether the immunity stems more from judges' sense of self-restraint than from any constitutional imperative in Article II is unclear, but the resulting deference would be the same.

Contrast *Mississippi v. Johnson* with the D.C. Circuit's approach one hundred years later in *NTEU v. Nixon*.[42] There, a federal employee union sued President Nixon to implement a pay increase that had been authorized by Congress. President Nixon had claimed the discretion not to authorize the increase for fear of further inflation. The court ruled for the plaintiff, despite the fact that the president was the named defendant. The court noted that "if it were possible for [plaintiff union] to enforce its rights by naming a defendant additional to or in substitution of the President, this Court would exercise its discretion" not to impose relief directly upon the president.[43] The court, however, declined to issue an order of mandamus, confining itself to declaratory relief "in order to show the utmost respect to the office of the Presidency."[44] No further relief was necessary because Nixon complied with the order. Some lower courts have continued to bar actions seeking coercive relief against the president; others have reached the merits of cases without commenting on the issue.[45]

The Supreme Court's reluctance to permit suit directly against the president, however, resurfaced later in a series of suits under the Administrative Procedure Act (APA),[46] the framework statute passed by Congress in 1946 to control administrative action generally. Pursuant to the APA, plaintiffs have filed suit challenging the constitutionality of a wide variety of executive branch actions, whether the Department of Housing and Urban Development's affirmative action policies, the Environmental Protection Agency's Superfund cleanup efforts, or the accuracy of Medicare benefits determinations. Courts under the APA have the power, with certain exceptions, to set aside executive branch conduct that is contrary to the Constitution or other law, or is "arbitrary [and] capricious."[47]

The Supreme Court decided in *Franklin v. Massachusetts,* however, that the president is not subject to the APA because he is not an "agency" within the meaning of the APA, which permits judicial review of only "agency" action.[48] That case arose because of a dispute as to how to allocate military personnel stationed abroad to states for the purpose of calculating the national census. The problem was that the military's records documenting the home state of such personnel were unreliable. Massachusetts, which lost one representative due to the allocation of military personnel overseas, claimed that the data underlying the assignment of personnel for purposes of the census were so untrustworthy as to be arbitrary and capricious under the APA. The Court asserted that it could review a constitutional challenge to the census act itself but not to the president's assigned role of transmitting census figures to Congress with a statement of the number of representatives to which each state is entitled.[49] According to the Court, Congress through the APA intended the Office of the President to be accorded more respect than other executive branch officials. As a consequence, Massachusetts under the APA could not challenge the legality of the president's determination.

Whether for reasons of constitutional principle or prudence, the Court has shielded presidents from direct legal challenge to their official acts. The Court has privileged executive initiative at the expense of subjecting presidents to greater accountability to the public through lawsuits. Perhaps courts have been skeptical as to whether such judicial oversight will result in greater accountability or rather would result in greater judicial power. Moreover, in most of such contexts plaintiffs could have found another route to effect the legal challenge without including the president in the suit, ensuring some recourse for those injured by presidential acts.[50] Nonetheless, no clear precedent exists as to whether the Constitution permits the president to be subject to direct judicial relief, though the Court has indicated its greater willingness to exercise review if constitutional claims are raised.

B. Executive Privilege

Congress throughout history has requested presidents to provide a wide variety of information within their control. Information may be highly relevant to congressional committees conducting oversight hearings or considering the need for new legislation. To many, democratic governance demands open government and the free flow of information. A government operating in the dark may breed resentment and fear. The clash between accountability to Congress and presidential initiative is brought into sharp focus. The resulting tension has both political and constitutional dimensions.

As with the question of immunity from suit, the Constitution nowhere explicitly provides for executive privilege to excuse the president from turning over information requested in the congressional investigations or judicial suits.[51] The question of privilege may cover a wide array of information, including confidential conversations with subordinates; deliberative-process materials generated within the executive branch; national security matters; or law enforcement investigatory materials. To the extent a privilege exists, it is either immanent in the "executive power" vested in the president under Article II of the Constitution, or derivative of some more specific power granted to the president, such as the power to "take care that the laws are faithfully executed." Other executive powers—such as the power to remove executive branch officials—long have been implied under Article II as well. A plausible but by no means overwhelming argument can be made that executive privilege is rooted in Article II.[52]

The absence of any textual recognition of privilege is troubling. Indeed, Article I, Section 5 provides that "[e]ach House shall keep a Journal of its Proceedings, and from time to time publish the same, excepting such Parts as may in their Judgment require Secrecy."[53] The lack of any comparable provision in Article II makes the case for executive privilege much more difficult. From a functional perspective, the case for executive privilege seems more convincing. Just as legislators or judges at times require secrecy in order to function effectively, so must presidents. Presidential initiative may hinge to a large extent on the ability to keep communications and plans secret. Presidents may not be able to negotiate or reach wise policy judgments if the confidentiality of their communications is compromised. Once conversations are forced into the open, adversarial positions may harden and subordinates may be less free with advice. Privilege may be critical to any chief executive, even if the president's accountability to both Congress and the public accordingly is compromised.

An additional functional consideration is warranted. Executive privilege not only affords presidents the ability to carry out their constitutional responsibilities more effectively, it also supplies a shield to *defend* the president under Article II from unwarranted intrusions from the coordinate branches. Congressional or judicial demands for information may threaten the executive's place within the constitutional scheme. By demanding sensitive information, Congress can disrupt the president's efforts to negotiate treaties, investigate covert groups, or prosecute lawbreakers. Publicizing ongoing executive enforcement initiatives or disclosing prior confidential sources and negotiations can hamstring execution of the law. Allowing a hostile Congress or judiciary a free hand to demand information or testimony might therefore alter too radically the balance of powers set forth in the Constitution and undermine the president's ability to take vigorous steps in the public's interest.

As a historical matter, presidents from the outset of the republic have asserted a privilege—based on any number of justifications—to keep information from prying eyes. Some presidents have been militant in raising presidential privilege to block requests for documents or testimony. Others have been more willing to reach an accommodation. Backroom deals have been struck, and information has been traded to secure strategic advantage. Conversely, congressional committees can withdraw or modify their requests for information once confronted by a presidential resolve not to cooperate. Much law of privilege is thus worked out in this political fashion.[54]

Courts nonetheless have become embroiled in a significant number of cases. The Supreme Court has determined that the executive's need to control information stems from Article II. Most notably, the Court in the *Nixon* tapes case held that executive privilege "can be said to derive from the supremacy of each branch within its own assigned area of constitutional duties."[55] As a later court summarized, "Nixon identified the President's Article II powers and responsibilities as the constitutional basis of the presidential communications privilege."[56] Yet, the Supreme Court has guarded its own terrain zealously by ensuring that the president not be placed beyond judicial process when information is highly relevant to a case or controversy. In contrast, the Court has been reluctant to require the president to turn over information to Congress except in unusual circumstances.

1. Demand from Congress

Congress has sought information from the executive throughout history. On the vast majority of occasions, presidents have complied.[57] President Reagan, in a memorandum to heads of executive departments, articulated a policy that almost every president has followed:

> The policy of this Administration is to comply with Congressional requests for information to the fullest extent consistent with the constitutional and statutory obligations of the Executive Branch. While this Administration, like its predecessors, has an obligation to protect the confidentiality of some communications, executive privilege will be asserted only in the most compelling circumstances, and only after careful review demonstrates that assertion of the privilege is necessary.[58]

Congress needs information to fashion policy in an informed manner and to monitor executive activities effectively. As Woodrow Wilson wrote, "It is the proper duty of a representative body to look diligently into every affair of government and to talk much about what it sees."[59]

Nevertheless, there have been occasions in which presidents have refused to accede to congressional demands. Presidents have couched their refusals on myriad grounds, including that Congress lacked jurisdiction to investigate the issue, or that disclosure would undermine the privacy rights of third parties, undercut needed confidentiality in communications or negotiations, or impair national security interests. In other cases, Congress and the president have come to an agreement after considerable political jockeying.[60]

Judges at times umpire disputes between the congressional and executive branches. Congressional demands for information ultimately may be resolved by judges attempting to balance any executive privilege against Congress's right to know. For example, courts have stepped in to review and generally uphold Congress's regulation of presidential papers.[61] In the rare instances in which courts have intervened, they have treated congressional demands for information as analytically akin to a demand for information from a president in the course of civil litigation.

But, despite the potential for resolution by a neutral third party, Congress's disputes with presidents over access to information generally are played out over the broader political terrain. Such clashes may form only an irritant in comparison to other sources of tension in executive-legislative relations. The clash over executive privilege may become a pawn in the larger battles over policy and prerogative. As a result, the executive privilege claim may be sacrificed at an early stage.

For instance, President Washington in 1792 discussed with his cabinet how to respond to a congressional request for information about the military fiasco of General St. Clair, whose troops had been beaten badly by Indians.[62] Thomas Jefferson, who was in the cabinet, recalled that the group determined "that the Executive ought to communicate such papers as the public good would permit, and ought to refuse those, the disclosure of which would injure the public."[63] Although Washington may have articulated this view informally to Congress, he complied with Congress's request to examine documents pertaining to St. Clair's expedition.[64] Washington, however, withheld information requested by the House relating to negotiation over the Jay Treaty, reasoning that the House had no constitutional role in treatymaking. Indeed, disclosure of such information, he stated, "might have pernicious influence on future negotiations or produce immediate inconveniences, perhaps danger and mischief to other powers."[65] Indeed, Washington explained that "the boundaries fixed by the Constitution between the different departments should be preserved, a just regard to the Constitution and to the duty of my office . . . forbids a compliance with your request."[66] President Washington, therefore, evidently was convinced of the constitutional underpinnings of his decision not to disclose secret information. Congress passed a nonbinding resolution in protest but took no further action.[67]

Shortly thereafter, Alexander Hamilton refused to comply with a congressional request about deposits into the Bank of the United States, arguing that he could not disclose the instructions that President Washington had relayed to him: "[T]hat question must, then, be a matter purely between the President and the agent, not examinable by the Legislature."[68] As pressure mounted, Hamilton acceded to the congressional request. Jefferson later refused to turn over to Congress all requested materials relating to the Burr conspiracy because "neither safety nor justice will permit the exposing [of] names."[69] President Monroe similarly refused to heed the request of the House of Representatives on another occasion for papers on the ground that disclosure might harm the privacy interests of a naval officer.[70]

Jackson further expanded the rationales for denying a request from Congress. He complained that a request for information about administration of the Bank of the United States intruded into confidential communications, and that subsequent requests interfered with his efforts under Article II to administer the laws: "Their continued repetition imposes on me, as the representative and trustees of the American people, the painful but imperious duty of resisting to the utmost any further encroachment on the rights of the Executive."[71] Tyler similarly asserted the right to withhold documents, particularly when they pertained to ongoing investigations and litigation.[72] Grover Cleveland withheld documents from the Senate relevant to a suspended official on the ground that the Senate lacked the power to investigate any act stemming from his constitutionally based removal authority. There is no "right of the Senate to sit in judgment upon the exercise of my exclusive discretion and executive function."[73] The Senate censured the president but ultimately approved Cleveland's nomination of a successor. Presidents therefore have relied on a variety of reasons to support refusal to turn over documents to Congress.

Clashes continued throughout the next hundred years, building in intensity with the advent of the Second World War and then the Cold War. The Roosevelt administration in 1939 rejected a request from a congressional committee for reports of investigations arising out of domestic "strikes [and] subversive activities."[74] President Truman refused to turn over information to the House Un-American Activities Committee.[75] President Eisenhower rejected calls for information from Senator Joseph McCarthy and his committee, instructing the secretary of defense that "it is essential to the efficient and effective administration that employees of the Executive Branch be in a position to be completely candid in advising with each other on official matters," and that "it is not in the public interest that any of their conversations or communications, or any documents or reproductions, concerning such advice be disclosed."[76] Eisenhower invoked executive privilege more than forty times during his term in office.[77] In fact, it was during his administration that the term "executive privilege" was first coined.[78] Congress's very requests for information may be shaped by the knowledge that the executive branch may withhold the information sought. Thus, the branches at times resolve disputes outside of court in the shadow of the Constitution.

Serious standoffs have on occasion arisen. For instance, a House committee investigating international commerce subpoenaed documents from

AT&T pertaining to warrantless wiretapping. The FBI had directed AT&T to help it place certain individuals under electronic surveillance. The Department of Justice sued AT&T to block compliance with the subpoena on the ground that national security would be jeopardized. Congress and the president came close to settling their dispute by agreeing to a procedure allowing members of Congress to inspect redacted copies. Negotiations, however, broke down over verification mechanisms, and the case proceeded. The court of appeals fashioned a compromise procedure under which background materials were disclosed to the congressional investigators with details excised. It reasoned that "where conflicts in scope of authority arose between the coordinate branches, a spirit of dynamic compromise would promote resolution of the dispute in the manner most likely to result in efficient and effective functioning of our governmental system."[79] The court seemed to endorse political resolution of subsequent disputes.

That goal, however, proved elusive. The question of executive privilege rose again to the forefront in Congress's effort to investigate the Reagan administration's efforts to clean up certain Superfund sites. The Oversight Committee of the House Committee on Public Works and Transportation sought files of the Environmental Protection Agency related to its enforcement of the Superfund Act.[80] The EPA refused on the ground that it could not disclose files pertaining to ongoing law enforcement investigations. After negotiations broke down, the committee subpoenaed the documents, and President Reagan responded by directing EPA Administrator Anne Gorsuch not to disclose documents from "open investigative files, [which] are internal deliberative materials containing enforcement strategy and statements of the Government's position on various legal issues which may be raised in enforcement actions."[81] Despite her reservations, Gorsuch acceded to the president's request, and she refused to comply with the congressional subpoena. The full House cited Gorsuch for contempt on December 16, 1982.[82]

That same day, the executive branch sued the House of Representatives for declaratory relief to determine the legitimacy of Administrator Gorsuch's refusal to disclose the papers.[83] The court, however, held the claim nonjusticiable, reasoning that "the Court should not address these issues until circumstances indicate that judicial intervention is necessary."[84] The court continued that the issue would be justiciable only upon appeal by Gorsuch from a criminal contempt citation, and it exhorted the parties instead "to settle their differences without further judicial involvement."[85] The parties subsequently settled, and the executive branch turned over the requested documents with some controls imposed to protect their confidentiality.[86] One individual implicated in the dispute, however, Rita Lavelle, was later convicted for lying to Congress about her role in the Superfund program. Ensuing conflicts between Congress and the president have largely ended with both sides agreeing to a compromise.[87] The extent to which Congress can demand information in the executive's possession remains unclear.

Congress has also sought to regulate disposition of presidential papers. Prior to the Nixon presidency, presidents leaving office customarily donated or destroyed their papers as they saw fit. In order to prevent President Nixon from destroying papers that might shed light on his conduct in office, Congress passed the Presidential Recordings and Materials Preservation Act.[88] The act vested control of presidential papers in the national archivist,[89] and directed the archivist to return any personal papers to the president. Former President Nixon challenged the act on several grounds, including that of presidential privilege, even though the Ford and Carter administrations supported the measure. He asserted that disclosure of communications made in confidence would chill future communications with the chief executive, and thereby impede the executive's ability to exert initiative and govern effectively.

The Supreme Court ultimately upheld the regulation in *Nixon v. Administrator of General Services*.[90] The Court acknowledged that "the privilege of confidentiality of Presidential communications derives from the supremacy of the Executive Branch within its assigned area of Constitutional responsibilities,"[91] and it recognized the regulation's potential impact on a president's ability to elicit frank and robust views from subordinates and visiting dignitaries. But, it ruled that the protections in the act were adequate to protect the president by taking into account "the need to protect any party's opportunity to assert any . . . constitutionally based right or privilege," and in light of the fact that "[t]he expectation of the confidentiality of executive communications . . . [is] subject to erosion over time after an administration leaves office."[92] The Article II interest in initiative must be accommodated with congressional policymaking.

Nonetheless, disputes over the duty of a current president to release prior presidential materials have continued. President George W. Bush sensibly asserted that a sitting president can block release of presidential records even if a former president waived the privilege. The privilege belongs to the office, not the individual. President Bush issued an executive order on November 1, 2001, however, blocking release of prior presidential records without articulating reasons for the refusal to comply with congressional terms, requiring requesters first to demonstrate some "specific need."[93] Whether motivated by principle or by the desire to protect presidential communications during his father's administration, the result at a minimum was a substantial delay in releasing the papers, contrary to Congress's direction in the Presidential Records Act.[94]

2. DEMAND ARISING FROM NEED FOR INFORMATION IN COURT CASES

Individuals' need to acquire information in the president's control may be as pressing as that of Congress. Information can help them protect their own rights in defending or pursuing a lawsuit. Disclosure of information in the president's control may help ensure that the president be more accountable to the public.

The first major incident in which a litigant demanded the testimony of a sitting president arose in the treason trial of Aaron Burr, who had been vice president during Jefferson's first term in office. Burr had attempted to obtain several letters in President Jefferson's possession written by General Wilkinson, one of Burr's principal accusers. Chief Justice Marshall, acting as a trial judge, ultimately issued several subpoenas for the letters. President Jefferson, who had narrowly defeated Burr in the 1800 election, objected, at least in part.[95] Jefferson had written to the United States attorney in charge of the prosecution that it was "the necessary right of the President of the United States to decide, independently, what papers coming to him as President, the public interest permit to be communicated, and to whom."[96] Marshall ruled that a subpoena could be directed to the president, although he acknowledged some limits if the subpoena was, for instance, burdensome or involved state secrets.[97] He wrote that the chief executive "may have sufficient motives for declining to produce a particular paper, and those motives may be such as to restrain the court from enforcing its production."[98] Jefferson never claimed the authority to ignore the subpoenas, and he furnished one of the letters and part of another.

The Supreme Court confronted the issue of privilege only after the Civil War. Individuals prior to that time may have considered seeking information from the president a waste of time, given the low likelihood of success, the resources needed for litigation, and the attendant delay. In the

Civil War case, however, the estate of a Union secret agent who operated behind Confederate lines sought back pay. The Supreme Court held that "public policy" excused the government from disclosing information necessary to maintaining the suit.[99] The Court's decision did not turn on the Constitution but relied on general policy concerns to excuse the executive branch from compliance.

One hundred years later, during the Eisenhower administration, a litigant challenged whether the president could justify ignoring a discovery request in a wrongful death action arising out of a crash of an Air Force bomber due to the fact that state secrets would otherwise be revealed. President Jefferson's claims regarding the Burr incident had not rested on state secrets *per se* but rather on a more general communication privilege. The Supreme Court in *United States v. Reynolds* ultimately upheld the state secrets privilege, describing the privilege as flowing from "an inherent executive power which is protected in the constitutional system of separation of powers."[100] The Court explained that, although a judge should not lightly accept a claim of state secrets, "even the most compelling necessity cannot overcome the claim of privilege if the court is ultimately satisfied that military secrets are at stake."[101] The privilege, based on the Constitution, is absolute. Since *Reynolds,* the state secrets privilege has been frequently litigated in civil cases, from constitutional tort suits over warrantless surveillance,[102] to suits alleging FBI forgery.[103] The privilege has become an accepted part of the authority exercised by the chief executive. The need for executive initiative in security matters outweighs the need for accountability to the public.

On the other hand, the government cannot rely on the state secrets privilege to excuse introducing inculpatory information during criminal prosecutions. The government must rely on evidence that it can disclose to defendants and their counsel. On rare occasions, the government must forgo a conviction against a suspected spy for fear of disclosing sensitive information. The privilege, however, may block a criminal defendant's effort to gain discovery from the government that might aid his or her case. Absent a strong showing of need, for instance, criminal defendants cannot obtain national security information from the government to benefit their defense.[104]

Other aspects of executive privilege remain more controversial. In particular, the question of the extent and scope of confidentiality for presidential communications—as raised in *Burr*—has drawn increasing attention with the scandals rocking the Nixon, Reagan, and Clinton administrations.[105] Executive privilege reached national stage during the Watergate crisis. The Watergate grand jury had returned an indictment against seven members of President Nixon's inner circle (but not Nixon) who either worked at the White House or with the Committee to Reelect the President. The charges covered both the break-in at the Watergate headquarters of the Democratic Party as well as the subsequent cover-up. The special prosecutor, whose predecessor had been fired pursuant to the president's orders, requested the production of tapes and papers relating to particular meetings between the president and others. The existence of secret taping of conversations in the Oval Office created quite a stir, to say the least, and the tapes fomented a legal and political battle between the president and the special prosecutor.

To justify his refusal to produce the tapes, the president asserted privilege to protect the confidentiality of presidential communications with subordinates. He asserted that the privilege was rooted in Article II; that it was absolute; and that it was up to the president alone to assess its scope.[106] He insisted that "the duty of every president to protect and defend the constitutional rights and powers of his office is an obligation that runs directly to the people of this country."[107]

The Supreme Court, after agreeing to hear the case on an expedited basis, concurred that "[c]ertain powers and privileges flow from the nature of enumerated powers; the protection of the confidentiality of Presidential communications has similar constitutional underpinnings."[108] Furthermore, it explained that confidentiality was necessary to ensure freedom for the president and those around him "to explore alternatives in the process of shaping policies and making decisions and to do so in a way many would be unwilling to express except privately."[109] The Court therefore reiterated that the privilege was "inextricably rooted in the separation of powers under the Constitution."[110] The Court continued that the "President's need for complete candor and objectivity from advisers calls for great deference from the courts."[111]

The Court, however, asserted the power for itself to determine the contours of the privilege. It was for the courts, not the president, in a properly drawn case or controversy to determine the scope of the privilege.[112] In examining that power, the Court claimed that, when the privilege depends solely on the broad, undifferentiated claim of public interest in the confidentiality of such conversations, a confrontation with other values arises."[113] Recognizing an absolute immunity—as in the state secrets context—"would place in the way of the primary constitutional duty of the Judicial Branch to do justice in criminal prosecutions."[114] Weighing the two values against each other, the Court concluded that the "generalized assertion of privilege must yield to the demonstrated, specific need for evidence in a pending criminal trial."[115] Accordingly, the Court ordered the tapes and papers released, at least for the purpose of *in camera* inspection by the trial court in order for that court to undertake the prescribed balancing. In part because of the ruling, President Nixon resigned on August 8, 1974.

Continuing controversies between presidents and independent counsels have sparked increased demands for information in the executive's possession. Several principles have gained widespread acceptance. First, the communications privilege is qualified. Assertions of such privilege are always balanced against the need for the information, as in *Nixon*. The balancing is particularly difficult, given that the damage to the integrity of the presidential office may be far more difficult to quantify than the need for critical information in a judicial proceeding. Second, courts make the initial privilege determinations and then attempt any needed balancing *in camera*. Courts may demand detailed statements from the president as to why the material merits privilege, and from the requesting party as to why the need for the information is so great. Third, the president personally must invoke executive privilege—the decision cannot be delegated.

Despite these areas of agreement, application of the principles remains difficult. For instance, in the wake of the Iran-Contra controversy, the district court denied Colonel Oliver North's effort to obtain the personal testimony of former President Reagan.[116] The court reasoned that testimony from a president would be compelled only if necessary to secure a fair trial, a standard not met in that instance.[117] Another district court judge determined that the standard was satisfied in the trial of former National Security Advisor John Poindexter, and former President Reagan complied.[118]

At times presidents have agreed to provide testimony without claiming privilege. For instance, President Ford gave a deposition in the criminal trial of his would-be assassin.[119] Presidents Grant and Carter also gave depositions in criminal proceedings.[120] President Reagan did not assert executive privilege initially to block access to his personal diaries during the Iran-Contra investigation.[121] President Clinton provided testimony in a number of cases arising out of investigations into his conduct in both the civil and criminal contexts.[122] Although he declined numerous invitations to appear before a grand jury investigating allegations that he obstructed justice and committed perjury in the Lewinsky matter, he relented after receiving a subpoena. Clinton agreed not to raise privilege contingent on the withdrawal of the subpoena. His videotaped testimony before the grand jury investigating whether he had committed perjury and obstruction of justice became a national event that riveted the public.[123]

A further clash arose during the independent counsel investigation of President Clinton's secretary of agriculture, Michael Espy, for accepting gratuities from companies that his agency was actively investigating.[124] The allegations against Espy also led the president to request White House counsel independently to investigate whether Espy's conduct warranted sanction. After an investigation and Espy's announced resignation, the White House counsel concluded that no further action was appropriate with respect to Espy's acceptance of the gifts but that steps be undertaken to alert other cabinet members to the ethical issues presented.

Meanwhile, the grand jury investigating Espy, at the independent counsel's direction, directed a subpoena to the White House counsel, requesting all information relevant to his prior investigation. The White House counsel complied but declined to produce eighty-five documents, all but one on the ground that they were protected by executive privilege, and one on the ground of the attorney-client privilege. The requested privileges covered communications between the president and subordinates, as well as predecisional documents that were issued prior to the final investigative report on Espy. The district court held an *in camera* proceeding, and concluded that the president had met his burden of demonstrating that the materials should be covered by executive privilege.[125]

On review, the court of appeals distinguished between claims of executive privilege based on communications with the president and those disclosing the deliberative process within the executive branch.[126] It reasoned that the communications privilege was broader in that entire documents could be protected in contrast to the deliberative process privilege, which would not protect parts of documents that reflected merely facts. The purpose of the so-termed deliberative process privilege "is to prevent injury to the quality of agency decisions" by encouraging vigorous debate of policy options outside the public eye.[127] Like the executive privilege claim addressed in *Nixon,* the deliberative process privilege is qualified and can be overridden by a strong showing of need for the information.

With respect to the communications privilege, the court first inquired whether discussions among subordinates for the purpose of preparing advice to the president would be protected even when the president never actually received the particular communication in question. The court noted that cases such as *Fitzgerald* had stressed the unique position of the president in our legal constellation, and thus that a strong argument could be made that the privilege should extend only when the president personally was involved.[128] Moreover, the broader the privilege, the less likely that important governmental information would be exposed to public view. Nonetheless, the court held that communications by immediate advisors to the president should be included in light "of the need for confidentiality to ensure that presidential decisionmaking is of the highest caliber, informed by honest advice and full knowledge."[129] But for the promise of confidentiality, presidential aides might "temper candor with a concern for appearances."[130] By recognizing a realm of privilege beyond the Office of the Presidency, the court embraced a goal of greater centralized administrative authority.

The court then turned to the question of how to balance what it termed the executive communications privilege against the public interest in disclosure. At least in the criminal context, it concluded that a party seeking to overcome a claim of privilege must demonstrate that each requested set of materials "likely contains important evidence," and also that the "evidence is not available with due diligence elsewhere."[131] Accordingly, the court remanded the case to the trial court to make a contextual determination of whether some documents should have been released to the Espy grand jury despite their privileged nature. The court's compromise reflects an admirable accommodation between the executive's need for secrecy and the public's need to hold the executive accountable for his actions.

The president also asserted presidential privilege to justify withholding various documents amidst the Whitewater investigation of his own conduct. During the independent counsel's investigation into the Lewinsky matter, the president raised privilege in the face of a subpoena directed to Bruce Lindsey, a White House advisor, that sought evidence of Lindsey's discussions with Clinton as to appropriate legal courses of action. The district court agreed that conversations between advisors and presidents can be cloaked with privilege even when the discussions cover private conduct. The president's private affairs readily become matters of public import. But the court reasoned that the independent counsel's need for the testimony in his investigation of Clinton was paramount.[132] The president declined to challenge this aspect of the court's decision.[133]

In a bizarre twist, the question of executive privilege reemerged at the conclusion of the independent counsel's investigation. In his referral to the House of Representatives of "substantial and credible" information "that may constitute grounds for an impeachment,"[134] the independent counsel asserted that one ground for impeachment was that "[t]he President repeatedly and unlawfully invoked the Executive Privilege to conceal evidence of his personal misconduct from the grand jury."[135] In other words, the independent counsel alleged that the president's efforts to protect his Article II power itself constituted a "High Crime and Misdemeanor."[136] Although a president conceivably could wrap himself in executive privilege to thwart an investigation, Clinton's invocations of privilege seem quite similar to those advanced previously by presidents from both parties. In fact, courts upheld much of President Clinton's contentions, and Clinton had acquiesced in the unfavorable decision on privilege in *Lindsey*. The House of Representatives rejected this particular article of impeachment.

The independent counsel's referral manifested a disregard for both the history and intellectual pedigree of presidential privilege. Presidents throughout history have defended their need to protect documents from public disclosure even when highly relevant to a judicial proceeding or congressional inquiry. Article II anchors presidential privilege not to comply with requests for certain types of information. Although the communications and deliberative process privileges are not absolute, their boundaries have been continuously reshaped through generations of give-and-take between courts and presidents. Full accountability to Congress and private litigants can come only with the price of diminished executive vigor.

Presidential control over information therefore is not complete. Only the state secrets privilege is absolute. Although courts have recognized other strands of presidential privilege under Article II, they have compelled testimony and production of information when highly material to a criminal and, even on occasion, civil proceeding. Presidents therefore must determine whether to comply with such requests—from Congress or the courts—in the shadow of at most a partial privilege. Control over information remains an important incident of executive power, but the interest in an energetic executive must be accommodated with the need of Congress and the public for that information. Judges attempt to forge such accommodations when individuals seek access to information in the executive's control, and conflicts between Congress and the president generally are resolved in the political arena.

5

The Pardon Power

The pardon power stands somewhat apart from other presidential authority under Article II. The president is the last resort for those convicted of criminal wrongdoing—he holds the keys to the prisons and can facilitate offenders' reintegration into society. Moreover, in contrast to the power to enter executive agreements, issue management circulars, or withhold information, the pardon power is textually explicit and its lineage easily traced to the Crown. Nonetheless, presidential exercise of the pardon power can displace Congress's policymaking province, and tensions have continuously surfaced. The constitutional framework presupposes that presidential initiative largely overrides concern for presidential accountability to Congress or to the public at large.

Article II empowers the president "to grant Reprieves and Pardons for Offences against the United States, except in Cases of Impeachment."[1] On its face, the clause seems entirely clear—the president may pardon anyone for transgressions, and the reasons for the pardon need not be disclosed. The only three restrictions are that the acts to be pardoned constitute offenses against the United States,[2] that no impeachment be involved, and that the offense already be committed. Indeed, the clause covers civil as well as criminal liability, and the form of the presidential pardon is immaterial. The president may remit fines and forfeitures, grant broad amnesty to a group of offenders, commute sentences, and grant pardons even prior to conviction.

Presidents have used the pardon power aggressively to further a wide array of goals. President Andrew Johnson's pardon of Jefferson Davis,[3] former president of the Confederacy, and President Ford's pardon of President Nixon represent two of the most controversial pardons in our history.[4] But there have been many more. President Washington pardoned many of the participants in the Whiskey Rebellion; President Lincoln pardoned Southern sympathizers, particularly those from his home state in

Kentucky; President Cleveland pardoned Mormons convicted of polygamy; President Harding pardoned the socialist leader Eugene V. Debs; President Carter pardoned Vietnam War draft evaders; the first President Bush pardoned former Secretary of Defense Caspar Weinberger, and President Clinton pardoned his brother as well as the fugitive financier Marc Rich.

Unlike with the exercise of the power to remove inferior officers or withhold documents, the pardon power as a textual matter appears beyond the reach of congressional revision or judicial oversight. As this chapter addresses, the pardon power cannot effectively exist if Congress or courts have too much oversight because the pardon power was designed to check legislative and judicial excesses in punishment. The pardon power vests in the president substantial power to temper justice with compassion, to check subordinate prosecutorial officials within the administration, and to assuage the fears of governmental opponents.[5] Yet, without any restraint, the president's exercise of the pardon power would escape accountability to Congress or the public. Accordingly, limited judicial review at least in the context of conditional pardons may be necessary to check executive discretion, to ensure that the president be accountable in some fashion for his pardon decisions. The pardon power thus presents an informative case study of authority exercised largely without the checks and balances constraining other executive action.

The roots of the pardon power in Article II can be found in prior English practice.[6] Kings could not only grant pardons to exonerate individuals for misdeeds, they could also use the power as an important aid to raising funds and armies. In exchange for a pardon, individuals would either contribute money to the royal purse or agree to serve in the army. By the middle of the sixteenth century, the royal power to pardon covered the "authority to pardon or remit any treasons, murders, manslaughters or any kind of felonies . . . or any outlawries for such offenses . . . committed . . . by or against any person or persons of this Realm."[7] The king enjoyed the flexibility to use the pardon for any purpose advantageous to his goals. The pardon power remained open-ended until Parliament constrained the king's power in the 1701 Act of Settlement to preclude utilization of the pardon power to frustrate attempted impeachments.[8] Under British practice, parliamentary impeachments included conventional punishment, and thus a royal pardon would directly impinge upon parliamentary prerogatives.

In the colonies, the royally appointed governors enjoyed similarly broad pardon powers. The governors could remit fines or exonerate convicted criminals as they saw fit, although there was some variation from colony to colony.[9] For instance, the colonial charter in Maryland vested the executive with the authority "to Remit, Release, Pardon, and Abolish, all Crimes and Offences whatsoever against such Laws, whether before, or after Judgment passed."[10] With independence, however, the newly enacted legislatures began to circumscribe the pardon power. For instance, the Georgia and New Hampshire legislatures vested the power in themselves, and Massachusetts restricted governors to pardoning after criminal conviction. Most state governments vested the power to pardon jointly in the governors and legislatures.[11] No less an authority than Blackstone had counseled that the pardon power should not exist in democracies "for there nothing higher is acknowledged than the magistrate who administers the laws: and it would be impolitic for the power of judging and pardoning to center in one and the same person."[12]

The Constitution restored the pardon power to much of its earlier breadth, despite Blackstone's views.[13] Efforts to condition the president's power on Senate consent, for instance, were defeated. According to Madison's notes, George Mason commented that "[t]he Senate ha[d] already too much power,"[14] and Madison himself stated that it would be improper to vest the pardon power in Congress "because numerous bodies were actuated more or less by passion, and might in a moment of vengeance forget humanity."[15] The Constitution vests the executive with the "Power to grant Reprieves and Pardons for Offences against the United States, except in cases of Impeachment."[16] The exception for impeachment tracks British precedent, preventing the president from nullifying congressional removal of executive or judicial officials through impeachment even though, unlike in the British system, the congressional impeachment power extends only to removal from office. As Justice Story commented, "[T]he Constitution has [] wisely interposed this check upon his power, so that he cannot, by corrupt coalition with favourites, or dependents in high offices, screen them from punishment."[17] With scant limits, therefore, the Constitution vests the president with broad discretion in determining when and why to grant pardons.

The Federalist Papers suggest that the Framers intended the pardon power to be a check on legislative control over punishments as well as a vehicle to pursue more strategic public concerns. For instance, Alexander

Hamilton defended the pardon power in *The Federalist No. 74* in conventional terms by explaining that "[h]umanity and good policy conspire to dictate that the benign prerogative of pardoning should be as little as possible fettered or embarrassed. The criminal code of every country partakes so much of necessary severity that without an easy access to exception . . . justice would wear a countenance too sanguinary and cruel."[18] The pardon power acts as a necessary safety valve in light of Congress's inability to foresee the particularities of every crime and the circumstances of every offender. Similarly, as James Iredell noted in the Constitutional Convention, "There may be instances where, though a man offends against the letter of the law, yet peculiar circumstances in his case may entitle him to mercy. It is impossible for any general law to foresee and provide for all possible cases that may arise."[19]

Hamilton also offered a less traditional justification, noting that

> in seasons of insurrection or rebellion there are critical moments when a well-timed offer of pardon to the insurgents or rebels may restore the tranquillity of the commonwealth. . . . The dilatory process of convening the Legislature or one of its branches, for the purpose of obtaining its sanction to the measure, would frequently be the occasion of letting slip the golden opportunity.[20]

And, James Iredell in the North Carolina ratifying convention noted a different strategic enforcement concern, explaining that the pardon power "is naturally vested in the President, because it is his duty to watch over the public safety; and as that may frequently require the evidence of accomplices to bring great offenders to justice, he ought to be intrusted with the most effectual means of procuring it."[21] The power to pardon can aid executive initiative in providing for the public safety.

From an early date, presidents have relied on the pardon power to issue general amnesties. President Washington issued a Proclamation of Amnesty to the Whiskey Rebels in 1795;[22] President Adams granted an amnesty to the Pennsylvania insurgents in 1800;[23] and President Madison granted a general pardon to the Barataria pirates in 1815.[24] President Lincoln in 1863 called for an amnesty to all Southerners who thereafter swore loyalty to the Union and afforded no further help to the Confederate States. President Carter issued a general pardon to those who had fled the country or hidden to escape the draft during the Vietnam War.

Pardons have also been extended to individuals whose misdeeds have been highly visible to the public. As mentioned previously, President Ford pardoned President Nixon for crimes he may have committed arising out of the Watergate break-in and cover-up. Presidents also have pardoned or granted clemency in thousands of less political cases as well, whether because of the ill health of prisoners or because of extraordinary evidence of rehabilitation.[25] As the Supreme Court summarized in *Knote v. United States,*

> A pardon is an act of grace by which an offender is released from the consequences of his offence, so far as such release is practicable and within control of the pardoning power, or of officers under its direction. It releases the offender from all disabilities [i]mposed by the offence, and restores to him all his civil rights. In contemplation of law, it so far blots out the offence, that afterwards it cannot be imputed to him to prevent the assertion of his legal rights.[26]

The effect of a pardon is to wipe away all collateral impact of a conviction, although Congress or administrative agencies can still impose some sanctions for the offender's behavior, just not for the fact of conviction.[27]

The incidence of pardons has varied with succeeding generations. The first President Bush granted the least number of petitions for pardon and clemency in the twentieth century, seventy-seven. President Harding granted the largest percentage of clemency applications,[28] and FDR granted the most applications for pardons and commutations of sentences, 3,687.[29] In the past ninety years, presidents have averaged roughly two hundred acts of clemency per year.[30] The number of individuals affected in amnesties has been much greater.

Exercise of the pardon power has also varied in light of operation of the surrounding criminal law system. First, as federal crime escalated in the Prohibition Era, the pardon process became more burdensome. Presidents such as Harding and Coolidge faced a growing number of pardon requests.[31] Considering such requests consumed an increasing amount of time, making pardons less attractive. Second, with passage of the federal parole and probation statutes in 1910[32] and 1925[33] presidents found less reason to offer pardons. Other statutory means existed to shorten punishment and help ensure that those released would be law-abiding. Moreover, parole boards could attain the same rehabilitative ends more effectively than presidential pardons. The boards could rely upon expert testimony as to each applicant's likelihood of recidivism. Indeed, part of the impetus for passage of the parole statute may well have been, as it was in some states, to prevent the inconsistent pardon practices of the chief executive.[34]

More recent rejection of parole and indeterminate sentencing, however, has brought us almost full circle. The federal government and most states have abolished parole, and Congress, through the sentencing guidelines, has deprived judges of much sentencing discretion. In an era of harsh and inflexible sentencing, the pleas of compassion may ring more powerfully.[35]

Despite its beneficial aspects, the president's pardon power can encroach on the powers of coordinate branches or directly threaten individual rights. The Framers anticipated the difficulty to some extent by precluding pardons in the case of impeachments. Otherwise, the president could counteract the legislative impeachment remedy and immunize those in the executive branch from the reach of Congress.

Nonetheless, several recurring conflicts among the branches have arisen. Congress (and at times the judiciary) has attempted to reign in or influence the president's exercise of the pardon power to preserve its own policymaking domain. First, Congress has attempted to limit the effect of presidential pardons; second, courts have questioned whether the president through the pardon power can interfere with the ability of Congress and the courts to protect their integrity through exercise of the contempt power; third, some have questioned whether the president can pardon subordinates for law violations when the president disagrees with the courts' interpretation of the underlying law; fourth, litigants have challenged both the process by which presidents reach pardon decisions and the very justifications for pardons granted; and fifth, courts have wrestled with the extent that a conditional pardon encroaches on individual rights.

A. Congressional Interference

The most heated clashes over the scope of the pardon power occurred in the aftermath of the Civil War. For one example, Congress in 1865 provided that no one would be permitted to practice law in a federal court before taking an oath asserting that he had never supported enemies of the Union. Garland, who had been a Southern sympathizer, received a pardon from President Johnson and accordingly sought to practice law. He argued that the pardon removed the taint of having supported the South, and that preventing him from practicing law would impermissibly interfere with the president's pardon power.

A narrowly divided court agreed.[36] The majority reasoned that a pardon "[i]f granted before conviction . . . prevents any of the penalties and disabilities consequent upon conviction from attaching."[37] Thus, according to the Court, barring Garland from practice would nullify part of the effect of the pardon. In dissent, Justice Miller may have been more persuasive in arguing that a pardon should not be equated with innocence: "The man who, by counterfeiting, by theft, by murder, or by treason, is rendered unfit to exercise the functions of an attorney or counsellor-at-law, may be saved by the executive pardon from the penitentiary or the gallows, but he is not thereby restored to the qualifications which are essential to admission to the bar."[38] Whether the case remains good law today is uncertain, but the decision's restriction of congressional ability to interfere with the president's pardon power has withstood the test of time.

Furthermore, President Johnson issued a general pardon in 1868 to enable Southern sympathizers to make a claim on property abandoned to federal troops during the war. Victor Wilson had marked six hundred bales of cotton as property belonging to the Confederate States of America to assure their transit. The cotton, however, was seized by Union agents. Legislation permitted any citizen of the Southern states who was loyal to the Union to recover seized property or its monetary equivalent. Wilson claimed that he was loyal and sought compensation, and after his death his administrator brought suit in the Court of Claims. The Court of Claims initially decided in favor of Wilson's estate, and upon motion from the government reconsidered. The court this time determined that Wilson had in fact been disloyal but refused to alter its $125,300 verdict on the ground that President Johnson's issuance of a blanket pardon to Wilson and others similarly situated forced the court to consider him loyal as a legal matter.[39]

Congress reacted in part by passing a statute providing that evidence of pardons, with some exceptions, could be admissible *against* a pardoned claimant. The 1870 statute provided that certain pardons "shall be taken and deemed . . . conclusive evidence that such person did take part in and give aid and comfort to the late rebellion."[40] All who had received a pardon by virtue of declaring loyalty in response to President Lincoln's

1863 amnesty were conclusively presumed disloyal. Furthermore, the statute required the Supreme Court to dismiss for lack of jurisdiction any Court of Claims decision granting compensation based on a pardon and order that the claim be dismissed.

The Supreme Court's decision reviewing the legislation in *United States v. Klein* is not a model of clarity.[41] The Court invalidated the statute, for the most part condemning Congress's effort to strip jurisdiction from the Supreme Court only in cases in which a claimant had prevailed against the United States. In so doing, however, the Court stated that the law could not be saved on the ground that Congress merely was attempting to redefine the consequences of a pardon because if viewed in that light, "[t]he rule prescribed is also liable to just exception as . . . infringing the constitutional power of the Executive."[42] Congressional acts undoing the effect of a pardon would violate Article II, and those attaching adverse consequences to acceptance of a pardon—as under the enactment in question—similarly violate Article II. Subsequent courts have understood the *Klein* analysis in like vein.[43]

Moreover, Congress cannot use the appropriations power to negate the effect of a presidential pardon. In 1977, Congress included in two appropriations bills a provision denying funds to President Carter to implement a pardon for draft evaders during the Vietnam War.[44] Although subsequent events largely mooted the controversy, Congress's directive should have been unenforceable. Congress cannot undermine the presidential prerogative under Article II to grant pardons.

B. General Separation of Powers Concern

Despite the breadth of the pardon power, the president's exercise of the pardon authority may infringe upon the powers of coordinate branches. First, if presidents can absolve individuals from contempt charges leveled either by the legislative or judicial branch, the pardons may undermine the ability of those branches to fulfill their constitutionally assigned functions. Otherwise, as Justice Story noted, the coordinate branches may be made "wholly dependent upon [the President's] good will and pleasure for the exercise of their own powers."[45] Second, the president through the pardon power may impermissibly intrude upon Congress's policy-making role in setting both the range and type of punishment to be served.

1. In *Ex parte Grossman* President Coolidge commuted the sentence of Grossman to a fine and time served.[46] Grossman had been enjoined from violating the Prohibition laws, and then held in criminal contempt for his return to illegal activities. Upon release from prison, however, Grossman was returned to prison in Chicago, on the ground that the president could not excuse a contempt before a court. From a judicial perspective, the prospect that a president could pardon someone convicted of flouting judicially imposed rules or decorum impermissibly undermined the independence of the judiciary.

The Supreme Court ultimately ordered Grossman released. It held that, despite the clash between branches, the president could pardon individuals convicted of criminal contempt, as for any other crime. Judicial independence did not turn on the ability to ensure that contemnors remained in prison. As the Court noted, "If we could conjure up in our minds a President willing to paralyze the courts by pardoning all criminal contempts, why not a President ordering a general jail delivery?"[47] The remedy for any abuse, the Court continued, should be impeachment.[48] Contumacious behavior before courts threatens that branch's discharge of duties no more than bribery or perjury. The same analysis should hold for pardons of criminal contempt of a congressional order.

Nonetheless, the Court in *Grossman* stated in dicta that pardons could not be used in the coercive contempt context. A coercive contempt order seeks to force the individual to take particular actions, whether disclosure of information or assets. Presidents cannot excuse individuals' obligation to abide by court orders. At that point, a presidential pardon would shade into an immunity for prospective violations. But, once the conduct becomes criminal, then a presidential pardon would be appropriate.

A problem similar to that of contempt might arise should a president pardon an individual charged with obstructing justice. The pardon can immunize criminal conduct only prior to the effective date of the pardon, not after. In other words, the president cannot shield anyone from the law's future commands, or wield a broad dispensation power. In general, however, pardons for criminal contempts of coordinate branches do not violate the separation of powers doctrine.

2. There is a broader concern under the separation of powers doctrine. Through offers of conditional pardons (as well as more traditional commutations of sentences), presidents can alter the congressionally determined range of punishments. Congress retains the power to set the parameters for punishment of federal crimes; it controls whether there should

be a death penalty, whether to order restitution, and whether to permit parole. Each exercise of the pardon power therefore could encroach on Congress's domain. Although not frivolous, such concerns are not ultimately persuasive.

The Supreme Court confronted the separation of powers claim in *Schick v. Reed.*[49] While stationed in Japan, Schick committed a grisly murder. After conviction and collateral challenge, Schick petitioned the president for a pardon or commutation of the sentence. The president commuted the sentence to life imprisonment "expressly . . . on the condition that the said Maurice L. Schick shall never have any rights, privileges, claims, or benefits arising under the parole and suspension or remission of sentence laws of the United States."[50] At that time, Congress had provided for sentences of only death and life imprisonment *with* the possibility of parole. Accordingly, Schick urged that, because the president could commute the sentence only to a congressionally approved sentence, the pardon condition failed. Otherwise, the president would invade the ambit of Congress's lawmaking province.[51]

The Court rejected Schick's argument. To reach the result, the majority relied on historical precedents and partly on a "greater includes the lesser" argument; namely, that if the president could permit Schick to be executed, certainly he could take the lesser step of offering the choice of life imprisonment without the possibility of parole. The majority dodged the separation of powers argument, noting only that the president's Article II power included the authority to impose conditions not recognized by Congress.

In dissent, Justice Thurgood Marshall addressed the separation of powers argument more directly. He argued that, "[w]hile the clemency function of the Executive in the federal criminal justice system is consistent with the separation of powers, the attachment of punitive conditions is not. Prescribing punishment is a prerogative reserved for the lawmaking branch of government, the legislature."[52] In Marshall's view, President Eisenhower had fashioned a punishment that Congress rejected. Absent a delegation from Congress, Marshall would have invalidated the condition as outside the president's Article II power.[53] Thus, according to Marshall, through the conditional pardon power, presidents can undermine Congress's prerogative to set the sentencing framework.

Although Justice Marshall's reasoning has some appeal, it is difficult to quarrel with the majority's "greater includes the lesser" argument. When the president commutes a death sentence to an eight-year sentence, no separation of powers problem arises even if Congress had prescribed a minimum ten-year sentence for the crime. The elimination of parole eligibility in *Schick* should be analyzed similarly, even if Congress has explicitly rejected the option of a no parole eligibility rule. As a necessary corollary to the pardon power, presidents can reduce sentences to those unauthorized by Congress.[54] President Clinton's last-minute commutation of sentences meted out to twenty-one drug offenders should be seen in a similar light, showcasing his disagreement with mandatory minimums for particular drug offenses.[55] Presidential action overrode Congress's specification of a minimum length for a sentence. The pardon power can blunt congressional policymaking.

A similar analysis should govern if the president imposes conditions other than reduction in sentences that Congress has neither authorized nor explicitly prohibited. For instance, consider that Congress may determine that supervised release is unavailable for a particular category of offenders. Can a president then commute the sentence of all such offenders contingent on their agreement to serve a term of supervised release? If one believes that Congress has the exclusive authority to prescribe the type of punishment, then the result, as the dissent suggested in *Schick,* is alarming. But the president, through the pardon power, shares authority with Congress over the length and type of punishment imposed. The Constitution vests the president with the authority to check the legislature's judgment in creating the framework for punishment.[56] The *Schick* majority, therefore, correctly brushed aside the separation of powers challenge: the presidential power to pardon can trump legislative policy.

C. Pardon Based on Legal Disagreement

Another area of uncertainty concerns whether presidents can issue pardons based on their belief that the law violated was unconstitutional. The president's power to interpret the laws contrary to the courts' interpretation raises a fundamental challenge to the courts' preeminence as law interpreter. Some might believe, therefore, that, although presidents may pardon an individual out of mercy or grace, they cannot predicate such pardon on disagreement with a legal interpretation of the courts.

Consider whether presidents could have pardoned anyone convicted after investigation and successful prosecution by an independent counsel on the ground that the Ethics in Government Act was unconstitutional. President Reagan had in fact challenged the act as unconstitutional, though the Court rebuffed the challenge in *Morrison v. Olson*.[57] In other words, could President Reagan have defied the Court's decision by predicating a pardon on his contrary interpretation of executive authority?

To be sure, presidents have no constitutional compulsion to disclose their reasons for pardon or clemency. But, if expressed, can the president's reasons for granting a pardon contravene constitutional principles and perhaps even become reviewable[58] if they are based on a constitutional view flatly repudiated by the courts?

The closest analogy rests with President Jefferson's pardons of individuals who had been convicted of violating the Sedition Act.[59] Jefferson had attacked the constitutionality of the act prior to the election, and then used his power subsequently to ensure that those convicted under what he believed to be an unjust law were exonerated. As he later explained in a letter to Abigail Adams,

> You seem to think it devolved on the judges to decide on the validity of the sedition law. But nothing in the Constitution has given them a right to decide for the Executive, more than to the Executive to decide for them. Both magistracies are equally independent in the sphere of action assigned to them. The judges, believing the law constitutional, had a right to pass sentence of fine and imprisonment; because the power was placed in their hands by the Constitution. But the executive, believing the law to be unconstitutional, were bound to remit execution of it; because that power has been confided to them by the Constitution.[60]

Presidents acting within the ambit of their constitutionally assigned functions may take steps based on views contrary to those adopted by the Supreme Court. Presidential refusal to abide by Supreme Court interpretations may invite criticism or even impeachment, but the president's oath to uphold the Constitution presupposes an independent duty to examine the constitutional text. That obligation may not excuse complying with a court decree in a particular case or controversy, but it does at a minimum entitle presidents to base pardons on their interpretation of the constitutional text, irrespective of any Supreme Court precedent to the contrary. Presidents may issue pardons for any reason, even if disagreement with the courts or Congress motivates the decision.

D. Scope of Judicial Review

Both offenders and third parties have gone to court to challenge the presidential exercise of the pardon power. Despite some judicial pronouncements to the contrary, no judicial review is appropriate of either the purposes or the processes by which the pardon decisions are made.

The political process checks the president's exercise of pardon authority, as it does almost every other presidential act. The public nature of the pardon offer ensures that public pressures can be brought to bear on the president. Although the Constitution does not itself mandate that the president publicize a record of all pardons, a strong tradition of publication exists.

The role of the press can be critical. The press anticipated and publicized President Ford's consideration of whether to pardon President Nixon,[61] President Bush's decision to pardon his former colleagues involved in the Iran-Contra investigation,[62] and President Carter's choice to pardon draft dodgers of the Vietnam era.[63] The clamor that followed President Clinton's pardon of fugitive financier Marc Rich further illustrates the importance of press oversight.[64] Publicity raises the stakes for the pardon decision.

Congressional oversight can be potent as well.[65] When President Clinton offered clemency to members of the Puerto Rican separatist group, the FALN, congressional committees demanded documentation and explanation as to why clemency was offered. Although President Clinton blocked the release of some information on grounds of executive privilege, Congress uncovered considerable background material that informed the public's view of the wisdom of the clemency decision.[66] Congress debated similar issues in the subsequent hearings over the propriety of the Marc Rich pardon.[67] Congress was vocal as well during the pardon deliberations for President Nixon and the Iran-Contra defendants. After President Ford's pardon of Richard Nixon, the Senate passed a resolution opposing any more pardons for Watergate defendants until their appeals had been exhausted. President Ford, indeed, testified before Congress about the pardon. Moreover, Congress in 1868 passed a resolution declaring that President Andrew Johnson's Christmas pardons, including that for Jefferson Davis, were unconstitutional.[68] Despite the discretion inherent in the exercise of the pardon power, traditional political checks of press and congressional oversight minimize the need for external review.

The president internalizes most of the costs of a pardon because he stands as the only elected official accountable to the entire electorate.[69] If the pardoned offender commits another crime,[70] then the president remains at least formally accountable for the pardon. Presidential motives for pardons may or may not be wise, but the president is unlikely to escape the adverse consequences from the pardon offer.[71] The furor that followed President Clinton's pardon in the Marc Rich and FALN cases amply demonstrates that presidents stand accountable to the public for their pardon decisions.

Judicial review would impose an additional check on the president's pardon power. Some believe that, if presidents wield the power for inappropriate ends or after insufficient consideration, then judges may be able to protect the offender's interest.

Despite the potential benefits from review, few presidential determinations seem as highly discretionary as the decision whether, and on what terms, to grant an offender a pardon. If judges could second-guess a president's *reasons* for granting a pardon, then judges could arrogate to themselves a substantial part of the executive's constitutionally grounded authority to exercise the pardon power. Consider the district court's decision in *Murphy v. Ford,* where the district court entertained a challenge to President Ford's decision to pardon Richard Nixon.[72] With reference to the historical context in which the Pardon Clause was enacted, the court seemingly suggested that the pardon was appropriate: "Under these circumstances, President Ford concluded that the public interest required positive steps to end the divisions caused by Watergate and to shift the focus of attention from the immediate problem of Mr. Nixon to the hard social and economic problems which were of more lasting significance."[73]

No constitutional or historical principles, however, demarcate permissible from impermissible reasons.[74] Presidents, not judges, should make the determination whether a pardon is warranted.

Judicial review similarly is precluded in other highly discretionary contexts. For instance, the textual commitment of the pardon power to the president resembles the textual commitment of the power to try impeachments to the Senate, as discussed previously. The Constitution plainly allocates authority to a particular branch in both cases, and judicial review in each might well end in judicial usurpation. Judges would decide what "trying" a case entails, and might determine the ends for which clemency can be used. Moreover, the Court in *Nixon v. United States* declined to intervene in the trial of the impeached judge, in part because of the impeachment process's role in checking judicial power. Indeed, Congress has few options other than impeachment to react to illegality or serious impropriety in the judiciary. Similarly, the pardon process allows the president to check the judiciary's power to impose punishments. Probing judicial review in general, and review of the *reasons* for pardons in particular, would intrude too sharply into the president's authority.

The possible assertion by individuals of constitutional claims arising from pardon decisions complicates the question. President Lincoln, for instance, allegedly showed favoritism to residents of Kentucky.[75] President Harrison may have granted pardons to Mormons who violated the laws but not to members of other religious sects.[76]

Two arguments, however, strongly suggest that courts should not even consider constitutional claims based on the failure to grant a pardon. First, the president's pardon power is constitutionally based. The strong presumption of judicial review that attaches to exercise of delegated authority does not hold. When Congress delegates authority to the president, it can condition that exercise on certain checks, including judicial review. The president's exercise of constitutionally based powers stands on a different footing. There is no presumption that there should be review of the president's exercise of the power to command the armed forces,[77] to issue internal management orders within the executive branch,[78] or to appoint ambassadors.[79] Similarly, there is no presumption that challenges to the president's exercise of the pardon power should be reviewed.

Second, the risk of judicial errors from entertaining such constitutional claims is unacceptably high. As discussed before, presidents need not provide reasons for their pardon decisions, and determining after the fact why the president granted pardons in some cases and failed to act in others is notoriously difficult.[80]

To be sure, one can imagine that some judges would strain to review serious allegations that a particular president refused to pardon anyone of a different race, or pardoned every white convicted of a hate crime but not those of other races. An equal protection violation might appear clear. But, even there, it would be impossible to assess the president's exercise of the pardon power without scrutinizing the reasons that underlay his decisions to grant or deny pardon requests. To probe the decisions any deeper risks insinuating judges into the decisionmaking process, and without the benefit of the president's experience in handling the thousands of prior pardon applications. Courts might insist that the president create an administrative record, might demand a list of explanations from the president, and might seek the president's testimony. The costs of attempting to ascertain the president's motives for not granting pardons may be too steep.

Whether courts should be able to second-guess the process by which presidents reach the pardon decision raises somewhat of a closer question. Often courts scrutinize the process that administrators use to reach decisions without reviewing the merits themselves. Under the Administrative Procedure Act, for instance, courts at times consider whether agencies follow the correct procedures even if various administrative law doctrines preclude review of a decision on the merits.[81] In that way, courts can help agencies reach better decisions merely by insisting upon greater deliberation, access from interested parties, more notice, and the like.

In *Ohio Adult Parole Authority v. Woodard* the Supreme Court considered whether judges could review challenges to the process by which a *governor* reached clemency decisions.[82] Earlier, in *Connecticut Board of Pardons v. Dumschat*[83] the Court, in rejecting a claim that the governor was obligated to provide an explanation for pardon decisions, asserted that "pardon and commutation decisions have not traditionally been the business of courts; as such, they are rarely, if ever, appropriate subjects for judicial review."[84] In *Woodard,* Chief Justice Rehnquist's opinion concluded that "[t]he Due Process Clause is not violated where, as here, the procedures in question do no more than confirm that the clemency and pardon power is committed, as is our tradition, to the authority of the executive."[85] To Rehnquist, clemency remained "a matter of grace."[86] A majority of the Court, however, would have exercised limited review under the Due Process Clause if "a state official flipped a coin to determine whether to grant clemency, or in a case where the State arbitrarily denied a prisoner any access to its clemency process."[87] The Court has left the door open to the possibility of limited judicial scrutiny of the pardon process in states to ensure that the pardon process will not be arbitrary.

But, in the presidential context, review of the president's process for issuing pardons robs the decisionmaker of too much discretion. The Constitution specifies no process and, as with the Senate power to try impeachments at stake in *Nixon,* implicitly vests the power to determine the appropriate procedures in a coordinate branch. Courts cannot readily second-guess the process by which presidents grant pardons without intruding at least somewhat into the decisionmaking itself.

Consider the decision by the Court of Appeals for the District of Columbia in *Yelvington v. Presidential Pardon & Parole Attorneys,* which preceded *Woodard* by almost twenty-five years.[88] There, the presidential pardon attorneys denied an offender's application for executive clemency on the ground that it "did not warrant consideration."[89] Accordingly, the attorneys did not forward the application to the president for his consideration. The court observed that "[i]t is doubtless true that the president intended that pardon applications should reach him in every case. . . ."[90] Yet, the court concluded that the presidential pardon power, "[t]he benign prerogative of mercy," should "be free of judicial control, even to the limited extent here proposed."[91] As a consequence, the court declined to review the charges.

There are many contexts in which a prisoner may raise such process claims. President Clinton, for instance, reportedly bypassed the Office of the Pardon Attorney in making many of the last-minute pardon decisions.[92] In addition, President Clinton reportedly failed to allow law enforcement officers or victims to present their case for why clemency should not have been granted to Marc Rich,[93] the FALN members,[94] and others. And, in granting a pardon to the former Teamster and reputedly mob leader James Hoffa, President Nixon allegedly departed from internal guidelines by inserting a pardon condition without consultation from the pardon attorney.[95] As in *Yelvington,* such claims should be rejected, despite the dictum in *Woodard.* Judges should stay their hands when confronting a challenge to either the merits of a pardon decision or the process by which a president reaches a decision. The dictum in *Murphy v. Ford,* suggesting judicial power to review pardons on their merits, and to a lesser extent that in *Woodard,* err in permitting to judges the power to second-guess presidential exercise of discretion in granting the pardons. Irrespective of whether the president is offering a pardon for reasons of compassion, international affairs, or domestic politics, no review should exist. The only checks are the disaffection of the electorate and possible impeachment by the House.

E. Conditional Pardons

Finally, the question of conditional pardons is quite vexing. Two questions of presidential power have arisen: first, whether an individual can reject an offer of conditional pardon; second, whether there should be judicial review of the appropriateness or legality of the condition imposed. The same analysis should hold whether the condition is attached to a pardon or commutation of sentence: in each, the presidential offer is made contingent upon certain action or omissions.[96]

1. The president has long enjoyed the power to grant pardons conditioned on certain conduct.[97] For instance, during the Civil War, the president offered a pardon if the former Southern loyalists swore an oath to uphold the Union. Similarly, presidents have conditioned pardons on offenders accepting lighter sentences,[98] agreeing to pay the costs of prior legal proceedings,[99] or returning lands taken from the government.[100] One would anticipate that a contract model would hold—that offenders could determine whether to accept the greater punishment or the reduced sanction with conditions attached.[101]

A conditional pardon resembles a bargained-for exchange. From the offenders' perspective, they are willing to accept conditions in return for the moderation of punishment, whether in terms of full pardon, commutation of sentence, or early release. As long as they can correctly gauge that the value of the diminution of punishment is greater than the value to them of honoring the new condition, then the exchange would be beneficial. From the perspective of the chief executive, early release can save the government money, manifest compassion, or further justice by recognizing the excessive harshness of a particular sentence. The condition attached to the offer of pardon, whether deportation or restriction on the right to associate, may be necessary to protect the public from future wrongdoing or may help the public in some other way.

One line of pardon decisions casts doubt on the validity of the bargaining model. The Supreme Court in *Biddle v. Perovich* held that an individual's consent was not required for a president to commute a death penalty to life imprisonment.[102] Justice Holmes, for the Court, asserted that the pardon power is "not a private act of grace from an individual happening to possess power. . . . When granted it is the determination of the ultimate authority that the public welfare will be better served by inflicting less than what the judgment fixed. . . . [T]he public welfare, not [the offender's] consent determines what shall be done."[103] The Court further explained,

> The opposite answer would permit the President to decide that justice requires the diminution of a term or a fine without consulting the convict, but would deprive him of the power in the most important cases

and require him to permit an execution which he had decided ought not
to take place.[104]

The *Biddle* analysis seems straightforward as applied to an uncondi-
tional pardon or commutation. But Attorney General Brownell later read
the case for much more. He advised President Eisenhower that the president could commute a death sentence to life imprisonment without the
possibility of parole, irrespective of the individual's consent. Unlike in
Biddle, the offer of pardon attached a condition: waiver of the right to parole that otherwise was guaranteed under the statutory scheme. Nonetheless, the attorney general concluded that the president "can validly attach
the condition that the prisoner foregoes parole . . . without obtaining the
prisoner's consent to the condition."[105] Attorney General Brownell por-
trayed the pardon power in legislative-type terms.[106]

Although Attorney General Brownell's analysis might be confined to
the death penalty context, the reasoning is far more broad. If viewed akin
to legislation, the pardon power might not brook any objections by the
offender, even if the offender subjectively believes he or she is better off
with the original sentence. Just as legislation can criminalize previously
lawful conduct (though not retroactively) or increase the tax rate for
prior transactions, so a president arguably can change punishment as
long as the new punishment—viewed objectively—is less severe. Thus,
even if an offender would prefer a longer sentence without the obligation
of restitution, a presidential condition of restitution would prevail. In Attorney General Brownell's words, "[T]he public welfare, not [the offender's] consent" would govern.[107]

Attorney General Brownell's views should be rejected. As an initial
matter, the pardon power resembles a legislative power only in that it permits the president to check legislative judgment. Although presidents indirectly may serve welfare goals through exercise of the pardon power,
the pardon authority itself does not embody a grant of substantive power
and never has. Second, the autonomy interests of those seeking pardons
should trump any presidential interest in furthering social goals through
pardons. The principal rationale for the pardon power has long been to
benefit the offender caught in the grasp of the criminal justice system. Individuals subjected to punishment should be permitted to determine
whether to accept "a new deal" predicated on different conditions. Even
if a proposed commutation appears from an objective perspective to be
more favorable, the subjective perspective should hold. Indeed, the

Supreme Court long before *Biddle* had declared that an offender retains the discretion to accept or reject the offer of pardon, for "the condition may be more objectionable than the punishment inflicted by the judgment."[108]

2. Individual consent is a necessary but not necessarily sufficient determinant of an offer of conditional parole. Even though offenders seemingly may benefit from accepting conditional pardons curtailing their future exercise of rights, we may wish to prohibit such bargains for a number of reasons. As Justice McLean stated when dissenting in *Ex parte Wells,*

> [T]he power of [conditional] commutation . . . substitutes a new, and, it may be, undefined punishment for that which the law prescribes a specific penalty. It is, in fact, a suspension of the law. . . . It is true that the substituted punishment must be assented to by the convict; but the exercise of his judgment, under the circumstances, may be a very inadequate protection for his rights.[109]

There are a number of reasons suggesting that we not place faith in the offender's ability to assess whether to accept the condition in exchange for the pardon or commutation. We might believe that offenders cannot accurately gauge when the benefits from the pardon outweigh the disadvantages flowing from acceptance of the condition attached. Or, we might block the bargained for exchange because certain rights are inalienable. The government, under this view, cannot coerce individuals to relinquish certain core rights. We may wish to prevent the bargained-for exchange because of the impact on society as a whole.

The paternalistic argument is perhaps easiest understood. We may opt for a rule that protects pardon seekers from their own zeal to escape prison. The desire for release may be so overwhelming that the offenders would welcome any condition as long as it resulted in less of a stay behind bars, even if accepting the condition is not in their long-range interest. Indeed, given the conditions in many prison facilities, few might turn down an offer of early release, irrespective of how draconian the conditions attached to the pardon offer.

Nonetheless, the paternalism argument does not make a strong case for taking the decision out of an offender's hands. The offender's great interest or need to accept the conditional offer is no reason to prohibit the offer.[110] The core difficulty rests with the background problem of the conditions of confinement or the length of the original sentence, and cannot be attributed to conditional offers. Coercion in a sense exists every time the government offers parole, probation, or a pardon. Offenders grasp the trade-off of more freedom immediately for less freedom in the future. Moreover, the information deficit is not likely to be large. The vast majority of conditions are relatively easy to understand. Offenders likely can—Attorney General Brownell's views notwithstanding—reject any condition they find unpalatable.

As a group, therefore, offenders are likely much better off determining for themselves whether to accept particular conditions than they are if certain conditions are taken off the table completely.[111] They benefit from a system allowing choice even if occasional injustices flow from the option of a conditional pardon. The paternalism argument may suggest the need to allow the offender time to consider the conditions fully, and perhaps the ability to contact counsel as well. But it does not convincingly suggest that conditional offers be prohibited.

Consider President Clinton's offer of clemency to sixteen convicted members of the FALN, the radical leaders of Puerto Rico's independence movement who had been involved in a series of bombings throughout the 1970s and 1980s. Although no one had died in the attacks, the bombings caused substantial damage and several police officers were seriously wounded. Clinton imposed several conditions on the offer, including that the offenders would have to renounce "violence for any purpose," could not associate with people with criminal records, and could not travel without permission of parole authorities. The impact of the conditions on civil liberties is clear: the conditions impinge upon rights to travel and association, as well as the First Amendment right to free expression. Indeed, the conditions seemingly preclude family members—two sisters were among those offered clemency—from maintaining any contact with each other.[112] Although two of the group in fact rejected the pardon offer, the others rationally agreed to the confining conditions in exchange for the greater freedom of movement. Thus, individuals should be able to accept conditions waiving their constitutional rights, whether to freedom of movement, association, or expression.

In addition to the potential harm to the individual offender, a bargained-for exchange between president and offender may jeopardize the Constitution's structural safeguards limiting presidential power. Presidents should be unable to gain authority through offers of conditional pardon that they otherwise cannot exercise under Article II of the Constitution. Judges therefore should not enforce conditions that would permit executive power in excess of that granted under the Constitution. For instance, a court should invalidate a condition imposed by the president that the offender attend Presbyterian services as a violation of the Establishment Clause and should invalidate a condition that the offender make payment to the president's reelection committee because the president lacks power to compel such partisan payments. Review may also be warranted to ensure that the condition does not violate the Tenth Amendment.[113] Judicial scrutiny helps prevent the president from attaining prohibited ends.[114]

Moreover, presidents have no authority to offer conditions that violate the Eighth Amendment's ban on cruel and unusual punishments. For instance, in 1730 one inmate in England was granted a pardon on the condition that he agree to experimental surgery at the hands of a famous physician.[115] In an analogous context, the judge in *State v. Brown* afforded the defendants, who had been sentenced to thirty years' imprisonment on a sexual misconduct offense, the option to undergo surgical castration instead.[116] Although the defendants evidently preferred the surgical option,[117] the appellate court invalidated their choice on the ground that the Eighth Amendment's prohibition against cruel and unusual punishments barred the government from offering that alternative.[118]

Whether the president can enhance punishments presents a somewhat different question. Consider whether the president can condition early release upon imposition of a longer sentence if the offender fails to meet certain conditions.[119] If an offender has served ten years of a twenty-year sentence, can a president order the offender released subject to a requirement that, if he violates certain conditions within the following ten years, the government would return the offender to jail for an additional twenty years? Or, what if the president offered early release predicated on the offender's agreement that he would be subject to presidential conditions for the rest of his life?[120]

From the offenders' perspective, it may be rational to agree to imposition of the condition that potentially prolongs their eventual discharge from prison. Offenders might reason that life outside custody is more valuable when they are younger, or might discount freedom later because of the risk of death or infirmity.

Nonetheless, the offender's consent to the potential increased punishment cannot remove any structural concern in the Constitution for limited governmental power.[121] The president lacks the power under the constitutional framework to enhance the punishment for crimes. The very rationale of the Pardon Clause is to empower a president to lessen, not increase, punishment. As the Supreme Court stated in *Schick v. Reed,* "Of course, the President may not aggravate punishment,"[122] for the Constitution authorizes only "an executive action that mitigates or sets aside punishment for a crime."[123] The offender's consent, therefore, should not permit the president to utilize the pardon power to enhance punishment.[124]

Thus, there should be no judicial review absent claims that the offer of a conditional pardon violates constitutional restrictions on presidential authority. This is true even though state court judges review whether the conditions offered by governors are moral and closely tied to purposes of the pardon system, as do federal judges reviewing challenges to conditions of probation.

Traditionally, most states have permitted limited judicial review of the conditions set by governors. For instance, in *Wilborn v. Saunders* the offender received a pardon on the conditions that he "conduct himself in the future as a good, law-abiding citizen," that he report to the clerk of court every month for four and one-half years, and that he thereafter not commit "a violation of the penal laws of the Commonwealth."[125] The Virginia Supreme Court, as had others,[126] reviewed the conditions to ensure that they "are not immoral, illegal, or impossible of performance."[127] Even though there are no limitations in the constitutional text, a common law can develop demarcating the permissible purposes of pardon conditions, just as there has developed a law of permissible conditions in the probation context. In this way, judicial review can ensure that pardon conditions serve the public interest.

Similarly, in the probation and parole context, federal and state courts scrutinize the conditions to ensure that they serve socially beneficial purposes, usually rehabilitation or public safety.[128] The conditions must be "reasonably related" to the purposes of probation or parole, namely, to protect the public and to facilitate rehabilitation.[129] Courts have upheld a wide variety of conditions, including constraints on free speech and association.[130] For instance, in *United States v. Stine,* the court upheld a condition on probation that defendant undergo psychological counseling despite privacy concerns,[131] and in *United States v. Tonry,* the court rejected a challenge to a condition that the offender not run for public office during the probation term.[132] Several conditions, however, have been struck down because the superintending court abused its discretion in imposing the condition.[133]

The germaneness inquiry in unconstitutional condition cases focuses similarly on the dangers of governmental manipulation. Consider, for instance, the president's conditional pardon in *Hoffa v. Saxbe*.[134] There, President Nixon granted a pardon to Jimmy Hoffa on the condition that he refrain from any "direct or indirect management of any labor organization for a number of years after release."[135] After accepting the pardon,[136] Hoffa contended that the presidentially imposed restriction swept too broadly, and accordingly he challenged the condition on First Amendment grounds. The district court asserted that the conditions imposed in a pardon must be "directly related to the public interest" and not "unreasonably infringe on the individual commutee's constitutional freedoms."[137] When the conditions are germane and "directly related" to the reasons for early release, there is less likelihood that the president has imposed them for improper reasons.[138] Given that the ban on involvement in union activities was so closely tied to the public interest, the court upheld the condition.[139]

The problem with the germaneness or "reasonably related" inquiry, however, is that it has no referent in the pardon context. There are no limitations as to permissible reasons for pardons. The presidentially imposed condition may seek ends completely unconnected to the traditional justifications for probation or parole, as with the former British practice of commuting sentences on the condition of banishment to the colonies or joining the navy. Presidents presumably can pardon individuals on the condition that they continue an art career started behind bars or sing "Happy Birthday, Mr. President." Almost every condition is germane to the reasons that a president may use in granting or denying a pardon because fulfillment of the condition may be a goal of the pardon.[140]

In attaching conditions to probation or supervised release, judges and parole boards are far more constrained than presidents, and appropriately so. First, the president's pardon power flows from the Constitution, unlike probation and parole, both of which are creatures of the legislature. Accordingly, legislation may specify the manner in which parole or probation conditions are to be imposed, including a grant of judicial review. Any similar effort to cabin the president's constitutionally based pardon authority would violate Article II.[141] Second, the "reasonably related" or germaneness test responds to the need to monitor lower-level officials, such as parole boards and trial judges, who are not as politically accountable as the president.[142] In contrast, we are reluctant to interfere with presidential discretion except in the rarest of circumstances. It is for the president and not the courts to assess whether a condition serves socially beneficial ends. As a consequence, the president's choice of conditions largely should escape judicial review. Conditions that seem overly harsh, such as banishment; that seem irrelevant, such as maintaining appropriate schooling for children; or that seem morally questionable can be imposed subject only to the offender's assent. The need for consent provides a critical check on presidential overreaching. We trust the president, in contrast to parole boards and trial judges, to exercise the pardon power judiciously, with the limited exceptions of conditions attached to pardons that violate some other constitutional provision such as the Establishment Clause.

Moreover, unlike with judges and parole boards, majoritarian forces largely should be adequate to check any president running amok. Members of Congress, and their constituents, should be able to pressure any president bent on offering problematic conditions. Congress has exerted such pressure before, and members of Congress may be as well positioned as judges to assess which conditions violate social values. Conditions that shock the conscience, therefore, are unlikely to escape congressional scrutiny and, if they violate the Constitution, they should be subject to review.

Finally, a more unique fundamental check constrains the conditional pardon power: Presidents cannot bind their successors. Any objectionable condition may be ignored or counteracted by a successor. For instance, a successor in office is not likely to enforce a condition imposed by a predecessor mandating that the offender vote Democratic. Nor is he likely to enforce a condition that the individual tithe to the former president's favorite charity. Presidents can easily undo the conditions imposed by their predecessors, limiting the reach of the conditional pardon power.[143]

Consider, for instance, President Andrew Johnson's offer of a pardon to one DePuy, who had been convicted and incarcerated for violating the revenue laws. President Johnson predicated the pardon on DePuy's agreement to pay a fine. When President Grant assumed the reins of power, he revoked the pardon, and the revocation was upheld on the grounds that the paperwork had yet to reach DePuy—the warden had the papers in his possession—at the time President Grant revoked the offer.[144] Although the timing of the revocation makes the *DePuy* case unusual, it highlights that presidents cannot control how their successors enforce conditions attached to pardons. Indeed, President George W. Bush's administration reportedly studied the feasibility of revoking the Marc Rich pardon for it was not clear whether the Clinton administration had completed all of the paperwork at the time Bush took office.[145] Thus, in light of congressional oversight and the additional check of successors in office, there should be no judicial review of either the nature or germaneness of the conditions attached to the pardons.

In short, presidents exercise near-unfettered authority in deciding whether to grant pardons and, if so, under what terms. The pardon power serves as an adjunct to the president's authority over criminal law enforcement. The chief executive can temper excesses of either legislators or judges through pardons, commutations of sentences, and remittances of fines. It is for the president to determine why, when, and to whom mercy should be shown. No court should sit in judgment on the reasons for the presidential decision to grant or deny applications for relief, and Congress should not fetter the president's discretion by attaching adverse consequences to those accepting the pardon offer.

On occasion, however, offer of a *conditional* pardon may violate some constitutional restriction on the president's authority, whether because of the limitations of the Pardon Clause itself (such as the impeachment limit) or in other provisions of the Constitution such as the Establishment Clause. The president's power to attach conditions subtly transforms the pardon power into a vehicle for accomplishing a wider set of governmental goals, including encouraging testimony and deporting undesirables. Limited judicial review helps ensure that the conditions offered do not violate any structural limitation in the Constitution. Otherwise, the president's exercise of discretion should not be second-guessed in court.

The pardon power, therefore, stands apart from the presidential power of law administration and the president's authority over foreign affairs. By design, the president's pardon power checks legislative and judicial power and thus largely can be exercised independently of congressional or judicial oversight. Presidential initiative through pardons can, to some extent, displace congressional policymaking. Congress can express its displeasure through informal means such as convening hearings or delaying appropriations, and the Senate can withhold consent for appointments. Congress's only formal option, however, is impeachment.

Conclusion

Article II sets forth the framework for executive powers. Although the text can be read in various ways, immanent in both the structure and the language of the Constitution is the blueprint for a vigorous, dynamic chief executive. Article II vests the "executive power" in a single president, charges the president with the responsibility "to take care that the laws are enforced faithfully," directs the president to serve as commander in chief of the armed forces, and authorizes him to appoint all higher-level executive and judicial officials. Commentary from the period both before and after the Founding confirm that the Constitution's choice of a single executive was deliberate; The Framers reacted to the instability during the Articles of Confederation period and the overreaching by Congress and state legislatures by instilling considerable authority in one president.

But the Constitution nowhere answers many questions of great import to administration of the nation. Although Article II lodges the appointment power in the president, it is silent about the power to remove executive branch officials. Although the president can propose and negotiate treaties, subject to the Senate's consent, the Constitution does not specify which entity can terminate treaties; nor does it plainly indicate whether the president can enter into "lesser" agreements with foreign powers that do not require consent from the Senate or from Congress. The president is commander in chief of the armed forces, but the extent to which he can commit troops in the absence of congressional authorization is unclear.

Not only is the Constitution conspicuously silent on fundamental matters of executive power, the president's powers under Article II potentially clash with those of Congress under Article I and the judiciary under Article III. No mechanism for resolving such tensions is apparent. For instance, Congress and the judiciary have legitimate need for information to carry out their constitutional functions under Articles I and III, but for the president to disclose information may undermine his ability to coordinate both domestic law enforcement actions and pursue foreign policy initiatives with dispatch. Congress can exercise the power of the purse, but if Congress withholds funds for implementing pardons, then the Article II pardon power would be seriously eroded. Furthermore, there is no consensus as to whether the president should be able to exercise any residual or protective power in emergency situations before Congress can weigh in.

The number of unresolved issues should not be that surprising. The Framers created a framework for government but could not have imagined all of the detailed implementation questions that would arise in the next generation, not to mention next centuries. Nor could they have anticipated the international and domestic pressures that would cry out for altering the means of governance.

Given the ambiguities in the text and history, flexible accommodations among the branches are needed. The Constitution can be a guide if not an answer sheet. Executive initiative must be balanced against Congress's constitutional authority to set the framework for national policy and determine within broad constraints how that policy should be implemented. Presidents must also be accountable to the public as a whole for their exercise of both constitutional and delegated authority.

Conflicts have flared between Congress and the president in particular; yet the lessons of such skirmishes are obscured because no enduring principles result from the political battles. Congress on some occasions may obtain desired information from the executive in exchange for greater funding for favored executive projects but not on others. Or, the president at times may divulge plans about troop landings to key members of Congress in return for a pledge that the War Powers Resolution not be invoked. The powers of the presidency are set, therefore, in part through the give-and-take of the political process, and few equilibria have been achieved.

Greater predictability has been gained only modestly through the courts. Judges hear isolated cases and controversies involving presidential powers, which culminate in judicial precedents expounding on Article II's scope. The lessons of history affect judges' decisions, yet courts independently assess the language and structure of the Constitution to demarcate the bounds of executive powers. Cases such as *Youngstown Steel, U.S. v. Nixon,* and *Morrison v. Olson* accommodate the seemingly expansive executive power under Article II with Congress's power under Article I and the judiciary's power under Article III. For instance, the president can commit troops in defending the nation in an emergency, but cannot take steps—such as seizing property—if Congress previously has directed the president to proceed otherwise; the president can withhold critical communications to protect the integrity of the presidency, but not if individual rights would thereby be infringed; the president can appoint all superior officers but, if Congress has determined that they should stand independent of the president's policymaking, the president can remove them from office only for cause. Thus, although presidents politically can exercise and have exercised sweeping powers both domestically and internationally, as a constitutional matter, courts have rejected absolutes. Courts have recognized vigorous executive initiative as just one constitutional goal among others to be accommodated within the Constitution's firmament.

Notes

NOTES TO THE INTRODUCTION

1. See Corwin, *The President: Office and Powers*; Milkis and Nelson, *The American Presidency*; Roche and Levy, *The Presidency*.

2. Wood, *The Creation of the American Republic*, 135, 201, 405; THE FEDERAL-IST No. 48, at 309 (James Madison) (Clinton Rossiter ed., 1961); Milkis and Nelson, *The American Presidency*, 4; Roche and Levy, *The Presidency*, 7.

3. Powell v. McCormack, 395 U.S. 486, 546–47 (1969).

4. McDonald, *The American Presidency*, 105–06.

5. Ibid., 98.

6. Ibid., 123.

7. Paine, *Common Sense*, 10.

8. Ibid., 20.

9. THE DECLARATION OF INDEPENDENCE para. 2 (U.S. 1776).

10. Ibid., para. 3.

11. Ibid., para. 25.

12. Ibid., para. 26.

13. Ibid., para. 28.

14. Ibid., para. 29.

15. Wood, *The Creation of the American Republic*, 442.

16. McDonald, *The American Presidency*, 133.

17. Thomas Jefferson, *Notes on the State of Virginia*, ed. Ford, 3:224.

18. THE FEDERALIST No. 48, at 309 (James Madison) (Clinton Rossiter ed., 1961).

19. ARTS. OF CONFED. art. IX, § 5 (1781).

20. Wood, *The Creation of the American Republic*, 404–07.

21. U.S. CONST. art. II, § 2, cl. 1.

22. Ibid.

23. U.S. CONST. art. II, § 2, cl. 2.

24. U.S. CONST. art. II, § 3.

25. U.S. CONST. art. II, § 1, cl. 1.

26. For instance, see Calabresi and Prakash, "The President's Power to Execute the Laws," 541; Monaghan, "The Protective Power of the Presidency," 20–24.

27. Storing, *The Anti-Federalist*, 310–11.

28. Kaminski and Saladino, eds., *The Documentary History of the Ratification of the Constitution*, 2:495.

29. Ibid., 9:1097–98.

30. Small, *Some Presidential Interpretations of the Presidency*, 14.
31. Hamilton, *Pacificus No. 1*, ed. Syrett et al., 15:33–43.
32. Ketcham, *Presidents above Party*, 106–07.
33. Jefferson, *The Writings of Thomas Jefferson*, ed. Ford, 8:244n1.
34. Milkis and Nelson, *The American Presidency*, 118.
35. Roche and Levy, *The Presidency*, 13.
36. Andrew Jackson, veto message, 10 July 1832, in *A Compilation of the Messages and Papers of the Presidents*, ed. Richardson, 3:1145.
37. Milkis and Nelson, *The American Presidency*, 136.
38. Binkley, *President and Congress*, 122–23.
39. Tourtellot, *The Presidents on the Presidency*, 399.
40. Milkis and Nelson, *The American Presidency*, 166.
41. Theodore Roosevelt quoted in Taft, *Our Chief Magistrate and His Powers*, 143.
42. Taft, *Our Chief Magistrate and His Powers*, 140, 144.
43. Ibid., 139–40.
44. Myers v. United States, 272 U.S. 52 (1926).
45. Milkis and Nelson, *The American Presidency*, 240–42.
46. Ibid., 248. Wilson, however, strengthened the hand of the presidency by augmenting the president's role within the political party structure. Ibid., 223.
47. Franklin D. Roosevelt, First Inaugural Address, 4 March 1933, in Jeffery A. Smith, *War and Press Freedom*, 143.
48. Franklin D. Roosevelt, Fireside Chat on the Plan for the Reorganization of the Judiciary, 9 March 1937, in Jeffery Smith, *War and Press Freedom*, 143.
49. Milkis and Nelson, *The American Presidency*, 283.
50. Harry Truman, Special Message to the Congress Reporting on the Situation in the Steel Industry, 9 April 1952, in Jeffery A. Smith, *War and Press Freedom*, 175.
51. Youngstown Sheet and Tube Co. v. Sawyer, 343 U.S. 579 (1952).
52. See discussion in Wald, "The Freedom of Information Act," 676 (addressing Cointelpro).
53. Milkis and Nelson, *The American Presidency*, 313.
54. Richard Nixon to David Frost, interview, in Jeffery A. Smith, *War and Press Freedom*, 188.
55. Milkis and Nelson, *The American Presidency*, 342.

NOTES TO CHAPTER 1

1. U.S. CONST. art. I, § 7, cl. 2.
2. Farrand, ed., *Records of the Federal Convention of 1787*, 1:139.
3. U.S. CONST. art. II, § 3.
4. Fisher, *Constitutional Conflicts between Congress and the President*, 146.
5. Binkley, *President and Congress*, 269.
6. Ibid., 115–19.
7. Congressional Quarterly, Inc., "Powers of the Presidency," 60.
8. INS v. Chadha, 462 U.S. 919, 947–948 (1983).
9. Presidents under the Constitution can also exercise a pocket veto. If the president fails to return a bill within ten days, it becomes law "unless the Congress by their Adjournment prevents its Return, in which Case it shall not be a Law." U.S.

CONST. art. I, § 7, cl. 2. Presidents therefore can effectuate a veto at times when Congress is not in session. Wright v. United States, 302 U.S. 583 (1938).

10. Fisher, *Constitutional Conflicts between Congress and the President,* 155–56.

11. 2 U.S.C. § 691 *et seq.* (Supp. II 1994).

12. Clinton v. City of New York, 524 U.S. 417, 421 (1998).

13. See generally McKay, "Presidential Strategy and the Veto Power," 447.

14. McGowan, "The President's Veto Power," 807.

15. U.S. CONST. art. II, § 1, cl. 1.

16. U.S. CONST. art. II, § 3.

17. U.S. CONST. art. II, § 2, cl. 2.

18. Printz v. United States, 521 U.S. 898, 922 (1997) (citation omitted).

19. Act of Sept. 29, 1789, ch. 24, 1 Stat. 95, 95.

20. Act of July 22, 1790, ch. 33, 1 Stat. 137, 137.

21. Yakus v. United States, 321 U.S. 414, 423 (1944).

22. National Broadcasting Co. v. United States, 319 U.S. 190, 216–17 (1943).

23. McDonald, *The American Presidency,* 164.

24. Quoted in Ketcham, *Presidents above Party,* 82.

25. U.S. CONST. art. I, § 8, cl. 18.

26. THE FEDERALIST No. 70, at 428 (Alexander Hamilton) (Clinton Rossiter ed., 1961).

27. Milkis and Nelson, *The American Presidency,* 4.

28. Census Bureau, "Federal Government Civilian Employment," http://www.census.gov/govs/apes/01fedfun.txt.

29. U.S. CONST. art. II, § 2, cl. 2.

30. See Harris, *The Advice and Consent of the Senate,* 6 ("The evils of legislative appointment of public officers were well known to members of the Constitutional Convention of 1787, who frequently referred to the intrigue, caballing, and irresponsibility which had marked the selection of officers by the state legislatures.").

31. See Gerhardt, *The Federal Appointments Process.*

32. Farrand, ed., *Records of the Federal Convention of 1787,* 2:314–15.

33. U.S. CONST. art. II, § 2, cl. 2.

34. THE FEDERALIST No. 77, at 461 (Alexander Hamilton) (Clinton Rossiter ed., 1961).

35. Ibid.

36. Tribe, "In Memoriam: William J. Brennan, Jr.," 43.

37. Smith and Beuger, "Clouds in the Crystal Ball: Presidential Expectations and the Unpredictable Behavior of Supreme Court Appointees," 132–35.

38. For a notable exception, see Jeff Zeleny and Naftali Bendavid, "2 Conservatives, 1 Democrat Named to Last Cabinet Posts," *Chicago Tribune,* sec. A5, Jan. 3, 2001.

39. The Senate blocked the first President Bush's nomination of John Tower to be secretary of defense, see Steve Daley, "Tower Rejected in Senate Vote in the End, Nunn's Stand Meant Most," *Chicago Tribune,* sec. A1, March 10, 1989, and President Reagan's choice of William Bradford Reynolds to be associate attorney general. "Reagan Justice Nominee Rejected," *Chicago Tribune,* sec. A1, June 28, 1985. President Clinton's first choice for attorney general was forced to withdraw, see Michael Tackett and Elaine S. Povich, "Baird Drops Attorney General Bid," *Chicago Tribune,* sec. A1, Jan. 22, 1993, as was his pick for assistant attorney general in charge of civil

rights. Mitchell Locin et al., "Clinton Dumps Nominee," *Chicago Tribune*, sec. A1, June 4, 1993.

40. Fisher, *Constitutional Conflicts between Congress and the President*, 38.

41. Washington, *The Writings of George Washington*, ed. Fitzpatrick, 373–74.

42. Gerhardt, *The Federal Appointments Process*, 51.

43. Congressional Quarterly, Inc., *Powers of the Presidency*, 19.

44. Ibid., 170–203.

45. Gerhardt, *The Federal Appointments Process*, 29–34.

46. Buckley v. Valeo, 424 U.S. 1, 126 (1976).

47. United States v. Hartwell, 73 U.S. (6 Wall.) 385, 393 (1867).

48. Freytag v. Comm'r of Internal Revenue, 501 U.S. 868 (1991).

49. Federal Election Campaign Act of 1971, 86 Stat. 3, *amended by* Federal Election Campaign Act Amendments of 1974, 88 Stat. 1263.

50. 2 U.S.C. § 437c(a)(1) (Supp. IV 1974), *amended by* 2 U.S.C. § 437c(a)(1) (1976); *Buckley*, 424 U.S. 1.

51. 2 U.S.C. § 437c(a)(1)(C) (Supp. IV 1974), *amended by* 2 U.S.C. § 437(c)(a)(1) (1976).

52. 2 U.S.C. § 437c(a)(1)(A–B) (Supp. IV 1974).

53. *Buckley*, 424 U.S. at 129.

54. Ibid., 143.

55. Metropolitan Washington Airports Auth. v. Citizens for the Abatement of Aircraft Noise, Inc., 501 U.S. 252 (1991).

56. Ibid., 260n5.

57. Ibid., 277. This aspect of the Airports Authority decision follows closely the Supreme Court's reasoning in INS v. Chadha, the legislative veto case. In INS v. Chadha, the Supreme Court limited Congress's ability to influence the exercise of delegated authority. 426 U.S. 919. Under the Immigration and Nationality Act, Congress vested the attorney general with the discretion to suspend deportation and grant permanent residence status to certain excludable aliens. Immigration and Nationality Act of 1952, McCarran-Walter Act, Pub. L. No. 82-414, ch. 477, 66 Stat. 163 (1952). After reviewing the relevant evidence, an immigration judge, on behalf of the attorney general, determined that Chadha met the requirements under the act and should be granted permanent residence status. Pursuant to the act's legislative veto provisions, either House could then have passed within the next two sessions a resolution vetoing the attorney general's findings and causing Chadha to be deported. Seven days before the end of the second session, the chairman of the relevant House committee offered a resolution against granting permanent residence status to six of 340 aliens considered, including Chadha. Without debate, the House passed the resolution and did not record any vote. Chadha sued to remain in the country.

In a sweeping decision that in effect nullified at least parts of more than two hundred statutes, the Court held that Congress could not participate in the execution of the law by reserving a veto for itself or constituent part: "Congress must abide by its delegation of authority until that delegation is legislatively altered or invoked." Ibid., 955. Any legislative act binding on those outside Congress must be preceded by agreement of both houses (bicameralism) and subject to the president's approval (presentment). With respect to bicameralism, the "division of the Congress into two distinctive bodies assures that the legislative power would be exercised only after opportunity for full study and debate in separate settings." Ibid., 951. With respect to presentment, the "decision to provide the President with a limited, qualified power to nullify proposed legislation by veto was based on the profound conviction of the Framers that the power conferred on Congress was the power to be most carefully circumscribed." Ibid., 947. Congress of course acts in many ways that affect those outside its branch. It conducts oversight hearings, passes hortatory resolutions, and issues reports on subjects that have a profound impact on many individuals, as well as on the coordinate branches. When those acts have the binding force of law, however, then Congress must abide by both the bicameralism and presentment requirements. Neither a veto by one nor two Houses of Congress comports with the constitutional structure.

    58. See Hechinger v. Metropolitan Washington Airports Auth., 36 F.3d 97 (D.C. Cir. 1994).

    59. Morrison v. Olson, 487 U.S. 654 (1988).

    60. 28 U.S.C. § 592(c)(1)(A) (2000).

    61. 28 U.S.C. § 593(e) (Supp. II 1978), *amended by* 28 U.S.C. § 593(e) (1988).

    62. 28 U.S.C. § 595(e) (Supp. II 1978), *amended by* 28 U.S.C. § 595(a) (1988).

    63. 28 U.S.C. §§ 593(b–c) (Supp. II 1978), *amended by* 28 U.S.C. § 593(b) (1988).

    64. *Morrison,* 487 U.S. at 671.

    65. Ibid.

    66. Ibid., 672.

    67. Ibid., 696.

    68. Ibid., 672, 696.

    69. Ibid., 719.

    70. Edmond v. United States, 520 U.S. 651 (1997).

    71. Ibid., 663.

    72. Ibid., 664.

    73. Ibid., 653.

    74. Ibid., 666.

    75. *Ex parte* Siebold, 100 U.S. (10 Otto) 371, 398 (1879).

    76. Morrison v. Olson, 487 U.S. 654, 676 (1988).

    77. 28 U.S.C. § 546(d) (2000).

    78. See generally Wiener, "Inter-Branch Appointments after the Independent Counsel: Court Appointment of United States Attorneys," 363.

    79. 19 U.S.C. § 1330(a) (2000).

    80. 28 U.S.C. § 505 (2000).

    81. Judiciary Act of 1789, ch. 20, § 35, 1 Stat. 73, 92.

    82. 1 Stat. 73.

    83. See for example restrictions on the International Trade Commission, 19 U.S.C. § 1330(a) (2000), the National Mediation Board, 45 U.S.C. § 154 (2000), and the Federal Election Commission, 2 U.S.C. § 437c(a)(1) (2000).

    84. See for example the composition of the IRS Oversight Board, 26 U.S.C. § 7802(b)(1)(D) (2000).

    85. 12 U.S.C. § 242 (2000).

    86. Omnibus Crime Control and Safe Streets Act of 1968, Pub. L. No. 90-351, title VI, § 1101, 82 Stat. 236, *amended by* Crime Control Act of 1976, Pub. L. No. 94-503, Title II, § 203, 90 Stat. 2427.

    87. For relatively recent examples see Statement on Signing the Cranston-Gonzales National Affordable Housing Act, 26 WEEKLY COMP. PRES. DOC. 1930, 1931

(Nov. 28, 1990); Statement on Signing the National and Community Service Act of 1990, 26 WEEKLY COMP. PRES. DOC. 1833, 1834 (Nov. 16, 1990); Statement on Signing the Intelligence Authorization Act, Fiscal Year 1990, 25 WEEKLY COMP. PRES. DOC. 1851, 1852 (Nov. 30, 1989).

88. See also Myers v. United States, 272 U.S. 52, 129 (1926), providing that Congress may set "reasonable and relevant qualifications and rules of eligibility of appointees."

89. 5 U.S.C. § 3110(b) (2000) (preventing a public official from appointing "any individual who is a relative of the public official" to a position in his or her agency). See Wulwick and Macchiarola, "Congressional Interference with the President's Power to Appoint," 625.

90. Cf. Olympic Fed. Sav. & Loan Ass'n v. Director, Office of Thrift Supervision, 732 F. Supp. 1183, 1193 (D.D.C. 1990), dismissed as moot, 903 F.2d 837 (D.C. Cir. 1990) (When Congress "abolished one agency and removed its three officers, yet designated one of the three as the head of the newly-created successor agency, Congress exercised the kind of decisionmaking about who will serve in Executive Department posts that the Constitution says it cannot.").

91. 19 U.S.C. § 1330(a) (2000).

92. 45 U.S.C. § 154 (2000); 2 U.S.C. § 437c(a)(1) (2000).

93. 28 U.S.C. § 251 (2000). Rappaport, Comment, "The Court of International Trade's Political Party Diversity Requirement," 1429.

94. The court of appeals in FEC v. NRA Political Victory Fund, 6 F.3d 821 (D.C. Cir. 1993), noted the question but declined to reach it. It did, however, rule that Congress's decision to place two nonvoting members on the FEC who were agents of Congress was unconstitutional.

95. See, e.g., Modernization Transition Committee, § 707(1)(A)(B), under Weather Service Modernization Act, 15 U.S.C. § 313 (2000); National Homeowner Trust, 42 U.S.C. § 12851(b) (2000); Agency for Health Care Policy & Research, 42 U.S.C. § 299 (2000).

96. 26 U.S.C. § 7802(b)(1)(D) (2000).

97. See Shoemaker v. United States, 147 U.S. 282 (1893); Olympic Fed. Sav. & Loan Ass'n v. Director, Office of Thrift Supervision, 732 F. Supp. 1183, 1192 (D.D.C.), dismissed as moot, 903 F.2d 837 (D.C. Cir. 1990).

98. Minnesota Chippewa Tribe v. Carlucci, 358 F. Supp. 973, 975–76 (D.D.C. 1973).

99. Ibid.

100. U.S. CONST. art. II, § 2, cl. 3.

101. Ibid.

102. 5 U.S.C. 3345–3349(d) (2000).

103. 5 U.S.C. 3345(a).

104. 5 U.S.C. 3347.

105. See generally Chanen, Comment, "Constitutional Restrictions on the President's Power to Make Recess Appointments," 191.

106. Carrier, Note, "When Is the Senate in Recess for Purposes of the Recess Appointments Clause?" 2213–14.

107. 33 Op. Att'y. Gen. 20 (1921).

108. S. Res. 430, 98th Cong. (1984).

109. The Supreme Court for its part has long held that "the power of removal [is]

incident to the power of appointment," but that analysis does not shed light on many important questions of power that lurk in the lacunae. *Ex parte* Hennen, 38 U.S. (13 Pet.) 230, 259 (1839).

110. THE FEDERALIST NO. 77, at 459 (Alexander Hamilton) (Clinton Rossiter ed., 1961) (Consent of the Senate "would be necessary to displace [public officials] as well as to appoint.").

111. For instance, Fisher Ames stated that "[t]he executive powers are delegated to the President, with a view to have a responsible officer to superintend, control, inspect, and check the officers necessarily employed in administering the laws. The only bond between him and those he employs, is the confidence he has in their integrity and talents; when that confidence ceases, the principal ought to have power to remove those whom he can no longer trust with safety." Ketcham, *Presidents above Party*, 216–17.

112. See discussion in Lessig and Sunstein, "The President and the Administration," 25–26.

113. Ibid., 27–28. For a different view, see Calabresi and Prakash, "The President's Power to Execute the Laws," 648–51.

114. Lessig and Sunstein, "The President and the Administration," 29–30; but see Calabresi and Prakash, "The President's Power to Execute the Laws," 655–58.

115. Milkis and Nelson, *The American President*, 94.

116. See discussion in Krent, "Executive Control over Criminal Law Enforcement," 275.

117. Myers v. United States, 272 U.S. 52, 163–64 (1926).

118. United States v. Perkins, 116 U.S. 483 (1886).

119. Gerhardt, *The Federal Appointments Process*, 53.

120. Milkis and Nelson, *The American President*, 164.

121. Ibid.

122. Ibid.

123. Ibid., 168–83.

124. President Grover Cleveland, Message to the Senate on the President's Power of Removal and Suspension, 1 March 1886, in Richardson, ed., *A Compilation of the Messages and Papers of the Presidents*, 4966.

125. Myers v. United States, 272 U.S. 52 (1926).

126. Act of July 12, 1876, ch. 179, § 6, 19 Stat. 78, 80.

127. *Myers*, 272 U.S. at 135.

128. Ibid.

129. Ibid., 133.

130. Ibid., 135.

131. Humphrey's Ex'r v. United States, 295 U.S. 602 (1935).

132. Ibid., 619.

133. 15 U.S.C. § 41 (2000).

134. *Humphrey's Ex'r*, 295 U.S. at 628.

135. Morrison v. Olson, 487 U.S. 654 (1988).

136. See generally Theodore H. White, *Breach of Faith: The Fall of Richard Nixon*, 268–73.

137. *Morrison*, 487 U.S. at 696.

138. Ibid., 691.

139. Ibid., 696.

140. Internal Revenue Service Restructuring and Reform Act of 1998, H.R. 2676, 105th Cong. (1998).

141. *Humphrey's Ex'r,* 295 U.S. at 629.

142. Bowsher v. Synar, 478 U.S. 714 (1986).

143. 2 U.S.C. § 901(b)(1) (Supp. III 1985), *amended by* 2 U.S.C. § 901(a)(2)(B) (Supp. V 1987).

144. 2 U.S.C. § 902(a)(3) (Supp. III 1985), *amended by* 2 U.S.C. § 902(a)(2) (Supp. V 1987).

145. *Bowsher,* 478 U.S. at 726.

146. Ibid.

147. Ibid., 733–34.

148. Ibid., 726. At the time, many questioned whether the comptroller general would act like an agent of Congress merely because of the congressional removal provision, which had never been exercised historically. See Elliot, "Regulating the Deficit after *Bowsher v. Synar*" 322; Entin, "The Removal Power and the Federal Deficit: Form, Substance, and Administrative Independence," 758–59. Under the second President Bush, however, the comptroller sued the executive branch to force disclosure of contacts between Enron and the vice president's Energy Task Force. Naftali Bendavid, "GAO Sues for Energy Panel Files," *Chicago Tribune,* sec. A1, Feb. 23, 2002. The comptroller's close ties to Congress seemed more clear.

149. Jefferson, *The Complete Jefferson,* ed. Padover, 306.

150. Kraines, "The President versus Congress," 5.

151. Pildes and Sunstein, "Reinventing the Regulatory State," 12.

152. Budget and Accounting Act, ch. 18, 42 Stat. 20 (1921).

153. Building and Construction Trades Dep't, AFL-CIO v. Allbaugh, 295 F.3d 28, 32 (D.C. Cir. 2002).

154. See, e.g., President Truman's Executive Order No. 9835, 3 C.F.R. 627 (1943–1948). See generally Cooper, *By Order of the President: The Use and Abuse of Executive Direct Action,* 25.

155. Executive orders often have covered critical policy terrain. President Truman used executive orders to start the fight against segregation. Even though Congress had not dismantled Jim Crow, he issued orders first to desegregate the military, Exec. Order No. 9981, 3 C.F.R. 722 (1943–1948), and then Presidents Eisenhower and Kennedy followed with Executive Order No. 10,925, 3 C.F.R. 448 (1959–1963) and No. 11,063, 3 C.F.R. 652 (1959–1963) to ensure that all contractors doing business with the federal government abided by principles of integration. Congressional Quarterly, Inc., *Powers of the Presidency,* 90. If Congress had directed that the military remain segregated, then President Truman's order plainly would have been invalid. Similarly, if Congress had directed that the president not apply any "public health or welfare" conditions to government contractors, then President Eisenhower's order would have been unlawful in that respect as well. But, in the absence of any conflicting legislation, the presidents' orders effected considerable change in the government, and fueled nationwide momentum toward integration. Presidents through executive orders nudged Congress toward the position of greater protection for civil rights.

156. Congressional Quarterly, Inc., *Powers of the Presidency,* 91.

157. Exec. Order No. 11,281, 3 C.F.R. 114 (1966).

158. *In re* Surface Mining Regulation Litig., 627 F.2d 1346, 1357 (D.C. Cir. 1980). Private parties cannot sue the agency directly for failure to comply with rules

or policy statements lacking the force of law. See, e.g., Haitian Refugee Ctr. v. Baker, 953 F.2d 1498, 1508 (11th Cir. 1992); Romiero De Silva v. Smith, 773 F.2d 1021 (9th Cir. 1985); Pasquini v. Morris, 700 F.2d 658, 662–63 (11th Cir. 1983).

159. For a compilation of many such orders and description of the procedures used by presidents in issuing executive orders, see Cooper, *By Order of the President.*

160. Editorial, "Mr. Ridge Goes to Washington," *New York Times,* sec. A16, Oct. 8, 2001.

161. See United States v. East Tex. Motor Freight Sys., Inc., 564 F.2d 179, 185 (5th Cir. 1977).

162. Exec. Order No. 12,954, 60 Fed. Reg. 13,023 (1995).

163. 29 U.S.C. § 151 *et seq.* (2000).

164. Chamber of Commerce of U.S. v. Reich, 74 F.3d 1322, 1335 (D.C. Cir. 1996). See also UAW-Labor Employment and Training Corp. v. Chao, 325 F.3d 360 (D.C. Cir. 2003) (rejecting challenge to Executive Order No. 13,201, which required large government contracts to include a provision informing employees of federal laws protecting them from being forced into a union).

165. *Environmental Defense Fund v. Thomas,* 627 F. Supp. 566 (D.D.C. 1986).

166. 42 U.S.C. § 6924 (2000).

167. Environmental Defense Fund, 627 F. Supp. at 571–72.

168. Exec. Order No. 11,281, 3 C.F.R. 114 (1966).

169. Exec. Order No. 12,044, 3 C.F.R. 152 (1979).

170. Exec. Order No. 12,291, 3 C.F.R. 127 (1982), *reprinted in* 5 U.S.C. § 601, 431 (1982).

171. Exec. Order No. 12,498, 3 C.F.R. 323 (1985), *reprinted in* 5 U.S.C. § 601, 40 (Supp. II 1994).

172. Morrison, "OMB Interference with Agency Rulemaking," 1065.

173. For an analysis of the impact of the rules, see Bruff, "Presidential Management of Agency Rulemaking," 533.

174. Morrison, "OMB Interference with Agency Rulemaking," 1062.

175. DeMuth and Ginsburg, "White House Review of Agency Rulemaking," 1084.

176. Portland Audubon Soc'y v. Endangered Species Comm., 984 F.2d 1534 (9th Cir. 1993).

177. Exec. Order No. 12,866, 3 C.F.R. 638 (1994), *reprinted in* 5 U.S.C. § 601 app. at 557–61 (1994). President Clinton's order followed President Reagan's initiatives with Exec. Order No. 12,291, 3 C.F.R. 127 (1982), *reprinted in* 5 U.S.C. § 601, at 431 (1982), and Exec. Order No. 12,498, 3 C.F.R. 323 (1985), *reprinted in* 5 U.S.C. § 601, at 40 (Supp. II 1984).

178. Exec. Order No. 12,866 § 3(f)(1).

179. Ibid., § 6(a)(3)(A).

180. Ibid., § 1(b)(7). The order also limited OMB's power to a certain extent by limiting the time in which OMB had to act before a proposed rule went into effect and by restricting the opportunities for ex parte contacts during the regulatory review stage.

181. Ibid., § 4(c)(2).

182. Ibid., § 6(b).

183. See McGarity, *Reinventing Rationality: The Role of Regulatory Analysis in the Federal Bureaucracy,* 282–83.

184. Exec. Order No. 12,866 § 6(b)(3).
185. Ibid., § 7.
186. Ibid., § 5.
187. Ibid., § 7.
188. Kagan, "Presidential Administration," 2287–88.
189. Office of Management and Budget, "Regulatory Matters," http://www.whitehouse.gov/omb/inforeg/qa_2-25-02.pdf.
190. Indeed, Congress itself may try to exercise a coordinating role. For instance, Congress adopted the Small Business Regulatory Enforcement Fairness Act of 1996, Pub. L. No. 104-121, Title II, 110 Stat. 857 (1996), to provide greater congressional review of agency regulations. Each agency is required to submit final and interim final rules for review by Congress and the General Accounting Office before the final or interim final rules can take effect. 5 U.S.C. § 801(a)(1)(A) (Supp. III 1997). In addition, the act requires agencies to submit a concise general statement relating to the rule, and (among other obligations) to make available upon request a cost-benefit analysis defending the rule. § 801(a). The GAO is then to prepare a report on the rule to Congress within fifteen days of receipt. § 801(a)(2)(A). In large part, the regulatory requirement affects only those rules that have an annual effect on the economy of one hundred million dollars or more, results in a steep increase in prices, or has a significant adverse effect on competition, jobs, investment or productivity. § 804(2). The Regulatory Enforcement Fairness Act in a sense mirrors OMB oversight under Executive Order No. 12,866, and indeed its definition of significant rule is congruent with the executive order's definition of regulation. Congress should have time to ensure both the efficacy of proposed rules and their consistency with congressional policy before the rules take effect. Through the procedures delineated, Congress will have greater information and ability to assess the impact of agency proposals and determine whether—subject to the usual lobbying—to reject the agency rule before it takes effect.
191. U.S. CONST. art. II, § 2, cl. 1.
192. For a more complete discussion, see Kagan, "Presidential Administration," 114.
193. See, e.g., http://www.whitehouse.gov/omb/inforeg/regpol.html.
194. President's News Conference, 2 PUB. PAPERS 1237 (Aug. 10, 1995).
195. Commencement Address at Grambling State University in Grambling, Louisiana, 1 PUB. PAPERS 836, 839 (May 23, 1999). The preceding examples are discussed in more detail in Kagan, "Presidential Administration," 2283–84. President Clinton also signed a variety of directives to help guide agency heads in the exercise of statutory delegation. For instance, he extended federal nondiscrimination policies to prohibit actions based on sexual orientation, parental status, and genetic information. Clinton probably used this tack to manage the executive branch more than any other president. His successor, President Bush, adopted the same approach soon after assuming the presidency. He directed all agency heads to review the executive orders issued by President Clinton at the end of his term in office that had yet to take effect. Ibid., 2319.
196. United States *ex rel.* Accardi v. Shaughnessy, 347 U.S. 260 (1954).
197. See generally Strauss, "Presidential Rulemaking," 965.
198. Myers v. United States, 272 U.S. 52, 135 (1926).
199. See Waxman, "Defending Congress," 1073.

200. See Judiciary Act of 1789, ch. 20 § 27, 1 Stat. 73, 87; see generally White, *The Federalists,* 411. Congress today has still vested state officials with some authority in terms of arrest. 18 U.S.C. § 3041 (2000).

201. The Framers evidently based the office upon a British model. Each colony utilized the services of an attorney general. See Clayton, *The Politics of Justice,* 11–15.

202. Judiciary Act of 1789, ch. 20, § 35, 1 Stat. 73, 93.

203. Congress in the 1789 Judiciary Act authorized the president to appoint in each district "a meet person learned in the law to act as attorney for the United States." Judiciary Act of 1789, ch. 20, § 35, 1 Stat. 73, 92.

204. See generally White, *The Federalists,* 164–66; Key, "The Legal Work of the Federal Government," 175–76. Indeed, Congress did not vest jurisdiction in the Supreme Court with the power to entertain direct review of criminal actions in capital cases until 1889. Act of Feb. 6, 1889, ch. 113, 25 Stat. 655, 656. Before that time, the Supreme Court heard criminal matters only through habeas corpus or when there was a division of opinion within the two-judge circuit court. Act of Apr. 29, 1802, ch. 31, § 6, 2 Stat. 156, 159–161. See generally Fairman, *History of the Supreme Court: Reconstruction and Reunion, 1864–1888, Part II,* 7:269. Thus the attorney general could wield little influence in shaping interpretation and application of criminal laws.

205. American State Papers, Misc. 10, 1, No. 25.

206. White, *The Federalists,* 168.

207. Ibid., 408. Thus, even the controversial attempted prosecution of Aaron Burr in Kentucky was apparently launched by the district attorney without any guidance from higher political officials. Tachau, *Federal Courts in the Early Republic,* 140. During the period of hostilities prior to the War of 1812, Secretary of the Treasury Albert Gallatin complained on several occasions that the district attorney in Massachusetts never returned his letters, and the port collectors under Gallatin's control were forced to rely on the services of private counsel. Leonard D. White, *The Jeffersonians,* 455.

At times, of course, the president did show special interest in particular prosecutions. See, e.g., Levy, *The Legacy of Suppression,* 241–42; Jeffery A. Smith, *War and Press Freedom,* 182–86; James Morton Smith, *Freedom's Fetters,* 182–86; Crosskey, *Politics and the Constitution in the History of the United States,* 2:768–84; Henderson, *Congress, Courts, and Criminals,* 198. Nonetheless, even the president's control over district attorneys, at least in the view of several attorneys general, was not complete. 2 Op. Att'y Gen. 53 (1827) (setting bounds on orders that president can give district attorney); 2 Op. Att'y Gen. 482 (1831) (president can only rarely interfere with district attorney's handling of cases).

208. Act of March 3, 1797, ch. 20, 1 Stat. 512.

209. Act of May 15, 1820, ch. 107, 3 Stat. 592. Indeed, Attorney General Wirt under President Monroe refused to respond to legal inquiries from the district attorney's office because such duties lay outside his statutory responsibilities. 1 Op. Att'y Gen. 608, 609–611 (1823). See also Leonard D. White, *The Jeffersonians,* 340–41.

210. Even the secretary of the Treasury wielded only limited control over the district attorneys. Attorney General Wirt commented that "[t]he Secretary of the Treasury is not necessarily a lawyer by profession. . . . It could never have been considered, therefore, as among the duties of that officer, that he should instruct and direct the district attorneys as to the mere technicalities of their profession. . . . [Imposing

such duties] would be . . . to confound and amalgamate duties which are separated by our laws, and to shift to the Secretary of the Treasury responsibilities which properly belong to the district attorneys." 1 Op. Att'y Gen. 608, 611–612 (1823).

211. Key, "The Legal Work of the Federal Government," 178. The solicitor had jurisdiction over most civil actions, including suits for penalties and fines. Creation of the new office of solicitor of the Treasury apparently arose out of two concerns: first that the attorney general would not be an effective legal officer if he needed to discharge too many administrative duties (see Learned, *The President's Cabinet*, 174); and second, that if such an office were not created, the demand for a new home department might have received greater congressional support. Ibid., 272.

212. See, e.g., 6 CONG. DEB. 323 (1830) (statement of Mr. McKinley) ("[I]n no country was the Law Department in so wretched a condition as in the United States.").

213. See, e.g., 6 CONG. DEB. 324 (statement of Mr. Webster) (no "good would result from the metamorphosis of the Attorney General into the head of a bureau.").

214. Richardson, ed., *A Compilation of the Messages and Papers of the Presidents*, 3:1090.

215. Key, "The Legal Work of the Federal Government," 179–81.

216. R.H. Gillet, Report of the Solicitor of the Treasury, Showing the Operations of that Office Since its Organization, May 29, 1830 to October 1, 1848 in 532 U.S. Congressional Serial Set (Congressional Documents and Reports) 30th Cong., 2d Sess. Senate, Exec. Doc. No. 36, at 13, referred to in President James Polk, Message from the President of the United States Communicating a Report Showing the Operations of the Office of the Solicitor General Since its Organization in Richardson, ed., *Messages and Papers of the Presidents*, 6:2539.

217. Langeluttig, *The Department of Justice of the United States*, 8. Even then, Congress still chose to vest some jurisdiction over criminal matters in the Department of the Treasury. See 20 Op. Atty. Gen. 714, 715–716 (1894).

218. The Supreme Court has more recently adverted to the congressional power to disperse decisionmaking responsibility, even as to criminal matters, within the executive branch. United States v. Providence Journal Co., 485 U.S. 693, 705n9 (1988) (recognizing that Congress may carve out exceptions to the solicitor general's litigating authority in the Supreme Court).

219. Act of July 22, 1870, ch. 150, 16 Stat. 162.

220. See Bell, "The Attorney General," 1056.

221. Clayton, *The Politics of Justice*, 75. In this period of history, the Supreme Court was more solicitous of the need for centralization than was Congress.

222. Executive Order No. 6166, June 10, 1933, *reprinted in* 5 U.S.C. § 901 (2000).

223. Exec. Order No. 6166, § 5.

224. Bell, "The Attorney General," 1056–57.

225. See Devins, "Unitariness and Independence," 264.

226. Bell, "The Attorney General," 1061.

227. See Olson, "Challenges to the Gatekeeper: The Debate over Federal Litigating Authority," 77–78.

228. Whistleblower Protection Act of 1988, S 508, 100th Cong., 2d Sess., 134 CONG. REC. S 15, (daily ed. Oct. 9, 1988); Memorandum of Disapproval for the

Whistleblower Protection Act of 1988, 24 WEEKLY COMP. PRES. DOC. 1377 (Oct. 26, 1988).

229. Devins, "Unitariness and Independence," 268.

230. Exec. Order No. 12,146, 3 C.F.R. 409 (1980).

231. Devins, "Unitariness and Independence," 277.

232. Bob Jones Univ. v. United States, 461 U.S. 574 (1983).

233. Local 28 of the Sheet Metal Workers' Int'l Ass'n v. EEOC, 478 U.S. 421 (1986).

234. Mail Order Ass'n v. United States Postal Serv., 986 F.2d 509 (D.C. Cir. 1993).

235. Ibid., 527.

236. President Andrew Jackson, for instance, dismissed Attorney General John Berrien for refusing to support Jackson's legal effort to dismantle the Bank of the United States. Clayton, *The Politics of Justice*, 8.

237. Bowsher v. Synar, 478 U.S. 714, 730 (1986).

238. Carter v. Carter Coal Co., 298 U.S. 238 (1936).

239. Bituminous Coal Conservation Act of 1935, ch. 824, §§ 1–23, 49 Stat. 991, *repealed by* Bituminous Coal Act of 1937, ch. 127, § 20(a), 50 Stat. 90, *codified at* 15 U.S.C. § 850 (1946).

240. § 3, 49 Stat. at 993–94.

241. *Carter,* 298 U.S. at 311.

242. U.S. CONST. art. I, § 10, cl. 3.

243. Holmes v. Jennison, 39 U.S. (14 Pet.) 540 (1840).

244. Ibid., 598.

245. The scheme of enumerated powers, provisions such as the individual election of senators, U.S. CONST. art. I, § 3, and the Ninth and Tenth Amendments reflect the role that the states were to play in the new constitutional system.

246. Banking Act of 1935, ch. 614, § 205, 49 Stat. 705, *codified as amended at* 12 U.S.C. § 263 (2000).

247. 42 U.S.C. § 1393x(f), (5) (1983), *repealed by* Deficit Reduction Act of 1984, Pub. L. No. 98-369, Title VII § 2340, 98 Stat. 1093 (1984); 42 U.S.C. § 1395bb (1983 & Supp. 1990), *amended by* Deficit Reduction Act of 1984.

248. Agricultural Marketing Agreement Act of 1937, 50 Stat. 246, 7 U.S.C. § 601 *et seq.* (2000).

249. 7 U.S.C. §§ 608c(8), 608 (c)(5)(B)(i) (2000).

250. The secretary must also certify that the order is "the only practical means of advancing the interests of the producers." 7 U.S.C. § 608c(9)(B) (2000).

251. 7 U.S.C. § 608e-1 (2000).

252. Act of July 26, 1866, ch. 262, § 1, 14 Stat. 251.

253. St. Louis, Iron Mountain & Southern Ry. Co. v. Taylor, 210 U.S. 281, 285–87 (1908).

254. United States v. Griswold, 26 F. Cas. 42 (D. Or. 1877).

255. Ibid., 44.

256. See United States v. Shapleigh, 54 F. 126, 134 (8th Cir. 1893) ("Where provision is made by statute for the punishment of an offense by fine or imprisonment, and also for the recovery of a penalty for the same offense by a civil suit, a trial and judgment of conviction or acquittal in the criminal proceeding is a bar to the civil suit,

and a trial and judgment for the plaintiff or defendant in the civil suit is a bar to the criminal proceeding.").

257. United States *ex rel.* Marcus v. Hess 317 U.S. 537, 549–52 (1943).

258. United States *ex rel.* Coates v. St. Louis Clay Products Co., 68 F. Supp. 902, 904–05 (E.D. Mo. 1946).

259. 31 U.S.C. § 3730 (2000).

260. Chemical Weapons Convention Implementation Act of 1998, 22 U.S.C. § 6723(b) (2000).

261. See generally Ku, "The Delegation of Federal Power to International Organizations: New Problems with Old Solutions," 71.

262. The increasing tension between unilateralism and global multilateralism can be observed in the recent tussling between the United States and Europe over the International Criminal Court. Tom Hundley, "It's U.S. vs. World on Global Tribunal; Bush Firm on War Crimes Court," *Chicago Tribune*, sec. A1, July 3, 2002.

263. U.S. CONST. art. I, § 9, cl. 7.

264. THE FEDERALIST NO. 58, at 357 (James Madison) (Clinton Rossiter ed., 1961).

265. Story, *Commentaries on the Constitution of the United States,* § 1348, 2:215. See also THE FEDERALIST NO. 24, at 157–58 (Alexander Hamilton) (Clinton Rossiter ed., 1961).

266. Reeside v. Walker, 52 U.S. (11 How.) 272, 291 (1851).

267. Hart's Case, 16 Ct. Cl. 459, 484 (1880), *affirmed* Hart v. United States, 118 U.S. 62 (1886).

268. Appropriations Act of 1789, ch. 23, 1 Stat. 95.

269. For a historical survey, see Sofaer, "The Presidency, War, and Foreign Affairs: Practice under the Framers," 16.

270. Schlessinger, *The Imperial Presidency,* 24.

271. See generally Shane and Bruff, *Separation of Powers Law,* 194–95.

272. Energy and Water Development Appropriations Act, Pub. L. No. 100-202, § 309, 101 Stat. 1329-126 (1987). See 133 CONG. REC. S16275–76 (daily ed. Nov. 13, 1987) (remarks of Sen. Shelby).

273. Binkley, *President and Congress,* 236.

274. 31 U.S.C. § 1349(a) (providing penalties for violating the Anti-Deficiency Act).

275. See generally Sidak, "The President's Power of the Purse," 1162.

276. 42 U.S.C. § 18560 (2000).

277. Departments of Labor, Health and Human Services, and Education, and Related Agencies Appropriations Act, 2002, Pub. L. No. 107-116, 115 Stat. 2177, 2208, § 303.

278. Energy and Water Development Appropriations Act, 1991, (Act of Nov. 5, 1990), Pub. L. No. 101-514, Title V, § 510, 104 Stat. 2074. 2098, *repealed by* Energy and Water Development Appropriations Act, 1996 (Act of Nov. 13, 1995), Pub. L. No. 104-46, Title V, § 501, 109 Stat. 402, 419.

279. Stith, "Congress's Power of the Purse," 1343.

280. THE FEDERALIST NO. 58, at 359 (James Madison) (Clinton Rossiter ed., 1961).

281. Richardson, ed., *A Compilation of the Messages and Papers of the Presidents,* 7:3129; 9 Op. Att'y Gen. 462, 468–69 (1860).

282. Fisher, *Constitutional Conflicts between Congress and the President,* 49–50.

283. Supplemental Appropriations Act, Pub. L. No. 95-26, Title III, § 306, 91 Stat. 61, 114 (1977) (prohibiting funds for implementing President Carter's pardon of draft evaders).

284. Indeed, Congress's efforts to accomplish major objectives through the appropriations process does not lend itself to the deliberations that are the hallmark of legislation. Congress itself will not typically consider and debate a measure as much if it is buried in an appropriation measure. Congress has long attempted to restrict its own efforts to enact substantive legislation in appropriation bills. Both the Senate and the House have passed internal rules that make it "out of order" in the main to introduce an amendment that increases an appropriation already contained in a bill, or that adds a new item of appropriation. Senate Rule XVI(2); House Rule XXI(2)(a); see Tiefer, *Congressional Practice and Procedure,* 972–78. Of course, these restrictions can be circumvented but not with great ease. There are apparently several reasons underlying such limitations. One is efficiency. If appropriations measures could be held up by wrangling over controversial riders, as they were by the Hyde amendment's restriction on funding for abortions, then the entire government might grind to a halt. Act of November 20, 1979, Pub. L. No. 96-123, § 109, 93 Stat. 923, 926; see also Tiefer, *Congressional Practice and Procedure,* 985. Because appropriation measures generally include a great mass of detailed items, sometimes numbering hundreds of pages, members of Congress are entitled to presume that only the level of funding is at stake, as opposed to the propriety of the unrelated enterprises. Enactments emerging through the appropriations process are not usually as thoroughly debated as those that emerge through the more typical congressional channels. To some extent, that may be as true with riders on appropriations as well as with appropriations themselves, particularly riders inserted at the eleventh hour. Another reason for concern is that enactment of substantive legislation in appropriations measures distorts the usual legislative process by divesting the congressional committee most expert in the substantive area, such as a foreign relations committee, from control over legislation and placing it instead in the hands of the pertinent appropriation committees. The committee on foreign relations might itself be subject to interest groups or lobbyists, but it at least has a more visible process for debating and considering the many foreign relations measures it disposes of each year.

285. See generally Fisher, *Presidential Spending Power,* 150.

286. Ulysses S. Grant, Message of August 14, 1876, in Richardson, ed., *A Compilation of the Messages and Papers of the Presidents* 10:4331, quoted in Fisher, *Presidential Spending Power,* 165.

287. Shane and Bruff, *Separation of Powers Law,* 199.

288. Ibid., 200.

289. Train v. New York, 420 U.S. 35 (1975).

290. Federal Water Pollution Control Act, June 30, 1948, Pub. L. No. 80-845, ch. 758, 62 Stat. 1155.

291. 92 CONG. REC. S18055 (Oct. 13, 1972).

292. Congressional Budget and Impoundment Control Act of 1974, 31 U.S.C. §§ 1301–1407 (Supp. IV 1974), *revised by* Pub. L. No. 97-258, § 1, 96 Stat. 877, *codified at* 2 U.S.C. §§ 621–88 (1982).

293. 2 U.S.C. § 683(a) (2000).

294. 2 U.S.C. § 684(a) (2000); 31 U.S.C. § 1403(b) (Supp. IV 1974), *amended by* 2 U.S.C. § 684(b) (1988).

295. City of New Haven v. United States, 809 F.2d 900 (D.C. Cir. 1987).

NOTES TO CHAPTER 2

1. Some, of course, would disagree, arguing instead that the Constitution vests principal responsibility in Congress. See, e.g., introduction to Adler and George, eds., *The Constitution and the Conduct of American Foreign Policy,* 1, 6 (arguing for legislative primacy); Ely, *On Constitutional Ground,* 143 (same). Others believe that the president's role is more critical. The Supreme Court has referred to "the very delicate, plenary and exclusive power of the President as the sole organ of the federal government in the field of international relations—a power which does not require as a basis for its exercise an act of Congress." United States v. Curtiss-Wright Export Corp., 299 U.S. 304, 320 (1936); Powell, "The President's Authority over Foreign Affairs: An Executive Branch Perspective," 527.

2. U.S. CONST. art. I, § 8.

3. U.S. CONST. art. II, § 2.

4. U.S. CONST. art. II, § 2.

5. Corwin, *The President: Office and Powers,* 201.

6. Congressional Quarterly, Inc., *Powers of the Presidency,* 106.

7. See generally Prakash and Ramsey, "The Executive Power over Foreign Affairs," 231.

8. Thomas Jefferson to Edmond Charles Genet, 22 November 1793, in Jefferson, *The Writings of Thomas Jefferson,* ed. Ford, 6:451.

9. Wilson, *Congressional Government,* xix–xx.

10. ANNALS OF CONG., 613–14 (1800).

11. Corwin, *The President: Office and Powers,* 209–10.

12. 18 U.S.C. § 960 (2000).

13. Little v. Barreme (The Flying Fish), 6 U.S. (2 Cranch) 170, 177–78 (1804).

14. Judicial invalidation of the president's action, however, need not result in an award of money damages against executive branch officials. The owners of the seized ship recovered damages from the captain of the boarding vessel. Congress, however, reimbursed the defendant, who had abided by the president's directive. Wilmerding, "The President and the Law," 324n6.

15. Congress has, at times, gained the upper hand. For instance, Congress directed President Harding to convene an international disarmament conference after conclusion of the First World War. Despite reluctance, he acceded to its request. Milkis and Nelson, *The American Presidency,* 242.

16. See, e.g., Crabb and Holt, *Invitation to Struggle,* 39, 40–41; Varg, *Foreign Policies of the Founding Fathers.*

17. See Thach, *The Creation of the Presidency,* 59–60.

18. Fisher, *Presidential War Power,* 11.

19. Ordinance of February 22, 1782, in *Journals of the American Congress,* 3:723; Thach, *The Creation of the Presidency,* 68.

20. Prakash and Ramsey, "The Executive Power over Foreign Affairs," 277.

21. Ibid., 274.

22. See Morris, *The Forging of the Union,* 97–108.

23. ARTS. OF CONFED. art. IV (1781).

24. Swaine, "Negotiating Federalism," 1193.

25. See, e.g., Rakove, "Solving a Constitutional Puzzle: The Treatymaking Clause as a Case Study," in *Perspectives in American History* 1:233; Marks, "Power, Pride, and Purse," 303; Swaine, "Negotiating Federalism."

26. THE FEDERALIST NO. 84, at 519 (Alexander Hamilton) (Clinton Rossiter ed., 1961).

27. *Elliot's Debates on the Federal Constitution* 4:127.

28. Prakash and Ramsey, "The Executive Power over Foreign Affairs," 289–91.

29. See Haggenmacher, "Some Hints on the European Origins of Legislative Participation in the Treaty-Making Function," 315.

30. U.S. CONST. art. II, § 2, cl. 2.

31. James Madison to George Nicholas, 17 May 1788, in Rutland et al., eds., *Papers of James Madison*, 11:48.

32. THE FEDERALIST NO. 64, at 392 (John Jay) (Clinton Rossiter ed., 1961).

33. Ibid., 393.

34. U.S. CONST. art. II, § 2, cl.2.

35. Whitney v. Robertson, 124 U.S. 190, 194 (1888).

36. Chae Chan Ping v. United States (Chinese Exclusion Case), 130 U.S. 581 (1889).

37. Story, *Commentaries on the Constitution of the United States*, § 1508, 2:325.

38. Geofroy v. Riggs, 133 U.S. 258, 267 (1890).

39. Reid v. Covert, 354 U.S. 1, 16 (1957).

40. Eric Schmitt, "Senate Kills Test Ban Treaty in Crushing Loss for Clinton; Evokes Versailles Pact Defeat," *New York Times*, sec. A1, Oct. 14, 1999 (characterizing the defeat as the first time the Senate had rejected a major international security agreement since the defeat of the Covenant of the League of Nations).

41. U.S. CONST. art. II, § 2.

42. Corwin, *The President: Office and Powers*, 239.

43. Ibid., 240.

44. See, e.g., Bestor, "'Advice' from the Very Beginning, 'Consent' When the End Is Achieved," 725–27; Henkin, *Constitutionalism, Democracy, and Foreign Affairs*, 50.

45. See Currie, *The Constitution in Congress*, 22–23.

46. Congressional Quarterly, Inc., *Powers of the Presidency*, 115.

47. Swaine, "Negotiating Federalism," 1184.

48. Crabb and Holt, *Invitation to Struggle*, 13, 273.

49. Barry M. Blechman, "The New Congressional Role in Arms Control" in Mann, ed., *A Question of Balance*, 126.

50. Department of Defense Authorization Act of 1984 (Tsongas amendment), Pub. L. No. 98-94 § 1235, 97 Stat. 614, 695 (1983) (*amended* 1983).

51. Blechman, "The New Congressional Role in Arms Control," in Mann, ed., *A Question of Balance*, 128–30.

52. Some executive agreements are reached pursuant to an explicit delegation from Congress. Such agreements draw little controversy, given Congress's principal role in initiating the process.

53. North American Free Trade Agreement Implementation Act, Pub. L. No. 103-182, 107 Stat. 2057 (1993) (*codified in scattered sections of* 19 U.S.C.).

54. Uruguay Round Agreements Act, Pub. L. No. 103-465, 108 Stat. 4809 (1994) (*codified in scattered sections of* 19 U.S.C.).

55. Johnson and McCormick, "Foreign Policy by Executive Fiat," 118–24. For a general constitutional defense, see Ramsey, "Executive Agreements and the (Non)Treaty Power," 133.

56. In United States v. Belmont, 301 U.S. 324 (1937), the Supreme Court recognized that presidents pursuant to Article II could extend recognition to foreign nations through executive agreements. In upholding the president's decision to recognize the Soviet Union, the Court stated that "[g]overnmental power over external affairs is not distributed, but is vested exclusively in the national government. And in respect of what was done here, the Executive had authority to speak as the sole organ of that government." Ibid., 330.

57. Fisher, *Presidential War Power*, 65.

58. Henkin, *Constitutionalism, Democracy, and Foreign Affairs*, 60.

59. See, e.g., Tribe, "Taking Text and Structure Seriously: Reflections on Free-Form Method in Constitutional Interpretation," 1221 (arguing that congressional-executive agreements like NAFTA and the WTO violate the Constitution); Paul, "The Geopolitical Constitution," 671.

60. United States v. Guy W. Capps, Inc., 204 F.2d 655 (4th Cir. 1953), *affirmed on other grounds*, 348 U.S. 296 (1955).

61. Michael Wines, "Clinton Corners Himself, Along with His Quarry," *New York Times*, sec. 4, p. 1, Sept. 18, 1994.

62. Douglas Jehl, "Showdown in Haiti," *New York Times*, sec. A, p. 1, Sept. 16, 1994.

63. Here, Congress bared its teeth at the president by threatening to cut off funding as a politically unpopular invasion loomed; indeed, a vote to do just that was scheduled for a few days after the prospective invasion. "Mission to Haiti," *New York Times*, sec. A13, Sept. 20, 1994. But Congress backed down quickly when it became clear that democracy had been restored to Haiti without an American shot having been fired. Ibid.

64. Douglas Jehl, "Showdown in Haiti," *New York Times*, sec. A, p. 1, Sept. 19, 1994.

65. In defense of his sending troops, see *Deployment of United States Armed Forces into Haiti*, 18 Op. Off. Legal Counsel 173 (1994).

66. William Neikirk and Terry Atlas, "At the Brink, Attack Averted; American Planes Turn Back as Envoys Secure Haiti Deal," *Chicago Tribune*, sec. A1, Sept. 19, 1994.

67. Michael Wines, "Clinton Corners Himself, Along with His Quarry," *New York Times*, sec. 4, p. 1, Sept. 18, 1994.

68. Henkin, *Foreign Affairs and the U.S. Constitution*, 184.

69. Ramsey, "Executive Agreements and the (Non)Treaty Power," 210.

70. See discussion in Henkin, *Foreign Affairs and the U.S. Constitution*, 219.

71. 1 U.S.C. § 112b(a) (2000).

72. Weinberger v. Rossi, 456 U.S. 25 (1982).

73. Ibid., 30n6.

74. Declaration of the Government of the Democratic and the Popular Republic of Algier, Dep't St. Bull, No. 2047, February 1981, at 1, 2, *reprinted in American Journal of International Law*, 75:418 (1981).

75. Dames & Moore v. Regan, 453 U.S. 654 (1981).
76. 50 U.S.C. § 1702 (2000).
77. *Dames & Moore*, 453 U.S. at 679.
78. Corwin, *The President: Office and Powers*, 236–37.
79. Congressional Quarterly, Inc., *Powers of the Presidency*, 125.
80. See Yoo, "Laws as Treaties?" 757. See generally Missouri v. Holland, 252 U.S. 416 (1920) (upholding treaty addressing migratory birds over objection that regulation of migratory birds violated the Tenth Amendment).
81. Henkin, *Foreign Affairs and the U.S. Constitution*, 180–82; Powell, "The President's Authority over Foreign Affairs," 561–62.
82. See Henkin, *Foreign Affairs and the U.S. Constitution*, 181.
83. United States v. Stuart, 489 U.S. 353, 375 (1989) (Scalia, J., concurring).
84. Damrosch, "The Role of the United States Senate Concerning 'Self-Executing' and 'Non-Self-Executing' Treaties," 515–16.
85. Henkin, *Foreign Affairs and the U.S. Constitution*, 206.
86. Patrick Cole, "U.S. Risks Losing Its Vote in U.N.; Congress Lobbied to OK Payment of Past Dues as Deadline Nears," *Chicago Tribune*, sec. A2, Oct. 30, 1999.
87. See *Constitutionality of Proposed Conditions to Senate Consent to the Interim Convention on Conservation of North Pacific Fur Seals*, 10 Op. Off. Legal Counsel 12, 17–18 (1986) (any reservation that "takes effect only after the scope of the legal obligations of all parties has been agreed upon" should not be enforceable).
88. Crabb and Holt, *Invitation to Struggle*, 78.
89. R. Jeffrey Smith, "Foreign Relations Panel Denounces Reinterpreting of ABM Treaty," *Washington Post*, sec. A10, September 21, 1987; Crabb and Holt, *Invitation to Struggle*, 80.
90. Henkin, *Foreign Affairs and the U.S. Constitution*, 182n32.
91. Act of July 7, 1789, ch. 67, 1 Stat. 578.
92. Henkin, *Foreign Affairs and the U.S. Constitution*, 212.
93. Pyle and Pious, *The President, Congress, and the Constitution*, 254.
94. Goldwater v. Carter, 617 F.2d 697 (D.C. Cir. 1979).
95. Ibid., 706. See also Kucinich v. Bush, 236 F. Supp. 2d 1 (D.D.C. 2002) (refusing, on justiciability grounds, to consider a challenge by members of Congress to President Bush's withdrawal from the 1972 ABM Treaty without approval of Congress).
96. But see Powell, "The President's Authority over Foreign Affairs," 563–64 (declaring question "unsettled" as against rights of other branches).
97. Act of July 7, 1798, ch. 67, 1 Stat. 578.
98. See also La Abra Silver Mining Co. v. United States, 175 U.S. 423, 460 (1899) ("It has been adjudged that Congress by legislation, and so far as the people and authorities of the United States are concerned, could abrogate a treaty made between this country and another country.").
99. Merchant Marine Act of 1920, Pub. L. No. 261, ch. 250, s34, 41 Stat. 988 (1920); Letter and Enclosure from Bainbridge Colby to Woodrow Wilson (Sept. 23, 1920) in Wilson, *Papers of Woodrow Wilson*, ed. Link, 66:136–37.
100. Japan Line, Ltd. v. County of Los Angeles, 441 U.S. 434, 449 (1979) (citation omitted).
101. Zschernig v. Miller, 389 U.S. 429, 436 (1968). See also Goldsmith, "Federal Courts, Foreign Affairs, and Federalism," 1617.

102. *Zschernig,* 389 U.S. at 432.

103. Holmes v. Jennison, 39 U.S. (14 Pet.) 540 (1840).

104. U.S. CONST. art. I, § 10.

105. Oscar Avila, "Macedonia Tells Illinois to Mind Its Own Business," *Chicago Tribune,* sec. A1, Aug. 13, 2002.

106. Swaine, "Negotiating Federalism," 113 1n8.

107. See John M. Kline, *United States' Federalism and Foreign Policy* in *States and Provinces in the International Economy,* Brown and Fry, eds., 223.

108. Bethlehem Steel Corp. v. Board of Comm'rs, 80 Cal. Rptr. 800, 802 (Cal. Ct. App. 1969), *invalidated by* Cal. Gov't. Code §§ 4300–4305; See Jackson, *The World Trading System,* 227–28.

109. Mass. Gen. Laws Ann., ch. 7, §§ 22G, 22H, 22I (West 1998).

110. See Michael S. Lelyveld, "Clinton Refrains from Intervening in Myanmar Case," *Journal of Commerce,* sec. 3A, Mar. 11, 1999.

111. National Foreign Trade Council v. Baker, 26 F. Supp. 2d 287, 291 (D. Mass. 1998).

112. Crosby v. National Foreign Trade Council, 530 U.S. 363, 376 (2000).

113. American Insurance Ass'n v. Garamendi, 539 U.S. 396, 2387 (2003).

114. Ibid., 2390.

115. U.S. CONST. art I, § 8. Letters of Marque and Reprisal are authorizations to private individuals to carry out reprisals against foreign interests when the foreign power has been acting with great injustice.

116. U.S. CONST. art. I, § 10, cl. 1.

117. Fisher, *Presidential War Power,* 1.

118. Story, *Commentaries on the Constitution of the United States,* § 1171, 2:87.

119. David Gray Adler, "Court, Constitution, and Foreign Affairs," in *The Constitution and the Conduct of American Foreign Policy,* eds. Adler and Larry N. George, at 19.

120. Ely, *War and Responsibility,* 3.

121. Lofgren, *"Government from Reflection and Choice": Constitutional Essays on War, Foreign Relations, and Federalism,* 36.

122. U.S. CONST. art. II, § 2, cl. 1.

123. U.S. CONST. art. II, § 1, cl. 1.

124. Yoo, "The Continuation of Politics by other Means," 196–241.

125. Farrand, ed., *Records of the Federal Convention of 1787,* 2:318–19.

126. Little v. Barreme (The Flying Fish), 6 U.S. (2 Cranch) 170 (1804).

127. See generally Fisher, "War and Spending Prerogatives," 12.

128. Crabb and Holt, *Invitation to Struggle,* 50.

129. Schlessinger, *The Imperial Presidency,* 37, 63.

130. For examples, see Presidential Power to Use the Armed Forces Abroad without Statutory Authorization, 4A Op. Off. Legal Counsel 185 (1980).

131. Fisher, *Presidential War Power,* 151–52.

132. Schlessinger, *The Imperial Presidency,* 39.

133. Richardson, ed., *A Compilation of the Messages and Papers of the Presidents,* 7:3225.

134. The Brig Amy Warwick (The Prize Cases), 67 U.S. (2 Black) 635, 670–71 (1863).

135. The Brig Amy Warwick, 67 U.S. (2 Black) at 693.

136. Letter to Congressional Leaders Reporting on Airstrikes Against Serbian Targets in the Federal Republic of Yugoslavia (Serbia and Montenegro), I PUB. PAPERS 459 (Mar. 26, 1999).

137. Gulf of Tonkin Resolution, Pub. L. No. 88-408, § 1, 78 Stat. 384 (1964) (*repealed* 1971).

138. Gulf of Tonkin Resolution, § 3.

139. Ely, *War and Responsibility,* 31.

140. Gulf of Tonkin Resolution, § 1.

141. Ely, *War and Responsibility,* 36–37.

142. Though more common in the 1990s, this type of justification for presidential action dates at least from 1950, when President Truman used it in connection with entering Korea. See Fisher, *Presidential War Power,* xii.

143. Letter to Congressional Leaders Reporting on the Airstrikes against Serbian Targets in the Federal Republic of Yugoslavia (Serbia and Montenegro), I PUB. PAPERS 459 (Mar. 26, 1999).

144. Yoo, "Kosovo, War Powers, and the Multilateral Future," 1685–86.

145. United Nations Participation Act of 1945, Pub. L. No. 79-264, ch. 583, 59 Stat. 619 (1945), *codified as amended at* 22 U.S.C. §§ 287–287(e) (1988).

146. Fisher, *Presidential War Power,* 80.

147. In addition to the Korean War, President Truman decided in 1951 to send ground troops to Europe to deter perceived Communist aggression. Ibid., 92.

148. Ibid., 97–101.

149. 99 CONG. REC. 55, 3283 (para. 6) (1951).

150. Foreign Treaty Multilateral TIAS 1964, 63 Stat. 2241, 2244 (1949).

151. 63 Stat. 2241, 2246.

152. See Van Alstyne, "Congress, the President and the Power to Declare War," 1.

153. 140 CONG. REC. 19,324 (1994).

154. Schlessinger, *The Imperial Presidency,* 184.

155. Ibid.

156. Ibid.

157. Ibid., 190.

158. Ely, *War and Responsibility,* 3–4.

159. War Powers Resolution of 1973, Pub. L. No. 93-148, 87 Stat. 555 (1973), *codified at* 50 U.S.C. 1541–48 (1994).

160. Ely, *War and Responsibility,* 115–16. See also Yoo, "Kosovo, War Powers, and the Multilateral Future," 1677–78.

161. Letter to the Speaker of the House and the President Pro Tempore of the Senate Reporting on United States Participation in the Multinational Force in Lebanon, II PUB. PAPERS 1238 (September 19, 1982).

162. Multinational Force in Lebanon Resolution, Pub. L. No. 98-119, 97 Stat. 805 (1983).

163. Letter to Congressional Leaders on United States Participation in the Multinational Force in Lebanon, II PUB. PAPERS 1367–68 (Sept. 27, 1983).

164. Address to the Nation Announcing United States Military Action in Panama, II PUB. PAPERS 1722–23 (Dec. 20, 1989).

165. Fisher, *Presidential War Power,* 148–51.

166. Intelligence Authorization Act, Fiscal Year 1991, Pub. L. No. 102-88, 105 Stat. 429, 441 (1991), *codified at* 50 U.S.C. § 413 (West Supp. 1996).

167. International Security Assistance and Arms Export Control Act of 1976, Clark Amendment (Angolan Assistance Limitation) Pub. L. No. 94-329, Title IV, § 404, 90 Stat. 729, 757; Fisher, *Presidential War Power,* 172–73.

168. International Security Assistance and Arms Export Control Act of 1976, Clark Amendment (Angolan Assistance Limitation) Pub. L. No. 94-329, Title IV, § 404, 90 Stat. 729, 757.

169. Department of Defense Appropriations Act, 1985, Pub. L. No. 98-473, § 8066(a), 98 Stat. 1837, 1935.

170. Similarly, Congress attempted to limit our use of troops in Somalia by passing in 1993 legislation prohibiting the use of any funds after March 31, 1994, for operation of our forces there. Department of Defense Appropriations Act, 50 U.S.C. § 1541, Pub. L. No. 103-139 § 8151(b)(2)(B), 107 Stat. 1418, 1476 (1994).

171. Departments of Commerce, Justice, State, the Judiciary, and Related Agencies Appropriations Act, Pub. L. No. 100-202, 101 Stat. 1329 (1988).

172. Crabb and Holt, *Invitation to Struggle,* 39.

173. Ibid.

174. As another example, in the nineteenth century, a rider attached to the Army Appropriations Bill of 1880 prohibited use of army personnel as poll watchers on election day. Act of May 1880, ch. 81, § 2, 21 Stat. 110, 113.

175. Helen Dewar, "Senate Approves $87 Billion for Iraq; Bush Gets Package Largely as Requested," *Washington Post,* sec. A1, November 4, 2003.

176. Department of Defense Appropriations Act, 1983, Pub. L. No. 97-377, § 793, 96 Stat. 1830, 1865.

177. Department of Defense Appropriations Act, 1985, Pub. L. No. 98-473, § 8066(a), 98 Stat. 1837, 1935.

178. Hughes-Ryan Amendment of 1974 to the Foreign Assistance Act, Pub. L. No. 93-559, § 32, 88 Stat. 1795, 1804–05, *codified at* 22 U.S.C. §2422 (1982), *(repealed 1991).*

179. As has been discussed, Congress has also used the appropriations process to ensure that no covert operations proceed abroad of which it disapproves. In 1976, for instance, it prohibited use of funds in an appropriations bill for "any activities involving Angola directly or indirectly." Foreign Assistance and Related Appropriations Act, 1976.

180. U.S. CONST. art. III, § 2, cl. 1.

181. U.S. CONST. art. III, § 2, cl. 2.

182. See Temistocles Ramirez de Arellano v. Weinberger, 745 F.2d 1500 (D.C. Cir. 1984) (en banc) (rejecting political question grounds in reversing dismissal of claim that government occupied property in Honduras for military training facility).

183. See Doe v. Bush, 323 F.3d 133 (1st Cir. 2003) (dismissing challenge to legitimacy of President Bush's decision to initiate war with Iraq).

184. Central Intelligence Agency Act of 1949, §§ 1 *et seq.* 10(b); 50 U.S.C.A. §§ 403(a) *et seq.* 403j(b).

185. U.S. CONST. art I, § 9, cl. 7.

186. United States v. Richardson, 418 U.S. 166 (1974).

187. Ibid., 175.

188. See, e.g., Henkin, *Foreign Affairs and the U.S. Constitution,* 143–48; Ely, *War and Responsibility,* 55–56.

189. Marbury v. Madison, 5 U.S. (1 Cranch) 137, 166, 166–70 (1803). Even ear-

lier, Justice Iredell stated in Ware v. Hylton, 3 U.S. (Dall.) 199, 260 (1796), that determining whether a treaty between England and the United States had been breached involved "considerations of policy . . . certainly entirely incompetent to the examination and definition of a Court of Justice."

190. Baker v. Carr, 369 U.S. 186, 217 (1962).

191. Nixon v. United States, 506 U.S. 224 (1993).

192. U.S. CONST. art. I, § 3, cl. 6.

193. *Nixon,* 506 U.S. at 229–30.

194. Ibid., 235.

195. U.S. CONST. art. II, § 3.

196. A federal court in 1855 stated that interpretation of a treaty should be reserved for the political branches and not "confided by the people to the judiciary." Taylor v. Morton, 23 F. Cas. 784 (C.C.D. Mass. 1855) (No. 13,799).

197. Goldwater v. Carter, 444 U.S. 996 (1979). There, a plurality of the Court held that President Carter's decision to rescind a treaty with Taiwan could not be examined in court. Even though the power to rescind a treaty was not explicitly granted the president in the Constitution, and even though that power could undermine the Senate's textually rooted authority to consent to treaties, four justices held the claim barred by the political question doctrine. The president's power in the foreign affairs arena is considerable, and the Court did not want to interfere with the president's strategic policy moves. Unlike the repeal of laws, the treaty rescission issue was a "dispute between coequal branches of our Government, each of which has resources available to protect and assert its interests." Ibid. See also Commercial Trust Co. v. Miller, 262 U.S. 51 (1923) (finding that the congressional determination that the war with Germany had ended in 1921 could not be second-guessed in court).

198. *Goldwater,* 444 U.S. at 1004.

199. Chicago & Southern Airlines, Inc. v. Waterman S.S. Corp., 333 U.S. 103 (1948).

200. Ibid., 111.

201. 22 U.S.C. § 1732 (1982).

202. Smith v. Reagan, 844 F.2d 195, 200 (4th Cir. 1988), *reversing* Smith v. Reagan, 637 F. Supp. 964 (E.D. N.C. 1986).

203. Consider, as well, the difficulties that judges would have faced in resolving the territorial dispute presented in Occidental of UMM al Qaywayn, Inc. v. A Certain Cargo of Petroleum, 577 F.2d 1196, 1205 (5th Cir. 1978) ("Because no law exists binding these sovereigns and allocating rights and liabilities, no method to judicially resolve their disagreements" exists) (emphasis omitted).

204. *Smith,* 844 F.2d at 199.

205. A similar dynamic arguably can be seen in cases challenging a presidential decision to abrogate a treaty. A judicial decision well after a presidential decree terminating a treaty might embarrass the nation's conduct of foreign policy. See Kucinich v. Bush, 236 F. Supp. 2d 1 (D.D.C. 2002).

206. See, e.g., Mitchell v. Laird, 488 F.2d 611 (D.C. Cir. 1973); Orlando v. Laird, 443 F.2d 1039 (2d Cir. 1971); Massachusetts v. Laird, 451 F.2d 26 (1st Cir. 1971).

207. Da Costa v. Laird, 471 F.2d 1146, 1155 (2d Cir. 1973).

208. Holtzman v. Schlesinger, 361 F. Supp. 553 (E.D.N.Y. 1973).

209. Holtzman v. Schlesinger, 414 U.S. 1304, 1313 (1973).

210. Ibid., 1316.

211. Holtzman v. Schlesinger, 414 U.S. 1316, 1321 (1973).
212. Holtzman v. Schlesinger, 484 F.2d 1307, 1311 (2d Cir. 1973).
213. United States v. Munoz-Flores, 495 U.S. 385, 390 (1990) (emphasis added).
214. Durand v. Hollins, 8 F. Cas. 111, 112 (S.D.N.Y. 1860).
215. Hamdi v. Rumsfeld, 124 S. Ct. 2633 (2004).
216. Harisiades v. Shaughnessy, 342 U.S. 580, 588–89 (1952).
217. *Hamdi.*
218. United States v. Curtiss-Wright Export Corp., 299 U.S. 304 (1936).
219. Ibid., 319.
220. Ibid., 320. Similarly, almost a century earlier, a court rejected a suit by a United States citizen whose property had been destroyed by wanton shelling of Greytown, Nicaragua. The court reasoned that the president's decision to use force "belonged to the executive to determine; and his decision was final and conclusive." Durand v. Hollins, 8 F. Cas. 111, 112 (S.D.N.Y. 1860).

NOTES TO CHAPTER 3

1. Locke, *Two Treatises of Government,* 392–98.
2. Quoted in Congressional Quarterly Inc., *Powers of the Presidency,* 94.
3. The extent of Locke's influence on the Framers is not clear. See Schlessinger, *The Imperial Presidency,* 8–9.
4. U.S. CONST. art. I, § 9, cl. 2.
5. Quoted in Schlessinger, *The Imperial Presidency,* 9.
6. Jefferson later wrote that "[t]he laws of necessity, of self-preservation, of saving our country when in danger, are of a higher obligation. To lose our country by a scrupulous adherence to written law would be to lose the law itself, with life, liberty, property. . . ." Thomas Jefferson to John B. Calvin, 20 September 1810, in *The Writings of Thomas Jefferson,* ed. Ford, 1231.
7. Cited in Jeffery A. Smith, *War and Press Freedom,* 113.
8. Corwin, *The President: Office and Powers,* 10.
9. Ibid., 174–75.
10. Jeffery A. Smith, *War and Press Freedom,* 92. Even then, Andrew Jackson's actions to suppress freedom of the press drew fire.
11. The Brig Amy Warwick (The Prize Cases), 67 U.S. (2 Black) 635 (1862).
12. United States v. Midwest Oil Co., 236 U.S. 459 (1915).
13. *In re Debs,* 158 U.S. 564 (1895).
14. Youngstown Sheet and Tube Co. v. Sawyer, 343 U.S. 579 (1952).
15. U.S. CONST. art. II, § 2, cl. 1.
16. Winterton, "The Concept of Extra-Constitutional Executive Power in Domestic Affairs," 31.
17. Ibid., 12.
18. Sheffer, "Does Absolute Power Corrupt Absolutely?" 259; see also Hirschfield, *The Constitution and the Court,* 136.
19. Sheffer, "Does Absolute Power Corrupt Absolutely?" 258; Hirschfield, *The Constitution and the Court,* 134.
20. Ibid.
21. Abraham Lincoln, message to Congress in Special Session, 4 July 1861, in *Collected Works of Abraham Lincoln,* ed. Basler, 4:430. Jefferson had articulated

much the same philosophy: "To lose our country by a scrupulous adherence to written law, would be to lose the law itself, with life, liberty, property and all those who are enjoying them with us; thus absurdly sacrificing the end to the means." Thomas Jefferson to John B. Colvin, 20 September 1810, in *The Writings of Thomas Jefferson,* ed. Ford, 9:279.

22. Schlessinger, *The Imperial Presidency,* 61.

23. Swisher, *History of the Supreme Court of the United States,* 5:885 (quoting the *Washington Republican,* Feb. 12, 1863).

24. The Prize Cases, 67 U.S. (2 Black) 635 (1862).

25. Ibid., 698.

26. Ibid., 688–89.

27. Ibid., 698.

28. Posse Comitatus Act, ch. 263, § 15, 20 Stat. 152 (1878); 18 U.S.C. 1385 (2000).

29. Posse Comitatus Act, § 15.

30. Brown v. Board of Educ., 349 U.S. 294 (1955).

31. 41 Op. Att'y. Gen. 313, 326 (1957).

32. 10 U.S.C. § 332 (2000).

33. 10 U.S.C. § 333 (2000).

34. 41 Op. Att'y. Gen. 313 (1957).

35. Indeed, Congress itself has authorized steps, such as the Alien and Sedition Acts and later the Espionage Acts (during World War I and then the McCarthy era), that likely violate the Constitution.

36. Exec. Order No. 9066, 3 C.F.R. 1092 (1938–1943).

37. Hirabayashi v. United States, 320 U.S. 81 (1943).

38. Ibid., 99.

39. Korematsu v. United States, 323 U.S. 214, 245–46 (Jackson, J., dissenting 1944).

40. Youngstown Sheet and Tube Co. v. Sawyer, 343 U.S. 579 (1952).

41. Marcus, *Truman and the Steel Seizure Case,* 126.

42. John Malcolm Smith and Cotter, *Powers of the President during Crises,* 135.

43. Schlessinger, *The Imperial Presidency,* 142.

44. *Youngstown Sheet and Tube Co.,* 343 U.S. at 587–88.

45. Ibid., 585.

46. Ibid., 584.

47. Ibid., 586.

48. Ibid., 660.

49. Ibid., 610.

50. Ibid., 635.

51. Ibid.

52. Ibid., 637.

53. Ibid.

54. Ibid.

55. Ibid., 640.

56. Ibid., 656.

57. Ibid., 655.

58. Ibid., 701.

59. Ibid., 703–04.

60. United States v. Montgomery Ward & Co., 150 F.2d 369 (7th Cir. 1945).
61. Ibid., 370.
62. Ibid.
63. Ibid., 375.
64. Ibid., 380.
65. Ibid.
66. Fair Labor Standards Act, Pub. L. No. 75-718, ch. 676, § 1, 52 Stat. 1060, 29 U.S.C. § 201 et seq. (2000) and War Labor Disputes Act, Pub. L. No. 78-89, ch. 144, § 3, 57 Stat. 163, 164 (1943).
67. War Labor Disputes Act, § 3.
68. United States v. Montgomery Ward & Co., 58 F. Supp. 408, 416 (N.D. Ill. 1945).
69. *Montgomery Ward & Co.,* 150 F.2d at 381.
70. Ibid.
71. Ibid.
72. Corwin, *The President: Office and Powers,* 166.
73. Story, *Commentaries on the Constitution,* §§ 1339 & 1342, 2:206 & 2:208.
74. *Baltimore American,* May 29, 1861, reprinted in Swisher, *History of the Supreme Court of the United States* 5:847; see also Rehnquist, *All the Laws but One,* 32–42.
75. *Ex parte* Merryman, 17 F. Cas. 144 (C.C.D. Md. 1861) (No. 9487).
76. President Lincoln in addition attempted to muzzle the press, as had President Polk during the War with Mexico. Jeffery A. Smith, *War and Press Freedom,* 98–102.
77. *Ex parte* Milligan, 71 U.S. 2 (1866).
78. Ibid., 127.
79. Ibid., 121.
80. Ibid., 119.
81. Ibid., 126.
82. Ibid., 120–21.
83. Editorial, *New York Times,* Jan. 3, 1867, quoted in Warren, *Supreme Court in United States History,* 2:429.
84. Proclamation No. 2561, 3 C.F.R. 309 (1938–1943).
85. After September 11, 2001, one court of appeals held that the logic of *Quirin* should not apply to the capture of terrorists who were U.S. citizens, Padilla v. Rumsfeld, 352 F.3d 695 (2d Cir. 2003), rev'd on other grounds 124 S. Ct. 2711 (2004) at least in the absence of congressional direction.
86. *Ex parte* Quirin, 317 U.S. 1, 35 (1942). The disregard for civil liberties reflected in the exclusion of Japanese Americans from the West Coast is far more striking, and the Supreme Court's role is well chronicled. Korematsu v. United States, 323 U.S. 214 (1944) (upholding the exclusion).
87. *In re* Yamashita, 327 U.S. 1, 25–26 (1946).
88. Military Order of Nov. 13, 2001, 66 Fed. Reg. 57,833 §§ (1e), 2(a)(1)(ii)–(iii).
89. Ibid., §§ 1(e), 2(a)(1)(ii).
90. See Paust, "Antiterrorism Military Commissions," 1–2; Neil A. Lewis, "A Nation Challenged: The Detainees; U.S. Is Seeking Basis to Charge War Detainees," *New York Times,* sec. 1, p. 1, April 21, 2002.
91. Katyal and Tribe, "Waging War, Deciding Guilt," 1284–85.

92. Military Order, § 7(b).

93. See Paust, "Antiterrorism Military Commissions," 21. The White House counsel backed off from the language in the order. Katyal and Tribe, "Waging War, Deciding Guilt," 1304–05.

94. *In re* Neagle, 135 U.S. 1 (1890).

95. Ibid., 6.

96. Ibid., 64.

97. Ibid.

98. Ibid., 67.

99. Ibid.

100. Ibid., 82–83.

101. *In re* Debs, 158 U.S. 564 (1895).

102. Ibid., 577.

103. Ibid., 581.

104. Ibid., 582.

105. Ibid., 586.

106. Dugan v. United States, 16 U.S. (3 Wheat.) 172, 181 (1818).

107. New York Times Co. v. United States, 403 U.S. 713 (1971).

108. Ibid., 743–44.

109. Ibid., 745–46.

110. Ibid., 753–54. President Nixon used extrastatutory means more widely to consolidate control over the nation. Few have defended either his unauthorized use of surveillance against potential domestic foes or his use of paramilitary operatives in the Watergate break-in.

111. United States v. Philadelphia, 644 F.2d 187 (3d Cir. 1980).

112. Heyman, "Foundations of the Duty to Rescue," 673.

113. *Philadelphia,* 644 F.2d at 195.

114. Ibid.

115. Ibid., 213.

116. Ibid., 225–26.

117. United States v. Midwest Oil Co., 236 U.S. 459 (1915).

118. Corwin, *The President: Office and Powers,* 142.

119. Monaghan, "The Protective Power of the Presidency," 44.

120. *Midwest Oil Co.,* 236 U.S. at 469.

121. Ibid.

122. Quoted in Monaghan, "The Protective Power of the Presidency," 69.

123. As the court explained further in Wilson v. New, "[A]lthough an emergency may not call into life a power which has never lived, nevertheless emergency may afford a reason for the exertion of a living power already enjoyed." 243 U.S. 332, 348 (1917).

124. 40 Stat. 411.

125. National Emergencies Act of 1976, Pub. L. No. 94-412, 90 Stat. 1255 (1976); 50 U.S.C. § 1601 *et seq.*

126. International Emergency Economic Powers Act, Pub. L. No. 95-223, Title II, 91 Stat. 1626 (1977), *amended by* Omnibus Trade and Competitiveness Act of 1988, Pub. L. No. 100-418, 102 Stat. 1107 § 2502(b)(1) (1988), *codified at* 50 U.S.C. § 1702 (1991).

127. 50 U.S.C. § 1703.

128. See Regan v. Wald, 468 U.S. 222 (1984) (upholding President Reagan's ban on travel to Cuba against a Fifth Amendment right to travel challenge).

129. See, e.g., Jeffery A. Smith, *War and Press Freedom,* 41 (describing how Congress prior to Watergate had delegated some aspects of emergency powers to the president on almost five hundred occasions).

130. 84 CONG. REC. 2854 (1939).

131. Schlessinger, *The Imperial Presidency,* 115.

132. 88 CONG. REC. 7044 (1942).

133. For a broader elaboration of this point, see Gross, "Chaos and Rules: Should Responses to Violent Crises Always Be Constitutional?" 1011.

NOTES TO CHAPTER 4

1. See, e.g., Stump v. Sparkman, 435 U.S. 349 (1978).

2. See generally United States v. Brewster, 408 U.S. 501 (1972); Eastland v. United States Servicemen's Fund, 421 U.S. 491 (1975).

3. U.S. CONST. art. I, § 6, cl. 1.

4. Ibid.; Powell v. McCormack, 395 U.S. 486 (1969); United States v. Johnson, 383 U.S. 169 (1966); Kilbourn v. Thompson, 103 U.S. (13 Otto) 168 (1880). Article III judges similarly have been cloaked with immunity despite any textual basis in the Constitution. Cf. Pierson v. Ray, 386 U.S. 547 (1967); Stump v. Sparkman, 435 U.S. 349 (1978).

5. U.S. CONST. art. I, § 6. For an argument that this clause provides grounding for a somewhat analogous presidential immunity from suit during office, see Amar and Katyal, "Executive Privileges and Immunities," 702–08.

6. See, e.g., Federal Courts Improvement Act of 1996, Pub. L. No. 104-317, 110 Stat. 3847, *codified at* 42 U.S.C. § 1983 (2000) (expanding immunity for judges).

7. Congress seemingly has sanctioned some executive privilege by legislating exceptions under the Freedom of Information Act, 5 U.S.C. § 552 (2000), to protect interagency deliberations and other confidential information.

8. See, e.g., Butz v. Economou, 438 U.S. 478 (1978); Scheuer v. Rhodes, 416 U.S. 232 (1974).

9. See, e.g., Harlow v. Fitzgerald, 457 U.S. 800, 807 (1982) (stressing the objective nature of the test).

10. Nixon v. Fitzgerald, 457 U.S. 731 (1982).

11. *Fitzgerald* relied on the theory of Bivens v. Six Unknown Named Agents of Fed. Bureau of Narcotics, 403 U.S. 388 (1971), to assert constitutional claims against the president.

12. Fisher, *Constitutional Conflicts between Congress and the President,* 89.

13. *Fitzgerald,* 457 U.S. at 749.

14. Ibid., 749; Story, *Commentaries on the Constitution of the United States,* § 1569, 2:372.

15. *Fitzgerald,* 457 U.S. at 751.

16. Ibid., 753.

17. Schlessinger, *The Imperial Presidency,* 32.

18. *Fitzgerald,* 457 U.S. at 750.

19. Ibid., 755.

20. Gerhardt and Smolla, "Mock Arguments in *Clinton v. Jones,*" 256n22.

21. Ibid., 256n23.
22. Clinton v. Jones, 520 U.S. 681 (1997).
23. *Fitzgerald*, 457 U.S. at 751.
24. *Jones*, 520 U.S. at 694 quoting *Fitzgerald*, 457 U.S. at 752n32.
25. *Jones*, 520 U.S. at 695.
26. Ibid., 698.
27. Ibid., 702.
28. Ibid., 704.
29. Ibid., 705. See discussion in Symposium, "United States v. Nixon," 1061.
30. For an analysis of the subsequent pressures on Clinton's term in office, see John F. Harris, "In the President's Legal Battle, a Tale of Two White Houses," *Washington Post*, sec. A21, May 20, 1998.
31. See Krent, "Reconceptualizing Sovereign Immunity," 1529.
32. State of Mississippi v. Johnson, 71 U.S. (4 Wall.) 475, 484 (1867).
33. Ibid., 501.
34. Marbury v. Madison, 5 U.S. (1 Cranch) 137, 166 (1803).
35. State of Mississippi v. Johnson, 71 U.S. (4 Wall.) at 501.
36. When informed that the Supreme Court had ruled his administration's forcible removal of the Cherokee Indians from Georgia to be unconstitutional, President Andrew Jackson reportedly responded, "Well, John Marshall has made his decision, now let him enforce it." Roche and Levy, *The Presidency*, 13.
37. In a subsequent case challenging the districts, the Court declined to reach the merits on the ground that the case presented a nonjusticiable political question. *Ex parte* McCardle, 74 U.S. (7 Wall.) 506 (1868).
38. Franklin v. Massachusetts, 505 U.S. 788, 802 (1992).
39. Kendall v. United States *ex rel*. Stokes, 37 U.S. (12 Pet.) 524 (1838).
40. To be sure, the decision in Mississippi v. Johnson might instead be viewed as part of the Supreme Court's overall strategy during the time of Reconstruction to avoid as many troubling legal questions as possible. The Constitution simply did not foresee the legal difficulties arising from a failed war of secession. See Siegel, "Suing the President," 1693–96.
41. *Franklin v. Massachusetts*, 505 U.S. 788 at 827.
42. National Treasury Employees Union v. Nixon, 492 F.2d 587 (D.C. Cir. 1974).
43. Ibid., 606.
44. Ibid., 616.
45. See discussion in Ray, "From Prerogative to Accountability," 789–98.
46. Administrative Procedure Act of 1946, Pub. L. No. 79-404, 60 Stat. 237, *now found at* 5 U.S.C. § 553, et seq. (2000).
47. 5 U.S.C. § 706 (2000).
48. Franklin v. Massachusetts, 505 U.S. 788 (1992).
49. See also Dalton v. Specter, 511 U.S. 462 (1994) (rejecting suit against president for his approval of military base closures on the ground that his action did not constitute agency action within the meaning of the APA).
50. Siegel, "Suing the President," 1622–44.
51. Some, of course, have argued that no such privilege exists. See Berger, *Executive Privilege: A Constitutional Myth*. See also Van Alstyne, "The Role of Congress in Determining Incidental Powers of the President and of the Federal Courts," 102; Prakash, "A Critical Comment on the Constitutionality of Executive Privilege,"

1143. Several presidents have not been convinced that they enjoyed such wide authority. See, e.g., Rozell, *Executive Privilege: Presidential Power, Secrecy, and Accountability,* 9 (describing President Polk's views).

52. Evidently, there was only limited debate about the need for presidential secrecy at the time of the Founding. Although the importance of secrecy was discussed, see Rozell, *Executive Privilege,* 24, discussions were not couched in constitutional terms.

53. U.S. CONST. art. I, § 5, cl. 3.

54. See Paulsen, "Nixon Now: The Courts and the Presidency after Twenty-Five Years," 1337.

55. United States v. Nixon, 418 U.S. 683, 705 (1974).

56. *In re* Sealed Case, 121 F.3d 729, 748 (D.C. Cir. 1997).

57. See Cox, "Executive Privilege," 1395–1405.

58. President Ronald Reagan to the Heads of Executive Departments and Agencies on Procedures Governing Responses to Congressional Requests for Information, memorandum, 4 November 1982, *reprinted in* H.R. Rep. No. 435, 99th Cong., 1st Sess. 1106 (1985).

59. Wilson, *Congressional Government,* 303. See also McGrain v. Daugherty, 273 U.S. 135, 175 (1927) (addressing legitimacy of congressional investigative powers).

60. For examples, see Bush, "Congressional-Executive Access Disputes," 735–44; see also Jeff Zeleny, "Bush Tells Energy to Release Papers," *Chicago Tribune,* sec. A8, Mar. 2, 2002 (addressing GAO's efforts to subpoena information covering communications from private energy companies to the president's task force on energy policy).

61. Nixon v. Administrator of General Services, 433 U.S. 425 (1977).

62. See Fisher, *Constitutional Conflicts between Congress and the President,* 185.

63. Ibid.

64. Ibid, 185–86.

65. Schlessinger, *The Imperial Presidency,* 17.

66. See Rozell, *Executive Privilege,* 31.

67. Ibid.

68. Hoffman, *Governmental Secrecy and the Founding Fathers,* 122.

69. Schlessinger, *The Imperial Presidency,* 44.

70. For an overview of nineteenth-century disputes, see Rozell, *Executive Privilege,* 32–37.

71. Schlessinger, *The Imperial Presidency,* 45–46.

72. Ibid., 46–47.

73. Binkley, *President and Congress,* 203.

74. Corwin, *The President: Office and Powers,* 129; Rozell, *Executive Privilege,* 38.

75. Rozell, *Executive Privilege,* 38.

76. Corwin, *The President: Office and Powers,* 130. See also Dwight D. Eisenhower to Secretary of Defense Directing Him to Withhold Certain Information from the Senate Committee on Government Operations, in PUB. PAPERS 483, 483–84 (1954).

77. Rozell, *Executive Privilege,* 39.

78. Ibid.

79. United States v. American Tel. & Tel. Co., 567 F.2d 121, 127 (D.C. Cir. 1977).

80. Comprehensive Environmental Response, Compensation, and Liability Act of

1980 (Superfund Act), Pub. L. No. 96-510, 94 Stat. 2767, *codified as amended* at 42 U.S.C. §§ 9601–9675 (2000).
81. H.R. Rep. No. 97-968, at 42 (1982).
82. Rozell, *Executive Privilege,* 101.
83. United States v. House of Representatives of the United States, 556 F. Supp. 150 (D.D.C. 1983). The United States attorney declined to bring the matter before the grand jury while the suit was pending. Rozell, *Executive Privilege,* 101. The grand jury later decided not to indict.
84. *House of Representatives of the United States,* 556 F. Supp. at 152.
85. Ibid.
86. The agreement, however, did not prevent further injury. Administrator Gorsuch resigned soon after and was forced to pay a fine arising out of her contempt sanction. Congress then requested an independent counsel to look into whether senior Department of Justice officials had perjured themselves in dealing with representatives from Congress during the documents process. An independent counsel was appointed, and that investigation of Theodore Olson, who was assistant attorney general in charge of the Office of Legal Counsel, resulted in a constitutional challenge to the independent counsel legislation, which was rejected in Morrison v. Olson, 487 U.S. 654 (1988).
87. Miller, "Congressional Inquests," 649–69.
88. Presidential Recordings and Materials Preservation Act, Pub. L. No. 93-526, 88 Stat. 1695, *codified as amended* at 44 U.S.C. § 2111 (2000).
89. Executive branch agencies have long been required to retain records under schedules formulated by the archivist. Under the Federal Records Act, each agency must "make and preserve records containing adequate and proper documentation of the organization, functions, policies, decisions, procedures, and essential transactions of the agency and designed to furnish the information necessary to protect the legal and financial rights of the Government and of persons directly affected by the agency's activities." 44 U.S.C. § 3101 (2000).
90. Nixon v. Administrator of General Services, 433 U.S. 425 (1977).
91. Ibid., 446.
92. Ibid., 450–51.
93. See David G. Savage, "Group Fights Shield on Executive Records," *Los Angeles Times,* sec. A31, Nov. 29, 2001; Editorial, "Citizens Fight Back," *San Francisco Chronicle,* sec. A18, Dec. 3, 2001.
94. Presidential Records Act of 1978, Pub. L. No. 95-591, 92 Stat. 252, *codified as amended at* 44 U.S.C. §§ 2201–2207 (1988).
95. For the conflicting legacy of the Burr trial, see Yoo, "The First Claim: The Burr Trial, *United States v. Nixon,* and Presidential Power," 1435.
96. Thomas Jefferson to George Hay, 12 June 1807, in *The Writings of Thomas Jefferson,* ed. Ford, 9:55.
97. United States v. Burr, 25 F. Cas. 30 (No. 14,692d) (C.C. Va. 1807).
98. Ibid., 191.
99. Totten v. United States, 92 U.S. 105 (1875).
100. United States v. Reynolds, 345 U.S. 1, 6n9 (1953).
101. Ibid., 11.
102. See Ellsberg v. Mitchell, 709 F.2d 51 (D.C. Cir. 1983); Halkin v. Helms, 598 F.2d 1 (D.C. Cir. 1978).

103. See *In re* United States, 872 F.2d 472 (D.C. Cir. 1989).

104. See discussion in Rovario v. United States, 353 U.S. 53 (1957). If the need is met, then the government must comply with the request for information or dismiss the indictment. The Justice Department in September 2003 announced that it was willing to have its indictment against the terrorist suspect Zacarias Moussaoui dismissed rather than comply with the defendant's request that he be allowed to interview captured terrorists from Al Qaeda. Philip Shenon, "In Maneuver, U.S. Will Let Terror Charges Drop," *New York Times,* sec. A1, Sept. 26, 2003.

105. President Eisenhower had stated that "when it comes to the conversations that take place between any responsible official and his advisers . . . expressing personal opinions on the most confidential basis, those are not subject to investigation by anybody; and if they are, will wreck the Government." Dwight D. Eisenhower, The President's News Conference, 6 July 1955, in PUB. PAPERS 665, 674 (1955).

106. Rozell, *Executive Privilege,* 62–63.

107. Ibid., 68.

108. United States v. Nixon, 418 U.S. 683, 705–06 (1974).

109. Ibid., 708.

110. Ibid.

111. Ibid., 706.

112. For a contrary view, see Paulsen, "Nixon Now: The Courts and the Presidency after Twenty-Five Years," 1368.

113. *Nixon,* 418 U.S. at 706.

114. Ibid., 707.

115. Ibid., 713.

116. United States v. North, 713 F. Supp. 1448 (D.D.C. 1989).

117. Ibid., 1450.

118. United States v. Poindexter, 732 F. Supp. 142, 147–48 (D.D.C. 1990).

119. United States v. Fromme, 405 F. Supp. 578 (E.D. Cal. 1975).

120. Rotunda and Nowak, *Treatise on Constitutional Law: Substance and Procedure* § 7.1, 1:574–75.

121. Rozell, *Executive Privilege,* 94.

122. See, e.g., United States v. McDougal, 934 F. Supp. 296 (E.D. Ark. 1996).

123. President Clinton objected, however, to the independent counsel's efforts to subpoena an attorney working in the office of the president on the ground of attorney-client privilege. The Court of Appeals for the District of Columbia held that a government attorney owes a duty of loyalty to the office and not to the officeholder, and thus that no privilege would attach. *In re* Lindsey, 158 F.3d 1263 (D.C. Cir. 1998).

124. A jury acquitted Espy of all charges, even though the company that had delivered gifts to him had pled guilty. Bill Miller, "Espy Acquitted in Gifts Case," *Washington Post,* sec. A1, Dec. 3, 1998.

125. See *In re* Sealed Case, 116 F.3d 550 (D.C. Cir. 1997) (referring to in camera proceeding).

126. *In re* Sealed Case, 121 F.3d 729 (D.C. Cir. 1997).

127. Ibid., 737. The deliberative process privilege often arises in litigation under the Freedom of Information Act. 5 U.S.C. § 552(b)(5) (2000).

128. *In re* Sealed Case, 121 F.3d at 748.

129. Ibid., 750.

130. Ibid., citing United States v. Nixon, 418 U.S. 683, 705 (1974).
131. Ibid., 754.
132. *In re* Grand Jury Proceedings, 5 F. Supp. 2d 21 (D.D.C. 1998)
133. He challenged the court's alternative holding that the documents were shielded by attorney-client privilege. The court of appeals rejected that claim. See *In re* Lindsey, 158 F.3d 1263 (D.C. Cir. 1998).
134. 28 U.S.C. § 595(c) (2000).
135. Referral to the United States House of Representatives Pursuant to Title 28, United States Code, § 595(c), submitted by the Office of the Independent Counsel, H.R. Doc. No. 105-310, at 586 (1998).
136. U.S. CONST. art II, § 4.

NOTES TO CHAPTER 5

1. U.S. CONST. art. II, § 2, cl. 1.
2. The president has no authority to pardon offenses against the states in light of our federalist system. Nor does the president have the right to intrude into private lawsuits to excuse a defendant from liability.
3. Case of Davis, 7 F. Cas. 63 (C.C.D. Va. 1867–1871).
4. Murphy v. Ford, 390 F. Supp. 1372 (W.D. Mich. 1975).
5. The pardon power can be abused as well. One governor was impeached for selling pardons to line his own pockets. 3 United States Department of Justice, The Attorney General's Survey of Release Procedures, 150–53 (1939).
6. See Duker, "The President's Power to Pardon," 475.
7. Act for the Continuing Certain Liberties of the Crown, 27 Hen. 8, ch. 24, § 1 (1535–36).
8. Duker, "The President's Power to Pardon," 495.
9. Ibid., 497–500.
10. Jensen, *The Pardoning Power in the American States*, 5.
11. Kobil, "The Quality of Mercy Strained," 590–91.
12. 4 Blackstone's Commentaries * 390.
13. Justice Joseph Story in his Commentaries on the Constitution turned Blackstone's argument on its head: "If the [pardon] power should ever be abused, it would be far less likely to occur in opposition, than in obedience to the will of the people. The danger is not, that in republics the victims of the law will too often escape punishment by a pardon; but that the power will not be sufficiently exerted in cases, where public feeling accompanies the prosecution, and assigns the ultimate doom to persons who have been convicted upon slender testimony, or popular suspicions." Story, *Commentaries on the Constitution of the United States*, § 1497, 2:320.
14. Madison, *Journal of the Federal Convention*, ed. Scott, 735.
15. Kaminsky and Saladino, eds., *The Documentary History of the Ratification of the Constitution*, 1380.
16. U.S. CONST. art. II, § 2, cl. 1.
17. Story, *Commentaries on the Constitution of the United States*, § 1501, 2:323.
18. THE FEDERALIST NO. 74, at 447 (Alexander Hamilton) (Clinton Rossiter ed., 1961).
19. James Iredell, Address in the North Carolina Ratifying Convention, *reprinted in The Founders' Constitution*, Kurland and Lerner, eds., 4:17.

20. THE FEDERALIST NO. 74, at 449 (Clinton Rossiter ed., 1961). Indeed, presidents have used the pardon power as well to prevent prisoners from becoming "martyrs," such as with Oscar Collazo, the Puerto Rican nationalist whose death sentence was commuted by President Truman, or generally take the wind out of a political protest (female suffragettes).

21. Kurland and Lerner, eds., *The Founders' Constitution*, 4:18.

22. President Washington in part explained that the pardon was appropriate because of "assurances" made to the population of Western Pennsylvania. 20 Op. Att'y Gen. 330, 339 (1892) (appendix).

23. President Adams declared that "[w]hereas the late wicked and treasonable insurrection against the just authority of the United States of sundry persons in the counties of Northampton, Montgomery, and Bucks, in the state of Pennsylvania . . . having been speedily suppressed, without any of the calamities usually attending rebellion . . . and the ignorant, misguided, and misinformed in the counties have returned to a proper sense of their duty . . . it is become unnecessary for the public good that any future prosecutions should be commenced." Ibid., 343.

24. President Madison justified the pardon on the grounds that "the offenders have manifested a sincere penitence" and had "exhibited in the defense of New Orleans unequivocal traits of courage and fidelity." Ibid., 344.

25. For a partial listing of reasons, see Humbert, *The Pardoning Power of the President*, 96–99.

26. Knote v. United States, 95 U.S. 149, 153 (1877).

27. See United States v. Noonan, 906 F.2d 952, 958–59 (3d Cir. 1990); Bjerkan v. United States, 529 F.2d 125, 128n2 (7th Cir. 1975); Effect of a Pardon on Statute Making Persons Convicted of Felonies Ineligible for Enlistment in the Navy, 39 Op. Att'y Gen. 132 (1898); Effects of a Presidential Pardon, 1995 OLC Lexis 4 (1995).

28. Ruckman, Jr., "Executive Clemency in the United States," 261.

29. Ibid.

30. P. S. Ruckman, Jr., "FALN Members Release Presidential Prerogative," *Rockford Register Star*, Sept. 26, 1999.

31. In 1908, for instance, there were 509 applications for clemency. By 1925, there were 1,799. Humbert, *The Pardoning Power of the President*, 98.

32. Act of June 25, 1910, 36 Stat. 819 (1910).

33. Federal Probation Act of 1925, 48 Stat. 1259 (1925).

34. See Messinger, "The Foundations of Parole in California," 73–76.

35. See Love, "Of Pardons, Politics and Collar Buttons," 1494–96.

36. *Ex parte* Garland, 71 U.S. (4 Wall.) 333 (1867).

37. Ibid., 380.

38. Ibid., 397.

39. See Young, "Congressional Regulation of Federal Courts' Jurisdiction and Processes: *United States v. Klein* Revisited," 1189.

40. Act of July 12, 1870, ch. 251, 16 Stat. 230, 235.

41. United States v. Klein, 80 U.S. (13 Wall.) 128 (1871).

42. Ibid., 147.

43. See, e.g., Armstrong v. United States, 80 U.S. (13 Wall.) 154, 155–56 (1871).

44. Act of May 4, 1977, Pub. L. No. 95-26, § 306, 91 Stat. 61, 114.

45. Story, *Commentaries on the Constitution of the United States*, § 1503, 2:324.

46. *Ex parte* Grossman, 267 U.S. 87 (1925).

47. Ibid., 121.

48. Ibid.

49. Schick v. Reed, 419 U.S. 256 (1974).

50. Ibid., 258.

51. See also Ross v. McIntyre, 140 U.S. 453 (1891) (upholding conditional pardon to similar effect offered by President Hayes to seaman convicted of murder on ship); *Ex parte* Wells, 59 U.S. (18 How.) 307 (1855) (similar).

52. *Schick,* 419 U.S. at 274–75.

53. Ibid., 279.

54. But see Boudin, "The Presidential Pardons of James R. Hoffa and Richard M. Nixon," 26–27 (arguing that presidents may not, as a matter of separation of powers, impose conditions that are not at least implicitly authorized by Congress).

55. Presidents should be able to offer such commutations despite the apparent clash with congressional policy. President Clinton acted more controversially in the case of Paul Prosperi, an attorney charged and convicted for swindling clients. While Prosperi was awaiting sentencing, Clinton commuted "any total period of confinement that has already been imposed or could be imposed in the future upon Arnold Paul Prosperi as a result of his conviction." Josh Gerstein, "Unanswered Questions," *ABC News,* Mar. 9, 2001, http://www.abcnews.go.com/sections/us/whitehousewag/wag010309.html. In essence, Clinton placed a cap on the sentence that Prosperi could receive. The cap not only departed from the applicable sentencing guidelines but seemingly undermined the court's role of exercising discretion in sentencing. Although the cap may well be consistent with the separation of powers doctrine, it can be seen as an affront to the dignity of the sentencing court. Clinton could not wait for sentencing, given the impending expiration of his term in office.

56. But see Cowlishaw, "The Conditional Presidential Pardon," 165 (arguing that the president should have the authority only to substitute punishments that have been "authorized by law").

57. Morrison v. Olson, 487 U.S. 654 (1988).

58. On occasion, courts have exerted the power to review otherwise unreviewable acts of executive officials on the ground that they disagreed with the legal reasons voluntarily proffered. See, e.g., International Union, United Automobile, Aerospace & Agricultural Implement Workers of America v. Brock, 783 F.2d 237 (D.C. Cir. 1986).

59. Milkis and Nelson, *The American Presidency,* 101.

60. Thomas Jefferson to Abigail Adams, 11 September 1804, in *The Writings of Thomas Jefferson,* ed. Ford, 8:310–11.

61. Anthony Ripley, "For Nixon: Indictment, Pardon or a Deal?" *New York Times,* sec. 4, p. 4, Sept. 1, 1974.

62. See, e.g., Neil A. Lewis, "Ex-Spy Chief Is Convicted of Lying to Congress on Iran-Contra Affair," *New York Times,* sec. 1, Dec. 10, 1992.

63. "Problems Pile Up Fast for Carter," *U.S. News & World Report,* p. 17, Nov. 22, 1976. The press also vilified President Lincoln's pardon policies during the Civil War for showing leniency to the Confederates and draft dodgers. See, e.g., Ruckman and Kincaid, "Inside Lincoln's Clemency Decision Making," 84; Dorris, *Pardon and Amnesty under Lincoln and Johnson.*

64. President Clinton issued 140 pardons. See "Those Pardoned by Clinton Range from the Unknown to the Famous," *St. Louis Dispatch,* sec. A4, Jan. 23, 2001;

"Narrow Pardon Probe Ignores Needed Reforms," *USA Today*, sec. 12A, Mar. 12, 2001; U.S. Dep't Justice, "Pardon Grants January 2001," http://www.usdoj.gov/opa/pardonchartlst.htm.

65. See e.g., David Johnston, "Federal Agencies Opposed Leniency for 16 Militants," *New York Times*, sec. A1, Aug. 27, 1999; Katharine Q. Seeyle, "Clinton Says Clemency Plan Was Unrelated to First Lady," *New York Times*, sec. B4, Sept. 10, 1999.

66. Neal K. Katyal, "Executive Privilege, Confidentiality, Trust; The Road to a Compromise between the White House and Congress," *Washington Post*, sec. A31, Sept. 24, 1999. In addition, Senator Hatch proposed a bill to regulate the pardon process to afford more voice to the offenders' victims and to law enforcement representatives. Cannon and Byrd, "The Power of the Pardon," 774.

67. See "U.S. House Panel Wants Clinton Library Fund Records," *Channel News Asia*, Feb. 10, 2001; Maxim Kniazkov, "U.S. Congressional Committee to Subpoena Rich's Bank Records," *Agence France Presse*, Feb. 10, 2001.

68. See Elizabeth Arnold, "Clinton Transition Progressing Slowly," *National Public Radio Broadcast*, Nov. 8, 1992 (discussing Iran-Contra defendants); Adler, "The President's Pardon Power," in Cronin, *Inventing the American Presidency*, 222 (addressing Watergate era pardons); See Johnson and Christopher E. Smith, "White House Scandals and the Presidential Pardon Power," 926 (addressing Jefferson Davis pardon).

69. See, e.g., Moe, "Political Institutions: The Neglected Side of the Story," 235–38.

70. The Willie Horton incident manifests the danger. Horton, who was released on furlough from Massachusetts prison, raped while on furlough. President Bush used Horton in an advertisement to paint his opponent, Michael Dukakis, as soft on crime. Anthony Lewis, "The Dirty Little Secret," *New York Times*, sec. A27, Oct. 20, 1988; Edward Walsh, "Clinton Charges Bush Uses Crime Issue to Divide," *Washington Post*, sec. A16, July 24, 1992.

71. Because President Clinton's term in office expired as he pardoned Marc Rich, Clinton did not have to worry about confronting any repercussions as president. But the hearings illustrate that the impact continued on his party as well as on President Clinton's reputation.

72. Murphy v. Ford, 390 F. Supp. 1372 (W.D. Mich. 1975).

73. Although the court rejected the challenge on other grounds, it implicitly assumed the responsibility to review the merits of the pardon decision. *Murphy*, 390 F. Supp. at 1374.

74. In fact, no judicial review of the pardon power apparently existed at all in England. See A. T. H. Smith, "The Prerogative of Mercy, the Power of Pardon and Criminal Justice," 432.

75. Dorris, *Pardon and Amnesty under Lincoln and Johnson*. Note, however, that no one is likely to have standing to challenge on constitutional grounds grants as opposed to denials of pardon.

76. See "Pardons by Our Presidents—A Remedy for Partisan 'Crimes,'" *Orlando Sentinel Tribune*, sec. G3, Jan. 3, 1993 (comparing Harrison's pardon of Mormon polygamists to Bush's lame duck pardon of Iran-Contra defendants).

77. See U.S. CONST. art. II, § 2, cl. 1.

78. See, e.g., Sur Contra la Contaminacion v. EPA, 202 F.3d 443, 449 (1st Cir. 2000); Indep. Meat Packers Ass'n v. Butz, 526 F.2d 228, 236 (8th Cir. 1975); cf. Dept. of the Treasury v. FLRA, 494 U.S. 922, 933 (1990).

79. U.S. CONST. art. II, § 2, cl. 2.

80. See, e.g., Heckler v. Chaney, 470 U.S. 821 (1985) (establishing a presumption that Congress did not intend judicial review over an agency's failure to act).

81. See, e.g., ibid., 825n2.

82. Ohio Adult Parole Auth. v. Woodard, 523 U.S. 272 (1998).

83. Connecticut Board of Pardons v. Dumschat, 452 U.S. 458 (1981) (rejecting a claim that governors were obligated to provide explanations for pardon denials).

84. Ibid., 464.

85. *Ohio Adult Parole Auth.,* 523 U.S. at 276.

86. Ibid., 281.

87. Ibid., 289.

88. Yelvington v. Presidential Pardon & Parole Attorneys, 211 F.2d 642 (D.C. Cir. 1954).

89. Ibid.

90. Ibid., 643.

91. Ibid., 644.

92. "Noted in Passing, Pardon Us?" *Fort Worth Star Telegram,* p. 16, Jan. 27, 2001; Susan Page, "Who Gets a Pardon," *USA Today,* sec. A7, Mar. 20, 2001.

93. See Debra J. Saunders, "Justice for the Non-Rich," *San Francisco Chronicle,* sec. S23, Jan. 31, 2001; Kevin Freking, "11th Hour Pardons Belie Clinton Campaign Talk," *Arkansas Democrat-Gazette,* sec. A1, Feb. 1, 2001.

94. See Cannon and Byrd, "The Power of the Pardon."

95. Such evidently was the case. See Boudin, "The Presidential Pardons of James R. Hoffa and Richard M. Nixon," 26–27.

96. The critical difference is that pardons remove the fact of conviction under the law, while commutations merely reduce the punishment.

97. British monarchs enjoyed a similar power. See 4 Blackstone's Commentaries * 394. Pardons were offered, for instance, on the condition that the individual relocate to the colonies.

98. *Ex parte* Wells, 59 U.S. (18 How.) 307 (1855).

99. Osborn v. United States, 91 U.S. 474 (1875).

100. Bradford v. United States, 228 U.S. 446 (1913).

101. See, e.g., Burdick v. United States, 236 U.S. 79 (1915).

102. Biddle v. Perovich, 274 U.S. 480 (1927).

103. Ibid., 486.

104. Ibid., 487.

105. 41 Op. Att'y Gen. 251 (1955). Attorney General Brownell later defended that result, asking, "Should the prisoner withhold his consent, is it to be supposed either that the death sentence must be carried out or the condition withdrawn? . . . [T]he public welfare, not his [the prisoner's] consent, determines what shall be done." Ibid. (Citation omitted).

106. See also *In re* Greathouse, 10 F. Cas. 1057 (No. 5741) (N.D. Cal. 1864) (asserting that a conditional pardon "is not a contract between equals, each receiving an equivalent for what he surrenders. It is an act of clemency, grace, and conciliation. Its

condition was intended not as a consideration, but merely to exclude from its benefits the obdurate.").

107. See also U.S. Department of Justice, *Survey of Release Procedures,* 3:202 ("It is submitted that the true rule should be that the convict has no more legal right to reject a conditional pardon than an absolute one.").

108. United States v. Wilson, 32 U.S. (7 Pet.) 150, 161 (1833).

109. *Ex parte* Wells, 59 U.S. (18 How.) 307, 319 (1855).

110. Any duress arises from the situation and not from the coercive or improper conduct on part of the promisor. See Restatement (Second) of Contracts § 175 (1988); see also Chouinard v. Chouinard, 568 F.2d 430, 434 (5th Cir. 1978) ("[A] duress claim . . . must be based on the acts or conduct of the opposite party and not merely on the necessities of the purported victim. Thus, the mere fact that a person enters into a contract as a result of pressure of business circumstances, financial embarrassment or economic necessity is not sufficient").

111. The Supreme Court in *Ex parte Wells,* 59 U.S. at 315, rejected the argument "that conditional pardons cannot be considered as being voluntarily accepted by convicts as to be binding on them, because they are made while under duress." Patricia Williams, however, provocatively has commented that "[t]he vocabulary of allowance and option seems meaningless in this context of an imprisoned defendant dealing with a judge whose power is, in effect, absolute as to his fate." Williams, "Commercial Rights and Constitutional Wrongs," 303. In her view, the contract terminology masks that it is the state that is exacting this toll. Ibid., 304–05. In addition, the ability to "purchase" freedom may result in vesting those more affluent in society with a better chance to bargain their way out of prison.

112. Consider as well the former practice in Oregon that conditioned a pardon upon agreement that the individual remain a law-abiding citizen, and if the governor determines that the individual has violated any state, federal, or municipal rule, he or she can revoke the pardon and send the individual back to prison. Jensen, *The Pardoning Power in the American States,* 69. The conditional pardon in this respect mirrors a traditional parole, but it evidently extends in perpetuity. The beneficiary of the pardon is not entitled to the traditional process protections of the criminal justice system before returning to jail.

113. Cf. United States v. Snyder, 852 F.2d 471 (9th Cir. 1988) (invalidating condition imposed as part of federal probation requiring suspension of state driver's license).

114. There is undeniably an overlap between individual rights and structural restraints in the Constitution. For instance, the First Amendment can be seen both as a protection for individuals and as a constraint on governmental authority, and the Equal Protection Clause can be viewed in similar light. This chapter does not suggest any new way to demarcate one set of rights from the other. Rather, it suggests that, although offenders can waive any individual right by accepting conditional offers of pardon, their assent cannot remove any concern for structural constraints in the Constitution.

115. U.S. Department of Justice, *Survey of Release Procedures,* 3:20.

116. For a discussion of a case in which a judge offered the option of Norplant use—a birth control device that can be implanted in a woman's arm—to a defendant convicted of child abuse, see Matthew Rees, "Shot in the Arm: The Use and Abuse of

Norplant; Involuntary Contraception and Public Policy," *New Republic,* p. 16, Dec. 9, 1991.

117. State v. Brown, 284 S.C. 407 (1985). See also Jamie Talan, "Castration Plan in Texas Raises Anew Questions from Science and Law over Treatment vs. Punishment for Rapists," *Newsday,* p. 59, Mar. 17, 1992 (describing another case in which the trial judge initially offered defendant a castration option).

118. *Brown,* 284 S.C. at 412.

119. Several states have apparently released prisoners through conditional pardons so that any future wrongdoing, even beyond the expiration date of the original sentence, can result in violation of the condition and return to prison for the time that was not served. See U.S. Department of Justice, *Survey of Release Procedures,* 3:197.

120. The hypothetical is not fanciful. Several state courts have upheld conditions that extend for the offender's natural life. See Crooks v. Sanders, 115 S.E. 760 (S.C. 1922); Spencer v. Kees, 91 P. 963 (Wash. 1907). President Cleveland may have imposed such a condition when he pardoned Michael Magruder, "an old, colored, wounded soldier" convicted of carrying a concealed weapon "so long as at any time hereafter he shall not be guilty of carrying a pistol or any other deadly weapon." 1894 Att'y Gen. Ann. Rep. at 160. In the probation context, the probation term cannot exceed the maximum sentence. See, e.g., Hirjee v. State, 487 S.E.2d 40 (Ga. Ct. App. 1997); State v. Watson, 535 So. 2d 1329 (La. Ct. App. 1988); Hartless v. Commonwealth, 510 S.E.2d 738 (Va. Ct. App. 1999).

121. Neither the president nor the offender has the incentive to limit presidential power, which suggests that consent does not remove concern for the allocation of powers among the three branches. The Court has held, for instance, that consent to resolution of a dispute by a non-Article III officer does not eliminate the Article III structural concern. See Peretz v. United States, 501 U.S. 923, 937 (1991); Commodity Futures Trading Comm'n v. Schor, 478 U.S. 833, 850–51 (1986) ("To the extent that the structural principle is implicated in a given case, the parties cannot by consent cure the constitutional difficulty."); Northern Pipeline Constr. Co. v. Marathon Oil Co., 458 U.S. 50, 58 (1982). Similarly, parties by agreement cannot confer subject matter jurisdiction on an Article III court.

122. Schick v. Reed, 419 U.S. 256, 267 (1974).

123. Nixon v. United States, 506 U.S. 224, 232 (1993).

124. Determining when a condition extends punishment may be daunting. No clear objective benchmark exists. One might look, however, to the total time likely to be spent in prison, or time in prison plus some fraction of time in recognition of restrictions imposed by the conditional offer. One might even discount time to be spent behind bars in the future.

125. Wilborn v. Saunders, 195 S.E. 723, 724 (Va. 1938).

126. See, e.g., Fuller v. State, 26 So. 146 (Ala. 1898); *Ex Parte* Hawkins, 33 S.W. 106 (Ark. 1895); State *ex rel.* Bailey v. Mayo, 65 So. 2d 721, 722 (Fla. 1953); State v. Horne, 42 So. 388 (Fla. 1906).

127. *Wilborn,* 195 S.E. at 725.

128. See, e.g., United States v. Schave, 186 F.3d 839, 842 (7th Cir. 1999); United States v. Albanese, 554 F.2d 543, 546 (2d Cir. 1977); Commonwealth v. Pike, 701 N.E.2d 951 (Mass. 1998); Wilborn v. Saunders, 195 S.E. 723 (Va. 1983).

129. See United States v. Ritter, 118 F.3d 502, 504 (6th Cir. 1997); United States v. Schiff, 876 F.2d 272 (2d Cir. 1989).

258 I Notes to Chapter 5

130. See United States v. Richey, 924 F.2d 857 (9th Cir. 1991) (reporting that condition prohibiting speaking out against the government had been imposed); *United States v. Schiff*, 876 F.24 272 (2nd Cir. 1989) (condition banning promotion of view of noncompliance with tax laws). Indeed, several courts imposed on violators of hazardous waste laws the probation condition that the offenders join the Sierra Club. See Levine, "'Join the Sierra Club!': Imposition of Ideology as a Condition of Probation," 1841–42.

131. United States v. Stine, 675 F.2d 69 (3d Cir. 1982).

132. United States v. Tonry, 605 F.2d 144 (5th Cir. 1979).

133. See, e.g., United States v. Smith, 972 F.2d 960 (8th Cir. 1992) (striking down limitation on siring children other than with wife); Rennie v. Klein, 653 F.2d 836 (3d Cir. 1981) (stating that conditions interfering with thought processes of offender should be invalidated); Higdon v. United States, 627 F.2d 893 (9th Cir. 1980) (holding that requirements that defendant perform charitable work and forfeit all assets were harsher than necessary to achieve rehabilitation or public protection); Porth v. Templar, 453 F.2d 330 (10th Cir. 1971) (striking down condition of probation that prohibited expression of opinion as to unconstitutionality of income tax laws); Sobell v. Reed, 327 F. Supp. 1294 (S.D.N.Y. 1971) (similar); Hyland v. Procunier, 311 F. Supp. 749 (N.D. Cal. 1970) (holding that condition barring parolee from speaking on college campuses was not related to the goal of rehabilitation); People v. Hackler, 16 Cal. Rptr. 2d 681 (Cal. Ct. App. 1993) (striking down condition that offender wear a T-shirt reading "I am on felony probation for theft"); Parkerson v. State, 274 S.E.2d 799 (Ga. Ct. App. 1980) (striking down condition that spouse must move); Commonwealth v. Pike, 701 N.E.2d 951 (Mass. 1998) (holding that banishment from Massachusetts was unwarranted).

134. Hoffa v. Saxbe, 378 F. Supp. 1221 (D.D.C. 1974).

135. The pardon attorney and Attorney General John Mitchell both recommended that the pardon be issued unconditionally. The condition apparently was inserted at the last minute on the insistence of Presidential Counsel John Dean. See Boudin, "The Presidential Pardons of James R. Hoffa and Richard M. Nixon," 21.

136. A dispute existed as to whether Hoffa had notice of the presidential condition. Ibid., at 22. The district court found acceptance in the fact that Hoffa did not reject the commutation, presumably after release. *Hoffa*, 378 F. Supp. at 1241–43.

137. *Hoffa*, 378 F. Supp. at 1236.

138. In unconstitutional conditions cases, courts have inquired whether the condition placed on the benefit is related to the reasons for withholding or granting the benefit. Thus, in South Dakota v. Dole, 483 U.S. 203 (1987), the Court asked whether the condition of raising the state's drinking age to 21 was related to the underlying purpose of why Congress might grant funds to states intent on road construction, which was presumably road safety. Ibid., 208. See also Jim C. v. United States, 235 F.3d 1079 (8th Cir. 2000) (reaffirming the importance of ensuring that a direct relationship between the condition and the federal goal exists).

139. The case was mooted on appeal by Hoffa's disappearance.

140. But see Cowlishaw, "The Conditional Presidential Pardon," 173–74 (arguing that a *Hoffa*-type germaneness test should be applied).

141. See United States v. Klein, 80 U.S. (13 Wall.) 128 (1871) (noting that congressional limitation of presidential pardon power would be unconstitutional); Armstrong v. United States, 80 U.S. (13 Wall.) 154, 155–56 (1871) (same); *Ex parte* Gar-

land, 71 U.S. (4 Wall.) 333, 380 (1866) (same); cf. Hart v. United States, 118 U.S. 62 (1886) (same).

142. Indeed, state appellate courts, in order to impose greater constraints, have held that the power to set conditions cannot be subdelegated to officials who are even less accountable. See, e.g., People *ex rel.* Perry v. Cassidy, 250 N.Y.S.2d 743 (N.Y. Co. Ct. 1964) (invalidating delegation to caseworker); *In re* Collyar, 476 P.2d 354 (Okla. Crim. App. 1970) (invalidating sentencing court's delegation to state department of corrections).

143. Conversely, subsequent presidents may attempt to enforce conditions far more strictly than the original president would have intended. Presidents attaching conditions to pardons must take into account that risk.

144. See generally *In re* De Puy, 7 F. Cas. 506 (S.D.N.Y. 1869) (No. 3814).

145. Saunders, "Justice for the Non-Rich," *San Francisco Chronicle,* sec. A23, Jan. 31, 2001.

Bibliography

Adler, David G. and Larry N. George, eds. *The Constitution and the Conduct of American Foreign Policy: Essays in Law and History.* Lawrence: University Press of Kansas, 1996.

Amar, Akhil Reed and Neal Kumar Katyal. "Executive Privileges and Immunities: The Nixon and Clinton Cases." *Harvard Law Review* 108 (1995).

Basler, Roy P., ed. *Collected Works of Abraham Lincoln.* 11 vols. New Brunswick, N.J.: Rutgers University Press, 1953–1990.

Bell, Griffin B. "The Attorney General: The Federal Government's Chief Lawyer and Chief Litigator, or One among Many?" *Fordham Law Review* 46 (1978).

Berger, Raoul. *Executive Privilege: A Constitutional Myth.* Cambridge: Harvard University Press, 1974.

Bestor, Arthur. "'Advice' from the Very Beginning, 'Consent' When the End Is Achieved." *American Journal of International Law* 83 (1989).

Binkley, Wilfred E. *President and Congress.* 3d rev. ed. New York: Vintage Books, 1962.

Boudin, Leonard B. "The Presidential Pardons of James R. Hoffa and Richard M. Nixon: Have the Limitations on the Pardon Power Been Exceeded?" *University of Colorado Law Review* 48 (1976).

Brown, Douglas M. and Earl H. Fry, eds. *States and Provinces in the International Economy.* Berkeley: University of California, Institute of Governmental Studies Press, 1993.

Bruff, Harold H. "Presidential Management of Agency Rulemaking." *George Washington Law Review* 57 (1989).

Bush, Joel D. Note. "Congressional-Executive Access Disputes: Legal Standards and Political Settlements." *Journal of Law & Policy* 9 (1993).

Calabresi, Steven G. and Saikrishna B. Prakash. "The President's Power to Execute the Laws." *Yale Law Journal* 104 (1994).

Cannon, Carl M. and David Byrd. "The Power of the Pardon." *National Law Journal* 32 (2000).

Carrier, Michael A. Note. "When Is the Senate in Recess for Purposes of the Recess Appointments Clause?" *Michigan Law Review* 92 (1994).

Chanen, Stuart J. Comment. "Constitutional Restrictions on the President's Power to Make Recess Appointments." *Northwestern University Law Review* 79 (1984).

Clayton, Cornell W. *The Politics of Justice: The Attorney General and the Making of Legal Policy.* Armonk, N.Y.: M.E. Sharpe, 1992.

Congressional Quarterly Inc. *Powers of the Presidency.* Washington, D.C., 1989.

Cooper, Phillip J. *By Order of the President: The Use and Abuse of Executive Direct Action.* Lawrence: University Press of Kansas, 2002.

Corwin, Edward S. *The President: Office and Powers, 1787–1984.* 5th rev. ed. New York: New York University Press, 1984.

Cowlishaw, Patrick R. Note. "The Conditional Presidential Pardon." *Stanford Law Review* 28 (1975).

Cox, Archibald. "Executive Privilege." *University of Pennsylvania Law Review* 122 (1974).

Crabb, Jr., Cecil V. and Pat M. Holt. *Invitation to Struggle: Congress, the President, and Foreign Policy.* 4th ed. Washington, D.C.: CQ Press, 1992.

Cronin, Thomas E. *Inventing the American Presidency.* Lawrence: University of Kansas Press, 1989.

Crosskey, William W. *Politics and the Constitution in the History of the United States.* 2 vols. Chicago: University of Chicago Press, 1953.

Currie, David P. *The Constitution in Congress: The Federalist Period, 1789–1801.* Chicago: University of Chicago Press, 1997.

Damrosch, Lori Fisler. "The Role of the United States Senate Concerning 'Self-Executing' and 'Non-Self-Executing' Treaties." *Chicago-Kent Law Review* 67 (1991).

DeMuth, Christopher C. and Douglas H. Ginsburg. "White House Review of Agency Rulemaking." *Harvard Law Review* 99 (1986).

Devins, Neal. "Unitariness and Independence: Solicitor General Control over Independent Agency Litigation." *California Law Review* 82 (1994).

Dorris, Jonathan Truman. *Pardon and Amnesty under Lincoln and Johnson: The Restoration of the Confederates to Their Rights and Privileges.* Chapel Hill: University of North Carolina Press, 1953.

Duker, William F. "The President's Power to Pardon: A Constitutional History." *William and Mary Law Review* 18 (1977).

Elliot, E. Donald. "Regulating the Deficit after *Bowsher v. Synar.*" *Yale University Journal on Regulation* 4 (Spring 1987).

Elliot, Jonathan. *Elliot's Debates: The Debates in the Several State Conventions on the Adoption of the Federal Constitution, as Recommended by the General Convention at Philadelphia in 1787.* 2d ed. 5 vols. Philadelphia: J. B. Lippincott Co., 1881.

Ely, John H. *War and Responsibility: Constitutional Lessons of Vietnam and Its Aftermath.* Princeton: Princeton University Press, 1993.

Ely, John H. *On Constitutional Ground.* Princeton: Princeton University Press, 1996.

Entin, Jonathan L. "The Removal Power and the Federal Deficit: Form, Substance, and Administrative Independence." *Kentucky Law Journal* 75 (1986).

Fairman, Charles. *History of the Supreme Court: Reconstruction and Reunion, 1864–1888 Part II.* New York: Macmillan, 1987.

Farrand, Max, ed. *Records of the Federal Convention of 1787.* Rev. ed. 4 vols. New Haven: Yale University Press, 1966.

THE FEDERALIST NO. 24 (Alexander Hamilton) (Clinton Rossiter, ed. 1961).

THE FEDERALIST NO. 48 (James Madison) (Clinton Rossiter, ed. 1961).

THE FEDERALIST NO. 58 (James Madison) (Clinton Rossiter, ed. 1961).

THE FEDERALIST NO. 64 (John Jay) (Clinton Rossiter, ed. 1961).

THE FEDERALIST NO. 77 (Alexander Hamilton) (Clinton Rossiter, ed. 1961).

THE FEDERALIST NO. 84 (Alexander Hamilton) (Clinton Rossiter, ed. 1961).

Fisher, Louis. *Presidential Spending Power*. Princeton: Princeton University Press, 1975.

Fisher, Louis. *Constitutional Conflicts between Congress and the President*. Princeton: Princeton University Press, 1985.

Fisher, Louis. *Presidential War Power*. Lawrence: University Press of Kansas, 1995.

Fisher, Louis. "War and Spending Prerogatives: Stages of Congressional Abdication." *St. Louis University Public Law Review* 19 (2000).

Gerhardt, Michael J. *The Federal Appointments Process: A Constitutional and Historical Analysis*. Durham, N.C.: Duke University Press, 2000.

Gerhardt, Michael J. and Rodney A. Smolla. "1996–97 Supreme Court Preview: Mock Arguments in *Clinton v. Jones*." *William & Mary Bill of Rights Journal* 5 (1996).

Goldsmith, Jack L. "Federal Courts, Foreign Affairs, and Federalism." *Virginia Law Review* 83 (1997).

Gross, Oren. "Chaos and Rules: Should Responses to Violent Crises Always Be Constitutional?" *Yale Law Journal* 112 (2003).

Haggenmacher, Peter. "Some Hints on the European Origins of Legislative Participation in the Treaty-Making Function." *Chicago-Kent Law Review* 67 (1991).

Hamilton, Alexander. *Pacificus No. 1*. Vol. 15, *The Papers of Alexander Hamilton*. Edited by Harold C. Syrett et al. New York: Columbia University Press, 1961–79.

Harris, Joseph P. *The Advice and Consent of the Senate: A Study of the Confirmation of Appointments by the United States Senate*. Berkeley: University of California Press, 1953.

Henderson, Dwight F. *Congress, Courts, and Criminals: The Development of Federal Criminal Law, 1801–1829*. Westport, Conn.: Greenwood Press, 1985.

Henkin, Louis. *Foreign Affairs and the U.S. Constitution*. 2d ed. Oxford, U.K.: Clarendon Press, 1956.

Henkin, Louis. *Constitutionalism, Democracy, and Foreign Affairs*. New York: Columbia University Press, 1990.

Heyman, Steven J. "Foundations of the Duty to Rescue." *Vanderbilt Law Review* 47 (1994).

Hirschfield, Robert S. *The Constitution and the Court: The Development of the Basic Law through Judicial Interpretation*. New York: Random House, 1962.

Hoffman, Daniel N. *Governmental Secrecy and the Founding Fathers: A Study in Constitutional Controls*. Westport, Conn.: Greenwood Press, 1981.

Humbert, William Harrison. *The Pardoning Power of the President*. Washington, D.C.: American Council on Public Affairs, 1941.

Jackson, John H. *The World Trading System: Law and Policy of International Economic Relations*. 2d ed. Cambridge: MIT Press, 1989.

Jefferson, Thomas. *The Complete Jefferson*. Edited by Saul K. Padover. New York: Duell, Sloan and Pearce, Inc., 1943.

Jefferson, Thomas. *Notes on the State of Virginia*. Vol. 3, *The Writings of Thomas Jefferson*. Edited by Paul L. Ford. New York: G. P. Putnam, 1882–1899.

Jensen, Christen. *The Pardoning Power in the American States*. Chicago: University of Chicago Press, 1922.

Johnson, Loch and James M. McCormick. "Foreign Policy by Executive Fiat." *Foreign Policy* 28 (Fall 1977).

Johnson, Scott P. and Christopher E. Smith. "White House Scandals and the Presidential

Pardon Power: Persistent Risks and Prospects for Reform." *New England Law Review* 33 (1999).

Kagan, Elena. "Presidential Administration." *Harvard Law Review* 114 (2001).

Kaminski, John P. and Gaspare J. Saladino, eds. *The Documentary History of the Ratification of the Constitution.* Vol. 2. Madison: State Historical Society of Wisconsin, 1984.

Katyal Neal K. and Laurence H. Tribe. "Waging War, Deciding Guilt: Trying the Military Tribunals." *Yale Law Journal* 111 (2002).

Ketcham, Ralph. *Presidents above Party: The First American Presidency, 1789–1829.* Chapel Hill: University of North Carolina Press, 1984.

Key, Sewall. "The Legal Work of the Federal Government." *Virginia Law Review* 25 (1938).

Kobil, Daniel T. "The Quality of Mercy Strained: Wresting the Pardoning Power from the King." *Texas Law Review* 69 (1991).

Kraines, Oscar. "The President versus Congress: The Keep Commission, 1905–1909: First Comprehensive Presidential Inquiry into Administration." *Western Political Quarterly* 23 (1970).

Krent, Harold J. "Executive Control over Criminal Law Enforcement: Some Lessons from History." *American University Law Review* 38 (1989).

Krent, Harold J. "Reconceptualizing Sovereign Immunity." *Vanderbilt Law Review* 45 (1992).

Ku, Julian G. "The Delegation of Federal Power to International Organizations: New Problems with Old Solutions." *Minnesota Law Review* 85 (2000).

Kurland, Phillip B. and Ralph Lerner, eds. *The Founders' Constitution.* 5 vols. Chicago: University of Chicago Press, 1987.

Langeluttig, Albert G. *The Department of Justice of the United States.* Baltimore: Johns Hopkins University Press, 1927.

Learned, Henry B. *The President's Cabinet: Studies in the Origin, Formation and Structure of an American Institution.* New Haven: Yale University Press, 1912.

Lessig, Lawrence and Cass R. Sunstein. "The President and the Administration." *Columbia Law Review* 94 (1994).

Levine, Jaimy M. Comment. "'Join the Sierra Club!': Imposition of Ideology as a Condition of Probation." *University of Pennsylvania Law Review* 142 (1994).

Levy, Leonard W. *The Legacy of Suppression: Freedom of Speech and Press in Early American History.* Cambridge: Belknap Press of Harvard University Press, 1960.

Locke, John. *Two Treatises of Government.* Cambridge: Cambridge University Press, 1967.

Lofgren, Charles A. *"Government from Reflection and Choice": Constitutional Essays on War, Foreign Relations, and Federalism.* New York: Oxford University Press, 1986.

Love, Margaret Colgate. "Of Pardons, Politics and Collar Buttons: Reflections on the President's Duty to Be Merciful." *Fordham Urban Law Journal* 27 (2000).

Lowrie, Walter and Walter S. Franklin, eds. *Miscellaneous American State Papers,* Class x, Vol. 1, No. 25, 2d Cong., 1st Sess. 46 (1834).

Madison, James. *Journal of the Federal Convention.* Edited by E. H. Scott. Chicago: Albert Scott, 1893.

Mann, Thomas E., ed. *A Question of Balance: The President, the Congress, and Foreign Policy.* Washington: Brookings Institution, 1990.

Marcus, Maeva. *Truman and the Steel Seizure Case: The Limits of Presidential Power.* New York: Columbia University Press, 1977.

Marks III, Frederick W. "Power, Pride, and Purse: Diplomatic Origins of the Constitution." *Diplomatic History* 11 (Fall 1987).

McDonald, Forrest. *The American Presidency: An Intellectual History.* Lawrence: University Press of Kansas, 1994.

McGarity, Thomas O. *Reinventing Rationality: The Role of Regulatory Analysis in the Federal Bureaucracy.* Cambridge: Cambridge University Press, 1991.

McGowan, Carl. "The President's Veto Power: An Important Instrument of Conflict in Our Constitutional System." *San Diego Law Review* 23 (1986).

McKay, David. "Presidential Strategy and the Veto Power: A Reappraisal." *Political Science Quarterly* 104 (1989).

Messinger, Sheldon L. et al. "The Foundations of Parole in California." *Law & Society* 19 (1985).

Milkis, Sidney M. and Michael Nelson. *The American Presidency: Origins and Development, 1776–1990.* Washington, D.C.: CQ Press, 1990.

Miller, Randall K. "Congressional Inquests: Suffocating the Constitutional Prerogative of Executive Privilege." *Minnesota Law Review* 81 (1997).

Moe, Terry M. "Political Institutions: The Neglected Side of the Story." *Journal of Legal Economics and Organization* 6 (1990).

Monaghan, Henry P. "The Protective Power of the Presidency." *Columbia Law Review* 93 (1993).

Morris, Richard B. *The Forging of the Union, 1781–1789.* New York: Harper & Row, 1987.

Morrison, Alan B. "OMB Interference with Agency Rulemaking: The Wrong Way to Write a Regulation." *Harvard Law Review* 99 (1986).

Olson, Susan M. "Challenges to the Gatekeeper: The Debate over Federal Litigating Authority." *Judicature* 68 (1984).

Paine, Thomas. *Common Sense* in *Collected Writings.* New York: Library of America, 1995.

Paul, Joel R. "The Geopolitical Constitution: Executive Expediency and Executive Agreements." *California Law Review* 86 (1998).

Paulsen, Michael Stokes. "Nixon Now: The Courts and the Presidency after Twenty-Five Years." *Minnesota Law Review* 83 (1999).

Paust, Jordan J. "Antiterrorism Military Commissions: Courting Illegality." *Michigan Journal of International Law* 23 (Fall 2001).

Pildes, Richard H. and Cass R. Sunstein. "Reinventing the Regulatory State." *University of Chicago Law Review* 62 (Winter 1995).

Powell, H. Jefferson. "The President's Authority over Foreign Affairs: An Executive Branch Perspective." *George Washington Law Review* 67 (1999).

Prakash, Saikrishna B. "A Critical Comment on the Constitutionality of Executive Privilege." *Minnesota Law Review* 83 (1999).

Prakash, Saikrishna B. and Michael D. Ramsey. "The Executive Power over Foreign Affairs." *Yale Law Journal* 111 (2001).

Pyle, Christopher H. and Richard M. Pious. *The President, Congress, and the Constitution: Power and Legitimacy in American Politics.* New York: Free Press, 1984.

Rakove, Jack N. "Solving a Constitutional Puzzle: The Treatymaking Clause as a Case Study." *Perspectives in American History* 233 (1984).

Ramsey, Michael D. "Executive Agreements and the (Non)Treaty Power." *North Carolina Law Review* 77 (1998).

Rappaport, Adam J. Comment. "The Court of International Trade's Political Party Diversity Requirement: Unconstitutional under Any Separation of Powers Theory." *University of Chicago Law Review* 68 (2001).

Ray, Laura Krugman. "From Prerogative to Accountability: The Amenability of the President to Suit." *Kentucky Law Journal* 80 (1992).

Rehnquist, William H. *All the Laws but One: Civil Liberties in Wartime.* New York: Knopf, 1998.

Richardson, James D., ed. *A Compilation of the Messages and Papers of the Presidents.* 18 vols. New York: Bureau of National Literature, Inc., 1917.

Roche, John P. and Leonard W. Levy. *The Presidency.* New York: Harcourt, Brace & Wood, 1964.

Rossiter, Clinton, ed. *The Federalist Papers.* New York: New American Library, 1961.

Rotunda, Ronald D. and John E. Nowak. *Treatise on Constitutional Law: Substance and Procedure.* 2d ed. 4 vols. St. Paul, Minn.: West Publishing Co., 1992.

Rozell, Mark J. *Executive Privilege: Presidential Power, Secrecy, and Accountability.* 2d rev. ed. Lawrence: University Press of Kansas, 2002.

Ruckman, Jr., P. S. "Executive Clemency in the United States: Origins, Development and Analysis (1900–1993)." *Presidential Studies Quarterly* 27 (1997).

Ruckman, Jr., P. S. and David Kincaid. "Inside Lincoln's Clemency Decision Making." *Presidential Studies Quarterly* 29 (1999).

Rutland, Robert A., et al., eds. *Papers of James Madison.* 8 vols. Chicago: University of Chicago Press, 1977.

Schlessinger, Jr., Arthur M. *The Imperial Presidency.* Boston: Houghton Mifflin, 1973.

Shane, Peter M. and Harold H. Bruff. *Separation of Powers Law: Cases and Materials.* Durham, N.C.: Carolina Academic Press, 1996.

Sheffer, Martin S. "Does Absolute Power Corrupt Absolutely?" *Oklahoma City University Law Review* 24 (1999).

Sidak, J. Gregory. "The President's Power of the Purse." *Duke Law Journal* 1162 (1989).

Siegel, Jonathan R. "Suing the President: Nonstatutory Review Revisited." *Columbia Law Review* 97 (1997).

Small, Norman J. *Some Presidential Interpretations of the Presidency.* Baltimore: Da Capo Press, 1932.

Smith, A. T. H. "The Prerogative of Mercy, the Power of Pardon and Criminal Justice." *Public Law* 398 (1983).

Smith, Christopher E. and Kimberly A. Beuger. "Clouds in the Crystal Ball: Presidential Expectations and the Unpredictable Behavior of Supreme Court Appointees." *Akron Law Review* 27, 115 (1993).

Smith, James Morton. *Freedom's Fetters; The Alien and Sedition Laws and American Civil Liberties.* Ithaca: Cornell University Press, 1956.

Smith, Jeffery A. *War and Press Freedom: The Problem of Prerogative Power.* New York: Oxford University Press, 1999.

Smith, John Malcolm and Cornelius P. Cotter. *Powers of the President during Crises.* Washington, D.C.: Public Affairs Press, 1960.

Sofaer, Abraham D. "The Presidency, War, and Foreign Affairs: Practice under the Framers." *Law and Contemporary Problems* 40 (Spring 1976).

Stith, Kate. "Congress's Power of the Purse." *Yale Law Journal* 97 (1988).

Storing, Herbert J. *The Anti-Federalist: Writings by the Opponents of the Constitution.* Abr. ed. Chicago: University of Chicago Press, 1985.

Story, Joseph. *Commentaries on the Constitution of the United States.* Reprinted with Introduction by Roland D. Rotunda and John E. Nowak. Durham, N.C.: Carolina Academic Press, 1987.

Strauss, Peter L. "Presidential Rulemaking." *Chicago-Kent Law Review* 72 (1997).

Swaine, Edward T. "Negotiating Federalism: State Bargaining and the Dormant Treaty Power." *Duke Law Journal* 49 (2000).

Swisher, Carl B. *History of the Supreme Court of the United States: The Taney Period, 1836–1864.* New York: Macmillan, 1974.

Symposium. "United States v. Nixon: Presidential Power and Executive Privilege Twenty-Five Years Later." *Minnesota Law Review* 83 (1999).

Tachau, Mary K. *Federal Courts in the Early Republic: Kentucky, 1789–1816.* Princeton: Princeton University Press, 1978.

Taft, William Howard. *Our Chief Magistrate and His Powers.* New York: Columbia University Press, 1916.

Thach, Charles C. *The Creation of the Presidency, 1775–1789: A Study in Constitutional History.* Baltimore: Johns Hopkins University Press, 1969.

Tiefer, Charles. *Congressional Practice and Procedure: A Reference, Research, and Legislative Guide.* New York: Greenwood Press, 1989.

Tourtellot, Arthur B. *The Presidents on the Presidency.* Garden City, N.Y.: Doubleday, 1964.

Tribe, Laurence H. "Taking Text and Structure Seriously: Reflections on Free-Form Method in Constitutional Interpretation." *Harvard Law Review* 108 (1995).

Tribe, Laurence H. "In Memoriam: William J. Brennan, Jr." *Harvard Law Review* 111 (1997).

Van Alstyne, William W. "Congress, the President and the Power to Declare War: A Requiem for Vietnam." *University of Pennsylvania Law Review* 121 (1972).

Van Alstyne, William W. "The Role of Congress in Determining Incidental Powers of the President and of the Federal Courts: A Comment on the Horizontal Effect of the Sweeping Clause." *Law & Contemporary Problems* 40 (Spring 1976).

Varg, Paul A. *Foreign Policies of the Founding Fathers.* East Lansing: Michigan State University Press, 1963.

Wald, Patricia M. "The Freedom of Information Act: A Short Case Study in the Perils and Paybacks in Legislating Democratic Values." *Emory Law Journal* 33 (1984).

Warren, Charles. *The Supreme Court in United States History.* 2 vols. Boston: Little, Brown, and Company, 1926.

Washington, George. *The Writings of George Washington: From the Original Manuscript Sources, 1745–1799.* Edited by John C. Fitzpatrick. Vol. 30. Washington, D.C.: U.S. Government Printing Office, 1931–44.

Waxman, Seth P. "Defending Congress." *North Carolina Law Review* 79 (2001).

White, Leonard D. *The Federalists: A Study in Administrative History.* New York: Macmillan, 1948.

White, Leonard D. *The Jeffersonians: A Study in Administrative History.* New York: Macmillan, 1951.

White, Theodore H. *Breach of Faith: The Fall of Richard Nixon.* New York: Atheneum, 1975.

Wiener, Ross E. "Inter-Branch Appointments after the Independent Counsel: Court Appointment of United States Attorneys." *Minnesota Law Review* 86 (2001).

Williams, Patricia J. "Commercial Rights and Constitutional Wrongs." *Maryland Law Review* 49 (1990).

Wilmerding, Jr., Luicius. "The President and the Law." *Political Science Quarterly* 67 (1952).

Wilson, Woodrow S. *Congressional Government* (1885).

Wilson, Woodrow S. *Congressional Government: A Study in American Politics.* Boston: Houghton Mifflin, 1925.

Wilson, Woodrow S. *Papers of Woodrow Wilson.* Edited by Arthur S. Link. 69 vols. Princeton: Princeton University Press, 1966–1994.

Winterton, George. "The Concept of Extra-Constitutional Executive Power in Domestic Affairs." *Hastings Constitutional Law Quarterly* 7 (1979).

Wood, Gordon S. *The Creation of the American Republic, 1776–1787.* Chapel Hill: University of North Carolina Press, 1969.

Wulwick, Richard P. and Frank J. Macchiarola. "Congressional Interference with the President's Power to Appoint." *Stetson Law Review* 24 (1995).

Yoo, John C. "The Continuation of Politics by Other Means: The Original Understanding of War Powers." *California Law Review* 84 (1996).

Yoo, John C. "The First Claim: The Burr Trial, *United States v. Nixon,* and Presidential Power." *Minnesota Law Review* 83 (1999).

Yoo, John C. "Kosovo, War Powers, and the Multilateral Future." *University of Pennsylvania Law Review* 148 (2000).

Yoo, John C. "Laws as Treaties? The Constitutionality of Congressional-Executive Agreements." *Michigan Law Review* 99 (2001).

Young, Gordon G. "Congressional Regulation of Federal Courts' Jurisdiction and Processes: *United States v. Klein* Revisited." *Wisconsin Law Review* 1189 (1981).

Index

Adams, John: general amnesty, use of, 192; on pardon power, 252n. 23; plenary removal authority, 39; removal authority, exercise of, 38; use of veto, 18

Administrative Procedure Act, 171–172, 204, 247n. 49

Agency: executive, 4, 49, 68; independent, 4, 40, 49, 55, 60, 65, 68; president as, 171–172; rulemaking and litigation, 48–69

Agricultural Marketing Agreement Act, 74

Alien and Sedition Acts, 243n. 35

American Insurance Ass'n v. Garamendi, 238n. 113

Anti-Deficiency Act, 79

Appointment power, 20, 23–36, 48, 79, 215, 217; congressional restrictions, 25, 31; cross-branch appointments doctrine, 30–32; extension of terms, 34; interest group restrictions, 27, 33; limits on congressional role, 24, 27–28; political party restrictions 27, 31, 33; senate advice and consent, 24–25, 30, 85; superior and inferior officers, 23–24, 26–31, 39, 217; of Supreme Court justices, 25; term restrictions, 31–34; with respect to non-governmental actors, 70–77. *See also* Appointments Clause; Removal authority of president

Appointments Clause, 23–24, 26–28, 32

Appropriations, 77–83, 121, 130, 140, 216, 233n. 284; infringement on presidential prerogative, 80–81; lump sum, 78; for military action, 115; pardon power, effect on, 196, 216; power over covert actions, 123; power over foreign affairs, 86, 121–123. *See also* Impoundment authority of president

Appropriations Act, 232n. 268

Armstrong v. United States, 252n. 43, 258n. 141

Arthur, Chester B., interpretation of executive power, 13–14

Articles of Confederation, 2, 8–10, 108, 215; central government, 9; foreign affairs, 90–91; need for independent executive, 85; power of Congress, 18

Baker v. Carr, 126

Banking Act, 231n. 246

Bethlehem Steel Corp. v. Board of Com'rs, 238n. 108

Biddle v. Perovich, 206–208

Bituminous Coal Act, 70

Bivens v. Six Unknown Named Agents of Fed. Bureau of Narcotics, 246n. 11

Bjerkan v. United States, 252n. 27

Black, Hugo L., in *Youngstown Steel*, 143

Blackstone: on executive power in foreign affairs, 86, 251n. 13; on pardon power, 191, 251n. 13

Bob Jones Univ. v. United States, 231n. 233

Boland Amendment, 122–123

Bowsher v. Synar, 47, 70

Bradford v. United States, 255n. 100

Brennan, William, appointment by Eisenhower, 25

Brig Amy Warwick et al. (Prize Cases), 138–140, 149, 152, 238n. 134, 242n. 11

Brown v. Board of Education, 140–141

Buchanan, James: on congressional infringement of presidential prerogative, 80; refusal to spend omnibus appropriations, 19

Buckley v. Valeo, 26–27, 34

Budget and Accounting Act, 50

ABOUT THE AUTHOR

Harold J. Krent is Dean and Professor of Law at the Chicago-Kent College of Law.

ACKNOWLEDGMENTS

I have benefitted greatly from the excellent research work of Donald Gordon, Michelle Brunsvold, and Lindsay DuVall. I am heartened by the promise of a new generation of such talented attorneys. Keith Stiverson provided excellent library assistance as she does for all of our faculty. Many colleagues in the academy have helped me define the unifying themes and particular illustrations in this book. In particular, I wish to thank Neal Devins, Bill Marshall, Sai Prakash, and Mark Rosen for their comments on early drafts. The wonderful collegial atmosphere of Chicago-Kent College of Law has been of immeasurable help.

Several pages of chapter 1 originally appeared in the *American University Law Review*, vol. 38, as "Executive Control Over Criminal Law Enforcement: Some Lessons from History," and a few pages originally appeared in the *Northwestern Law Review*, vol. 85, as "Fragmenting the Unitary Executive: Congressional Delegations of Administrative Authority Outside of the Federal Government." A portion of chapter 5 first appeared in the *California Law Review*, vol. 89, as "Conditioning the President's Conditional Pardon Authority." I am grateful to the law reviews for their permission to reprint the pages here.

Finally, writing this book would not have been possible without the support and patience of my wife Nancy and the joys and challenges of our daughters Miriam, Stephanie, and Mollie.